Mary Rowland

The Fidelity

A Fidelity Publishing Book/Fireside
Published by Simon & Schuster
New York * London * Toronto * Sydney * Tokyo * Singapore

Guide to Mutual Funds

A Complete Guide
to Investing
in Mutual Funds

Fireside
Simon & Schuster Building
Rockefeller Center
1230 Avenue of the Americas
New York, New York 10020

First Fireside Edition 1991

FIRESIDE and colophon are registered trademarks
of Simon & Schuster

Designed by Irving Perkins Associates, Inc.
Manufactured in the United States of America

10 9 8 7 6 5 4 3 2 1
10 9 8 7 6 5 4 3 2 1 (pbk)
Library of Congress Cataloging in Publication Data

Rowland, Mary.
The Fidelity guide to mutual funds : a complete guide to investing in mutual funds /
Mary Rowland.
p.   cm.
''A Fidelity Publishing book.''
1. Mutual funds.   I. Title.
HG4530.R68   1990
332.63'27—dc20   89-27708
                                                                          CIP

ISBN 0-671-66104-3
ISBN 0-671-73331-1 (pbk)

Grateful acknowledgment is made for permission to reprint: *Mutual Fund Values*
(page 267), © 1989 Morningstar, Inc., Chicago, Illinois.

Tax information in Chapter 13 from *The 1990 Mutual Fund Tax Guide.* © 1989
Strategic Advisers/Fidelity Publishing.
''Using Moving Averages to Time Your Mutual Fund Investments'' from *The Independent Investor*, 1986.

Special thanks to Peggy Malaspina, who had the idea for this book, saw it through, and became my friend.

To Bo

Contents

Introduction

I have a friend whom I'll call John because we wouldn't be friends anymore if I used his real name in this book. He earns a lot of money and puts away a good portion of it every month in mutual funds. He's one of those people who stays on top of the current wisdom in investing because he makes his living writing and editing stories about business and personal finance.

A couple of years ago, John mentioned to me that a particular mutual fund had caught his attention. Its name kept appearing on the top of everyone's favorite funds lists. A consistent record winner for performance, it had achieved an average annual return of over 20 percent a year over the past decade. The fund manager was quoted everywhere and his company was well respected. So, in September of 1987, John plunked down all his retirement money—$45,000—in the fund. He bought his shares at $58 each. I remember feeling a little envious at the time. Not only did John have the knowledge, but he had the money to invest.

I started writing this book shortly after the markets took a dive on that infamous day in 1987 that was quickly baptized ''Black Monday.'' Many mutual fund investors were in a tailspin. They didn't know what to do about their investments. I decided to check in with John. He was knowledgeable. He'd made a well-researched decision. And I figured that he'd put Black Monday in perspective. I gave him a call to ask how his fund weathered the crash.

Actually John wasn't in. He was seeing his psychiatrist. Like most other investors I'd interviewed, he was panicked. His $58 shares had plunged to $35, reducing his retirement nest egg by 40 percent, to $27,155. John couldn't square what had happened to him with his conservative upbringing. He'd been raised in a staunch Midwestern family in which prudence was a virtue and gambling was a sin. (You had to cross state lines to do it, for one thing.) And what, he thought, had he been doing if not gambling?

More to the point, though, was his dilemma about what to do next. Should he sell? Should he wait? Should he turn his back on his Midwestern roots, throw caution to the wind and up the ante? After all, if the fund had been a good investment at $58, it must be a fabulous buy at $35. What about that ten-year track record, and all the stories he'd read about the fund? What were the financial sages saying about his investment now? Should he look to them for advice? Or had that been his original downfall?

John confessed that he developed something of a split personality. On one hand, he still saw himself as an affluent, knowledgeable investor. On the other, he was forced to confront his uncertainty. The events of October brought him face to face with the unpredictability of the financial markets for the first time, and he felt demoralized, even guilty. Maybe mutual fund investing was too complicated, even for someone with his knowledge and sophistication.

The specifics of John's situation may strike you as unusual, but his story is not untypical. No particular type of person has a monopoly on confusion when it comes to investing. In the years that I've been writing about business and personal finance, I've received hundreds of questions from exasperated readers from all walks of life, from all age groups, those with lots of money to invest and those with only the bare minimum savings. How do I save? they want to know. How do I invest? What's the best type of mutual fund for me? Should I pick my own funds or go to a broker? How can I sort through the fees and charges? When should I buy a fund? When should I sell? What is a mutual fund, anyway? And lately, since the crash, one plea dominates these letters—''Help! I've lost money. What do I do now?''

If you have asked yourself these same questions, this book can help you find the answers. Because understanding mutual funds is not impossible, and throwing in the towel is the worst choice of all. In this book I'll cover the basics of mutual fund investing and clear away some of the confusion. I think I can convince you that with a little bit of knowledge, you can invest with confidence.

You will learn something about yourself and what kind of investor you are. Then this book will help you set goals and develop strategies for mutual fund investing. It will help you sort out and evaluate the choices among mutual funds and the companies that provide them. It will show you how people who might resemble you solved their specific investment problems—problems that you'll probably recognize, because they are typical of the problems that most people encounter. It will show you how to put together a portfolio of mutual funds and how to stay on top of it. And most of all, it will help you master the skills that can result in improved investment performance.

By the way, John decided to stick with his mutual fund. Was that the right decision? Read on and judge for yourself.

PART I

Mutual Fund Basics

Chapter 1

Mutual Funds—What They Are, How They Work

I f you have ever thought about buying stocks but decided against it because you didn't know enough to make a good decision, you're in good company. If your eyes light up at the thought of earning a 20 percent annual return on a junk bond, only to glaze over when you find out that you've got to ante up $25,000 for a minimum investment, you're not alone. If you've got a chunk of money, say $5,000, and you want to see it grow faster than the rate of inflation but you're afraid to risk it all on a real estate deal that will tie it up for years and then perhaps fizzle, welcome to the club. These are some of the reasons why people choose to invest in mutual funds.

Most of us don't know enough about the markets to invest on our own. And we don't have enough money to hire a personal investment counselor. Nor do we have the necessary assets to set up a well-diversified portfolio of individual stocks, bonds, and other **securities.** By pooling the money of many people with similar financial goals, a mutual fund can do this for you. It can put your money in the hands of investment professionals who do the research and make the tough decisions on what stocks to buy and when to sell them; who figure out when the bond market looks like a good bet and calculate which foreign markets are likely to take off.

Securities Publicly traded financial instruments such as stocks, bonds, and shares of mutual funds or limited partnerships. Securities are regulated by the Securities and Exchange Commission.

In addition to professional management, you get instant diversification. It doesn't take a lot of money to invest in a mutual fund. And when you buy a piece of just one mutual fund, you own shares of many different securities, gaining clout in the market you couldn't manage on your own. No matter how small your mutual fund investment is, it is spread across dozens of different stocks and bonds. That reduces the risk that you'll lose money. Even if one or two stocks in the fund turn out to be duds, there may be dozens of others that hold their own and several more that turn in spectacular performances.

Investing in a mutual fund saves time, too. You don't have to research individual stocks or bonds. But you do have to research the fund itself. How do you that? Let's start at the beginning. You need to know something about what a mutual fund is as well as the various kinds of funds and how they can be expected to perform. You also need to know yourself, to get a handle on your own "investment personality" before you can determine the fund or funds that are right for you. After that, it's really pretty simple. Mutual fund investing can give you a personal edge in today's volatile financial markets. Once you find the fund for you, you can simply monitor its performance monthly or even quarterly.

WHAT IS A MUTUAL FUND?

If you looked up "mutual fund" in a financial dictionary, you might learn that it is a "diversified portfolio of securities, registered as an open-end investment company, which sells shares to the public at an offering price and redeems them on demand at net asset value." If that clears it up for you, you can probably skip the rest of this chapter. If not, read on.

A mutual fund pools the money of many people and invests it in stocks, bonds, money market instruments and other securities. Funds set a minimum amount that you can invest. Sometimes it's $1,000 or more; sometimes as little as $250; but it can even go as low as $50 if you're willing to invest on a regular monthly basis. The money you invest is pooled with that of other investors and is used to purchase stocks, bonds, or money market securities in the U.S. financial markets or other financial markets around the globe. Investors share in the fund's gains, losses, income, and expenses on a proportional basis.

There are thousands of mutual funds, but each one has a stated investment objective. This is your guide to what kind of investments the

STOCK SENSE

Buying stock means you become part owner of a company. You share in its prosperity and your investment suffers during its hard times.

Most companies pay dividends on their common stock. Whether you buy stock on your own or through a mutual fund, your fortunes become those of the companies you own. If the company has a great year, it may raise the dividend and the share price may go up. If it is the object of a huge lawsuit, it might cancel the dividend and the share price might nosedive. The major advantage of buying stock through a mutual fund is that a professional is picking the stocks for you and diversifying your assets among a large group of stocks.

Professional money managers have a broad range of theories on how to beat the market. Some take a top-down approach, looking first at broad economic trends, deciding which industries might prosper, and finally picking stocks of individual companies in those industries. Others are bottom fishers, always looking for stocks they consider underpriced, regardless of the industry or the economic climate. Still others are contrarians, determining first what most investors seem to be doing and then taking off in the opposite direction. Some are fundamental analysts, ignoring everything but the fundamentals of the company. Others are technical analysts, who value stocks based on their previous trading patterns. And some are market timers. They move in and out of the market based on how they expect it to perform.

When you buy stock through a mutual fund, you must make two basic decisions. You have to decide what kind of stock fund you want, and you have to decide whether you want to get into the stock market for the long haul or do a little market timing of your own, moving out of a stock fund and into a cash or money market position when you think the stock market has peaked.

manager intends to make with your money. The fund's objective is one of the most important pieces of information for the investor. It tells you whether the manager is going to invest some or all of the fund in the stock market or in bonds or in money market instruments or some combination of these. It tells you whether the investments will be made in steady, predictable securities or aggressive high flyers in a single industry. Sometimes the name of the fund suggests the objective, like the Oppenheimer Global Bio-Tech Fund. But you can't rely on the name alone to form a sound investment decision. Understanding the fund objective requires some work on your part. This will be explained in Chapter 12.

When you invest in a mutual fund, you buy "shares" at a price that is recalculated every business day. Today you might invest $1,000 in

According to the Investment Company Institute, as of 1989, there were more than 2,800 mutual funds registered in the United States.

BOND BASICS

When you invest your money in a bond, your goal is to earn income and preserve principal. A bond is an investment that produces income at a specified rate and returns your principal at a specified time.

The easiest way to understand how bonds work is to think about what happens when you go to a bank to borrow money. The bank looks over your credit history. If it likes what it sees, you get the loan. For your part, you agree to pay a set rate of interest and to repay the loan over a specified period of time. When a large institution wants to borrow money, it may go to a bank the same way that you do. Or it may borrow from investors by issuing a bond, a transaction in which the investor essentially becomes the banker.

When you invest in a bond, you are making a loan to a corporation or a government agency. The institution that issues the bond promises to pay a set rate of interest, which is also called the coupon. And it agrees to repay the principal at a specific time. (You probably have to make monthly payments on your bank loan, but the bond issuer repays his loan in one lump sum when the bond matures, a date specified when the bond is issued.)

Your concerns as a bond investor are the same as those of the bank that loans you money: the first is the ability or willingness of the issuer to repay the money. Bonds are assigned letter grades that indicate creditworthiness by Moody's Investor Service and Standard & Poor's Corporation as well as other rating agencies. These letter grades serve the same purpose as your personal credit history; they give the lender, in this case the bond investor, an objective evaluation of the institution's ability to repay. The top rating goes to the U.S. government, then come corporations with a AAA rating, ranging down to those with a D rating, which means they are in default, and those that are classified as NR because they have no rating. The higher the credit rating, the lower the risk for the investor, and the lower the interest that the institution will offer to pay on its bond. Bonds issued by companies with a low rating or no rating are called "high yield" or "junk" bonds. They offer the highest interest rate of all because the investor assumes a higher level of risk.

The second concern for a bond investor is what a change in the direction of interest rates will do to his investment. Because the interest rate of your bond is locked in, the price of your bond—what you could sell it for on the open market—will fluctuate to reflect the change in interest rates. When interest rates rise, the price of the bond you hold falls.

When you buy a single bond, you are totally exposed to both credit risk and interest rate risk. One way of minimizing your risk is to invest in a bond mutual fund. The fund manager buys and sells bonds daily, spreading credit risk over a large number of issues. Since it is unlikely that all the companies whose bonds are in the portfolio will default, the investor gains a large measure of protection with the diversification offered by a bond fund. And when interest rates change, the fund manager will adjust the fund's average maturity to take advantage of the changing rates. This keeps the investor from being locked into a lower rate when rates are rising.

CASH—IT'S NO LONGER LOOSE CHANGE

Time was when people talked about cash, they meant the coins jingling in their pockets or the bills at home in the cookie jar. In the early 1930s, cash referred to cold, hard currency that you knew you could count on and that you could spend in the next 15 minutes if you wanted to.

In those days, money in the bank wasn't cash. But after Franklin D. Roosevelt signed the Banking Act of 1933 and created the Federal Deposit Insurance Corporation, which put a government guarantee behind bank deposits, Americans gradually began to accept banks and bank accounts, too, became cash.

Today, though, when investors talk about cash, they mean something entirely different from money in their pocket or even in a guaranteed bank certificate of deposit. When an investor says he is "in cash," he means he's not invested in the stock or bond markets. Instead, he's moved his money into a money market fund to earn short-term rates of interest and wait for a good opportunity to buy. "Cash" still means that the money is safe, liquid, easy to get to. But few savvy investors consider the cookie jar a sensible depository.

No matter how short-term their needs, most investors prefer to keep "cash" in a money market fund where they can write checks on it and earn interest until the day the check clears. Many keep their money market account in a fund family that also allows them to move the cash quickly into other investments if they choose.

Today a cash position is part of most balanced individual portfolios. An investor who is very conservative or who may need to tap his investments in a short time probably keeps more of his portfolio in cash. An aggressive investor who is very optimistic about the market may be "fully invested," meaning he has none of his money in cash.

A cash position is also essential in a market timing program, no matter how rudimentary. Some investors attempt to time even the slightest moves in the market, moving their investments from stocks to bonds to cash. Others, even though they don't consider themselves market timers, may move out of an investment and into cash to protect their gains if they become nervous about what's happening in the stock or bond markets.

Big institutional money managers use cash the same way individuals do—to balance their portfolios and to play their hunches. There's a great deal of interest in how much these money managers keep "in cash" because it's an indication of their expectation of market movements. If they have a high percentage of their portfolios in cash, it indicates that they don't like the current prospects for the stock and bond markets.

a mutual fund and pay $10 a share, getting 100 shares for your $1,000. Tomorrow the price might be $10.05 or $9.95. The share price changes each day with the value of the investments in the fund.

Perhaps you figure your net worth once a year, calculating everything you own and everything you owe. A mutual fund has to go

Net asset value (NAV)
Market value of one share of
a mutual fund. It is
calculated at the close of
each business day by taking
the value of all the fund's
assets, less expenses, and
dividing by the number of
shares outstanding.

through this exercise every business day. The fund calculates the value of all its investments—every share of every stock that it owns, plus the value of its bond holdings and how much it has in cash. Then all the fund expenses—salaries, services, and administrative costs—are subtracted from its assets. The final amount is divided by the number of shares in the fund, and the result is the value of a single share—the **net asset value** or **NAV.** (It is listed in the daily newspaper under these initials.)

$$\frac{\text{Current value of total fund assets} \quad minus \quad \text{Fund liabilities and expenses}}{\text{Total number of shares owned}} = \text{Net Asset Value (NAV)}$$

Management fee   Annual
fee paid by an investment
company to the managers of
a mutual fund, which usually
ranges from .5 percent to
1.5 percent of all the assets
in the fund. For income
funds, management fees can
be considerably lower. For
specialized sector funds,
they may be considerably
higher.

Mutual funds charge for their services. Funds charge a **management fee** to cover salaries and administrative expenses. On a per share basis, the management fee is usually quite small, because it is spread over thousands or millions of shares. These fees are sometimes expressed as an **expense ratio,** or a percentage of the fund's assets that is paid out in expenses. And there are a variety of other fees that are used in various combinations to compensate the fund's sales representatives or pay for the fund's marketing program. Many funds charge a sales fee when you put your money into the fund or a redemption fee when you take money out. Some get you both coming and going.

A fund company has an obligation to redeem your shares (give you your money back) *on demand.* The catch here is that your original investment may be worth more or less than when you made it. Remember, the share value is recalculated every day.

Expense ratio   Percentage
of a fund's assets that is
paid out in expenses.
Expenses include
management fees and all
fees associated with
distributing shares and
literature and administration
of the fund. The expense
ratio for most funds ranges
from as low as .2 percent of
the fund's assets to around
2.5 percent. Expenses can
go higher for funds that do
an extraordinary amount of
trading, but these exceptions
are few.

The Internal Revenue Service considers trading and selling mutual fund shares a taxable transaction. Doesn't Uncle Sam always find a way into these stories? There are special tax rules that govern mutual fund investments, so before you invest, you should familiarize yourself with them. We'll cover the fundamentals in Chapter 13 and elsewhere in the book, but you may want to consult your tax adviser or invest in a good tax book before you jump into the fray.

Investing in a mutual fund is much like buying a condominium. You pick your style, you buy your unit (your "share" of the place), and someone else manages it, for a fee, of course. However, such investments are more problematic to both buyers and sellers than condos or most other products you buy. Mutual funds are advertised and promoted like products. But when you buy a car or a pound of coffee, the manufacturer can be pretty specific about what you can expect for your money. (He can also add a little advertising pizzazz.)

Your demands can be pretty specific, too. If the car doesn't run, you return it. If the coffee doesn't fulfill its promise to start your day off right, you don't buy it again. But a mutual fund can't make the same kind of promises of performance. One of the reasons is that mutual fund companies don't know what the performance of the fund will be. Another is that mutual funds are stiffly regulated by the **Securities and Exchange Commission,** which doesn't allow them to promise anything that they can't deliver for certain. An automobile company can tell you that under normal driving conditions you will get 30 miles to a gallon of gas, because the company has done tests to prove it. But because no one knows exactly how the economy or the securities markets will perform, the sellers of mutual funds can't promise you a 15 percent return—or any return. That's important to remember when you consider investing: *Investments with the potential for significant returns offer no guarantees.* Still, mutual funds have several basic advantages over other investments with good potential return.

• *Safety.* Safety is a relative term when it comes to investing. If you value safety first and foremost, you can save your money in a bank where it will be insured by an agency of the federal government. Unlike a bank, mutual funds cannot guarantee a specific return, nor guarantee that your **principal** (the amount you invest) will never decrease in value. But mutual funds, which are sold by investment companies, are one of the most highly regulated of investments. A mutual fund must file a registration statement with the SEC. It must provide you with a **prospectus,** a booklet that gives you all the details about the fund.

The SEC requires that you receive complete and accurate information about your investment, that all mutual fund shareholders be treated equitably, and that no major changes in operation be made without their approval. Mutual funds must also disclose all fees, commissions, and other charges. Nevertheless, you take some risk when you invest in a mutual fund.

• *Liquidity.* The problem with many investments is that you can't get your hands on your money without a lot of red tape. There's no open market for many types of investments. Or, to use the language of

Securities and Exchange Commission Federal agency that regulates the securities industry. The SEC regulates the investment companies that manage mutual funds as well as the securities they offer and the salespeople who sell them.

Principal Amount of your original investment. If you invest $1,000, that amount is your principal.

Prospectus A formal, written offer to sell a security. The prospectus is required to disclose important information about the security. A mutual fund prospectus, for example, discusses the fund's history, investment objectives, performance, and management. Every mutual fund is required to publish a prospectus, which is offered free to anyone who requests it.

the financial community, these investments aren't *liquid*. If you want to sell your grandmother's antique brooch, for example, you have to find your own buyer. Mutual funds are a very liquid form of investment, as liquid as a checking account. You can take your money out of a mutual fund by making a phone call, by writing a check, or by having the money wired to your bank. Most of these transactions take less than a day.

• *Convenience.* You can invest in a mutual fund by mail, by telephone, or in person. You can make regular investments by having the money deducted from your bank account or paycheck. Most funds send you regular statements of all your account activity, including the forms you need to figure your taxes. You can reinvest the money earned in your mutual fund account or you can receive your income in a separate check. You can find out the value of your investment by calling the mutual fund company—in some cases, you can call 24 hours a day. And you can set up all sorts of special accounts, such as Individual Retirement Accounts, Keoghs, or custodial accounts for your children.

• *Professional management.* Information and experience are the keys to investment success. Unfortunately, most of us have little of either. That's why we need professional money managers. If you're lucky enough to have a nest egg in the millions, you'll have no trouble finding a private investment counselor to manage your account. If, like most of us, your savings are more modest, you can still get professional investment management by investing in a mutual fund. By pooling their assets, small investors can afford the services of a top-notch pro.

Today as much as 90 percent of the trading volume on the exchanges comes from life insurance companies, large corporate and public pension funds, and mutual funds—the so-called **institutional investors.** With millions, even billions in their care, these big money managers can move the market by buying or selling large blocks of stock. When you buy mutual fund shares, you move from being the little guy up against the market monoliths with their sophisticated trading techniques to being on one of the big guy's teams.

Professional money managers are among the first to gain access to the latest information on securities. They can call top executives at a company to find out what's going on behind the scenes and act on the

Institutional investor
Investor that manages large amounts of money for a big organization. Some examples of institutional investors are mutual funds, insurance companies, and pension funds. These investors account for the bulk of trading on the major exchanges.

INVESTMENT COMPANIES

There are two types of investment companies that invest the pooled funds of investors. Best known is the open-end company or mutual fund. A mutual fund actively buys and sells securities on behalf of its investors, based on the manager's outlook for the market. The value of the shares and the number of shares fluctuate from day to day as the value of the securities changes and the number of investors (shareholders) increases or decreases. The open-end investment company is prepared to sell and redeem, or buy back, shares on demand every day.

A closed-end investment company or investment trust differs from an open-end mutual fund in a couple of ways. First, it issues a fixed number of shares that are priced and traded like stocks on the major exchanges. The shares may trade at a discount (below) or a premium (above) the net asset value. Like the shares of individual stocks,

trading prices of closed-end funds are determined by a variety of things, including supply and demand. Although the investment company does not adjust the net asset value of the shares, it makes periodic reports of the value of the underlying securities.

A unit investment trust is a type of closed-end investment company that has both a fixed number of shares and a fixed portfolio, usually composed of bonds. The portfolio is not traded; it remains fixed until the securities in the portfolio mature. An investor purchases a slice of the portfolio and gets a proportionate share of both the income and any appreciation in the securities. It is usually possible for an investor in a unit trust to resell the shares to the dealer he bought them from, though he frequently takes a loss in the process. Unit trusts are designed to produce the best performance when held to maturity.

information quickly. And they have the leverage to make big trades quickly and at negotiated prices. It's like buying wholesale. Because the fund manager is buying and selling securities in bulk, the transaction costs are much lower than you would pay as an individual investor.

• *Low minimum investment.* If you've checked the price of Digital Equipment Corporation stock lately, you may have noticed that even at $95 (give or take a few dollars), you can't buy much for $1,000. In the stock market, if you purchase fewer than 100 shares, which is called a **round lot,** you pay a higher commission. Furthermore, if you buy Digital, change your mind, sell it, and buy American Express, you've just paid three sets of commissions. Even if you use a discount broker, that's a lot of loose change.

The average investor fares much better with a mutual fund. Most have fairly low initial minimums, say $1,000, and they allow you to

Round lot   Stock purchase of 100 shares. Other securities, like bonds, also have round-lot trading units, but mutual fund shares do not. When you invest in a mutual fund you decide how much money you want to invest and the fund company allots you shares and fractional shares depending on the price of the fund.

make subsequent investments in increments of about $250. These amounts are lower for retirement accounts and certain types of investing plans. If you pay a sales charge on your investment, you usually don't have to pay it again if you decide to move from a stock fund to a bond fund within the same company. Once you're in, you're in, and you can reshuffle your portfolio without paying additional fees.

Odd lot   Unit of stock that is sold in other than 100-share lots. For example, 25 shares of IBM is an odd lot. Investors pay a higher commission on odd lots.

• *Diversification.* What can you do if all you have is $1,000 to invest? If you buy just one stock and it hits the skids, you can lose most of your investment. Realistically, you can't buy three or four different stocks, even if you buy an **odd lot** of less than 100 shares. You would have only a handful of shares of each and the commission would be prohibitive. It's true that you could buy a bond for $1,000. But you might make a bad choice, and the issuer might default. You get the picture. Diversification is to investing what location is to real estate. It's just about everything. If you have a diversified portfolio, you don't get caught holding the bag if one security—or one market—goes in the tank. Diversification means you're prepared to weather the storms.

A mutual fund offers instant diversification. With one investment, you can own a slice of perhaps a hundred different stocks. You can protect yourself from an unhappy surprise in one particular company because you are the owner of lots of companies. If your mutual fund owns a hundred stocks and one company goes belly up, you know there are 99 more that may be doing a whole lot better.

• *Reinvestment.* If you buy an individual stock, stock dividends are paid in cash. That means they sit in your brokerage account earning no interest—or they may be invested in a money market account earning interest at market rates. But when you invest in a mutual fund, you can elect automatic reinvestment of dividends and capital gains in your mutual fund. When the fund pays dividends or distributes capital gains, the mutual fund manager immediately invests this money in more securities. There's no cost. It's convenient. And your money compounds much more quickly.

WHERE MUTUAL FUNDS CAME FROM

Mutual funds have been around for a long time, at least since King William I set one up in the Netherlands in 1822. But they haven't always offered all the advantages they do today. The first mutual fund, or *open-end fund*, the Massachusetts Investors Trust, was started in this country in 1924 and it still exists. But in the frenetic investment environment of the 1920s, mutual funds were overshadowed by *closed-end funds*, which were highly leveraged speculative accounts. Unlike open-end mutual funds, these closed-end funds are not required to post regular share prices or a net asset value each day. During the 1920s, many investors bought shares of closed-end funds by depositing as little as 20 percent of their total value, a practice that was allowed at the time. When the market collapsed in 1929, these speculators suffered heavy losses.

This unsavory practice gave all mutual funds a black eye. And, if there were any investors around in the 1930s, they weren't much interested in stocks—or in mutual funds. Toward the end of the Great Depression, the SEC began a lengthy investigation into some of the closed-end companies. The result was the passage of the **Investment Company Act of 1940,** which regulates the fund industry today.

The stock market started to pick up steam in the 1950s. But it was during the prosperous decade of the sixties that mutual funds evolved from a stodgy investment for the unimaginative to an exciting new investment vehicle with the opportunity for growth rather than just preservation of capital. A "new breed" of money manager—people like Gerry Tsai and Fred Carr—emerged as growth managers. Tsai's Capital Fund, which focused on big glamour stocks, gained 50 percent in 1965. Carr's Enterprise Fund, which looked for small, emerging growth companies, racked up a gain of over 117 percent in 1967.

Just as these successes whetted the appetite of investors, the 1969–70 bear market scared them away from stocks. But now mutual fund companies were willing to be innovative. They knew they couldn't rely solely on the stock market; they had to offer something for all kinds of market environments. One brilliant solution was the money market fund, which represented a safe harbor from stocks and an attractive investment when interest rates were high. When fund companies saw how money funds caught on, they began to look for ways to package all kinds of new investment products into mutual funds. For periods of falling interest rates, they came out with new kinds of bond funds. They introduced funds that invest in gold and precious metals and in the real estate industry, in international stocks and bonds and funds that invest in a single country or a single industry. Today the mutual fund

Investment Company Act of 1940   Federal law that regulates investment companies. The act requires registration with and regulation by the Securities and Exchange Commission. It requires investment companies to provide investors with complete and accurate information about mutual funds and other investment company products and protects them from abuses.

WALTER L. MORGAN AND THE WELLINGTON FUND

As a young investor in the early 1920s, Walter L. Morgan lost a lot of money by investing in a wildcat oil scheme and buying stock on margin in a utility merger that bombed. He took his lumps, became a Certified Public Accountant, and joined an accounting firm that is today known as one of the "Big Eight."

The ambitious young CPA bridled at the firm's bureaucracy, though, and soon left to set up his own accounting firm. Morgan & Company opened its doors in Philadelphia in 1925. He had some early luck: He signed up one of the city's wealthiest families, the Ludingtons, as well as one of its largest banks, First Pennsylvania.

But Morgan wanted to do more than line up rows of numbers. As people came to him for tax advice, he looked over their investments and advised them to sell one stock and buy another. It still wasn't enough to satisfy him. "There must be a better way to handle investment management than to advise a large number of individual accounts," he recalls thinking. "There must be a better way to diversify investments than the purchase of only a few securities."

Morgan found a stockbroker and an investment manager and at the end of 1928 set up one of the early open-ended investment companies that we know today as mutual funds. Industrial and Power Securities Company, later to be renamed The Wellington Fund, opened for business on July 1, 1929, with $100,000 in assets. Wall Street was enjoying one of its greatest bull markets. From a low of 65 in 1921, the Dow Jones Indus-

trial Average had risen to 300 by the end of 1928, Morgan recalls.

But from his own investing mistakes, Morgan knew that investments could go down as well as up. Most of the early investors had contributed securities to the fund rather than cash. And Morgan quite promptly sold the stocks. He remembers that he accepted Curtis Publishing at $123 a share and sold it at $124. It later plunged to $1 before the company declared bankruptcy, Morgan says. He sold U.S. Steel at $258 and watched it plummet to $24 within three years. Guaranty Trust was sold at $679; it plunged to $179.

Morgan might have had a good idea, but mutual funds were still a tough sell. "It was terrible to try to get going in those early days," he says. "Dealers were not interested in selling mutual funds. They wanted to trade customer's accounts. I had to sell the first million dollars myself."

Morgan is one of the few pioneers in the business who was still investing during the 1987 stock market crash. He took the same approach that year that he did in 1929—he got out of the stock market and into bonds or cash. Yet Morgan doesn't expect a repeat of the investment climate of the 1930s, when the Dow hit a low of 41. "In 1929 everything was leveraged at 10 percent margin," he says. "This time things are much more rational." And Morgan believes, despite the two market crashes he observed, that stocks are still the best investment bet. "No matter what stock you bought in the 1930s or 1940s, you're rich today," he says.

investor can choose among 2,800 funds offered by about 350 fund groups. No matter how old you are, how affluent, how aggressive or cautious, there is a mutual fund today to meet your needs and help you reach your goals.

POINTS TO REMEMBER

• Investing in mutual funds saves you time and gives you access to professional management and instant diversification for a small initial investment.

• Mutual funds pool the money of many different people and invest it in stocks, bonds, and other securities. Each fund has a specific investment objective.

• The share price of a mutual fund is recalculated every business day so you know exactly what your investment is worth. The company is obligated to buy back your shares at the current price whenever you choose to sell.

• Mutual fund investments are not risk-free. But the companies that sell them are highly regulated.

• Mutual funds are convenient. You can invest by mail or by telephone. And you can take your money out by making a phone call, writing a check, or having it wired to your bank.

• With the range of mutual funds available today, there's one to meet any investment goal.

Chapter 2

Coming to Terms with Risk

B efore you invest your first dollar in a mutual fund, you must think about risk. It's true that investing is risky. But so is not investing. If you stick your money in the mattress, it could be lost or stolen. If you simply save your money rather than invest it, your risk is that it will be eaten up by **inflation.** In other words, whatever you do with your money can be risky. If you want to get ahead of inflation, investing is the best option. But before you invest, think about how much investment risk you'll be comfortable with. That will help determine which *types* of investments are best for you.

When financial people talk about risk, they may mean a few different things. One is market risk, or the chance that your investment will be affected by what the markets are doing in general. Another is interest rate risk, the chance that your investment will be affected by a rise or decline in interest rates. Or they may mean credit risk, which is the chance that your investment will be affected by a change in the creditworthiness of the institution that backs your investment.

But when you think about risk, it's probably much more straightforward. For most of us, risk comes down to two questions. The first question is, how likely is it that we will get our money back, or: *What is the risk to my principal?* In other words, if you put $1,000 in a mutual fund, you wonder whether you will ever see that $1,000 again. Will part of it disappear in some mysterious way? But that's not your only concern. You don't invest just to get your money back. If you did,

Inflation   Increase in the price of goods and services, most commonly measured by the Consumer Price Index (CPI). The average annual rise in the CPI from 1973 through 1988 was 6.6 percent. But during that period, it was as high as 13.3 percent in 1979 and as low as 1.1 percent in 1986.

you'd be shopping around for the bank with the sturdiest vault. So the second question is: *What is the likely return on my investment?*

Coming up with the answers to these questions is not an exact science. But there are some things you should keep in mind.

Risk and reward go hand in hand. OK, you've heard this a hundred times. But it's not an old wives' tale. The evidence is abundant. It's the first principle you need to grapple with. If you had invested in a high-technology mutual fund between 1981 and mid-1983, you could have made a lot of money. If you invested in the same sector of the market before the market decline of 1987, you probably lost a lot, maybe even more than the market lost on average. And your investment dollars probably continued to shrink in 1988. Investing in a narrow segment of the market that is made up of small, untested companies with big growth potential is a high-risk gambit. When investors take on a lot of risk, they expect the potential rewards to be commensurate. But the downside of an investment with high potential returns is not that you could earn nothing, but that you could lose principal. So before you invest in a mutual fund, you need to assess the risk-reward relationship of your investment.

Money market fund

Mutual fund that invests in short-term debt obligations of governments and corporations. These accounts pay a market rate of interest that fluctuates from day to day. They always maintain a share price of one dollar. They are not insured, but they are extremely safe. They are also very liquid, which means you can get your money out quickly either by writing a check on the account or by transferring money into your bank account.

Sometimes this exercise is pretty straightforward. A **money market fund** is a low-risk investment. It's about as low in risk as a mutual fund investment can be, because the securities in the fund are backed by solid institutions and they have very short maturities. No investor has ever lost principal in a money market fund. The return is also likely to be relatively low, in line with current interest rates. As you move across the spectrum of risk, you should expect a higher return. The potential return should be worth the extra risk.

Consequently, the first question you must ask yourself before you invest is: "What will I do if the value of my investment principal declines?" Say you put $1,000 into an aggressive stock mutual fund. Six months later, the market declines and it's worth only $850. If the fundamentals of the fund remain unchanged and you find yourself thinking about pulling your money out, you probably weren't comfortable with the risk level of that fund in the first place. Think through that exercise before you make the investment, and especially consider whether you are prepared to ride out the possibility of early losses in your investment.

That said, it's worth noting that over time, the investor who is

THE FIRST MONEY MARKET FUND

In 1968, Bruce Bent went into business for himself, opening a Wall Street firm to help raise capital for corporations. But the following year, "interest rates went through the roof," Bent recalls, "which means they went to 8 percent." No one was willing to borrow money because it was too expensive. That meant Bent didn't have any business.

What to do? "I didn't want to go back to work for someone else," Bent says. So he put on his thinking cap. How could he turn the situation to his advantage? Because he didn't have much overhead, he could probably offer a higher rate of interest to depositors than they could get from a bank, loan the money out at a little less than the market rate, and still make a profit. All he needed to do was pay, say, 7 percent to depositors and turn around and loan the money out at 7.5 percent.

But here Bent ran into a major stumbling block—the Federal Reserve Board's Regulation Q, which imposed a 5.25 percent cap on the interest banks could pay on savings accounts. In order to offer a higher rate of interest, Bent needed to find a way around "Reg Q" or "make an end run on it," as he says. First he checked all 50 states to see if he could find any banks that weren't required to follow the regulation. There were a couple, but they had other peculiar and limiting rules.

Bent was stymied. "We needed a vehicle through which you could funnel money without Reg Q," he says. One day it came to him. Why not a mutual fund? The fund would accept money from depositors and turn around and make short-term loans to government and big corporations in the money markets, just like a bank did. But, because it wasn't a bank, it wouldn't be subject to Reg Q and it could pass the market rate of interest along to shareholders. Like other mutual funds, it would make money by charging depositors a management fee.

In February 1970, Bent filed his registration statement for a money market fund with the Securities and Exchange Commission. In November 1971, the SEC approved it. Bent set up The Reserve Fund, the first money market fund and an investment vehicle that would shake the financial services industry to its core and alter the way nearly everyone in America thought about money. It was the first mutual fund to offer instant access to money with same-day telephone redemption.

But the fund initially attracted little interest, picking up only $300,000 in assets during the first year. Then in January 1973, Bob Hershey of *The New York Times* wrote a half-page story for the Sunday edition under this headline: "Mutual Fund for Overnight Money." Bent's money market fund took off. "On Monday we got 100 phone calls," Bent says. "It was tough with only two guys to answer the phone." By the end of the month, the fund had $1.8 million in assets. By the end of the year, it had $100 million.

By this time, lots of other companies had noticed the money market fund. And by 1974, Bent no longer had the field to himself. The big mutual fund companies quickly introduced money funds. And they offered new twists: check writing, switching among other funds in the family, and wire transfers to banks. Investing would never be the same.

willing to assume more risk historically has been rewarded with a higher return. Over time, the stock market has provided the best average annual return. But it's also been the most volatile. For example, it fell 25 percent in 1930 and another 43 percent in 1931, but it gained 53 percent in 1954 and piled on another 32 percent in 1955.

Because the stock market provides the best returns, it follows that stock mutual funds have a higher risk/reward ratio than other types of mutual funds such as bond or money market funds. A review of the financial markets over the past ten years moving down the spectrum of risk would show that capital appreciation mutual funds (growth stocks) provided an average annual return of 16.2 percent. Growth and income funds, a more conservative investment in stocks *and* bonds, grew at an average annual rate of 15.6 percent. U.S. government bond funds, a still more conservative investment, provided an average annual return of 10.5 percent, and money market funds returned an average of 9.9 percent per year.

How do you determine the risk/reward relationship of a particular mutual fund? By law, the fund must spell out the elements that will influence the fund's stability and performance. But sometimes it can be difficult to wade through the technical language in its sales literature. For example, here is a fairly simple risk statement from the prospectus of a fund that invests in the stocks of solid, established companies: ''The fund focuses on quality blue chip companies that have good earnings prospects, in the belief that their stocks will grow in value.''

You notice that there is no promise that you will make money or even that you will not lose money. But you probably know what blue-chip stocks are: The stock of companies like IBM, American Express, Exxon, AT&T, General Electric. If you invest in the stock market, blue chips are the safest investment; they offer the lowest risk. If the economy prospers and the stock market advances, blue-chip stocks should do well.

But here is another example, a risk statement for a fund that invests in bond markets all over the world: ''As with any bond investment, the fund's yield and share value may be positively or negatively affected by changes in interest rates or by the market's perception of the creditworthiness of the issuers the fund invests in. Because most securities of foreign issuers are not rated by U.S. rating services, their selection depends to a great extent on our firm's credit analysis. In addition, the

THE FOUR "R'S" OF INVESTMENT RISK

Many people think of investment risk as the chance that their investment decision will result in the loss of part or all of their money. That's true, but it's really too narrow a definition of risk.

When you're investing, you need to think of at least three more risks: inflation risk, opportunity risk, and reinvestment risk.

Inflation is a general and continual increase in the prices of the things you need to buy. The cost of housing, clothing, medical care, and food all increase. At some times prices rise more quickly and at other times more slowly. But rarely do the prices of basic goods and services go down. Obviously you need to make more money in order to pay for the things you need to buy. You risk losing your money to inflation if you don't invest at all or if the investments you choose don't earn enough to keep pace with inflation.

Say you have $10,000 that you plan to use for a down payment on a house in five years. If you keep it in your checking account and earn no interest and inflation averages 3 percent over those five years, your $10,000 will have real purchasing power of $8,626.09 at the end of that period. If you put it in a passbook account and earn 5.25 percent, you will have $11,141.01 after inflation.

You know what opportunity is. The risk here is that you will tie up your investable dollars in a ho-hum investment and lose the chance to put them into something with real growth potential. Most often, opportunity risk has to do with the changing investment environment. Say you buy a five-year certificate of deposit with an interest rate of 8 percent. One year later, interest rates shoot up to 11 percent. Because you've locked up your money over the long term, you've lost the opportunity to put it somewhere more attractive. You can't get out of the CD unless you pay a penalty.

Reinvestment risk also has to do with the changing investment environment. When you make an investment decision today, you face the uncertainty of whether you can reinvest dividends, earnings, or even your principle at the same earnings rate next month or next year.

For example, if you invest $10,000 in a bond that matures in five years and pays 8 percent, you will earn 8 percent on that $10,000 until the bond matures. But you have no guarantee that you will be able to reinvest the earnings at 8 percent. Perhaps interest rates will fall and you will only be able to reinvest the interest at 5 percent. Furthermore, you have no idea what the market rate of interest will be when your bond matures in five years. Perhaps you will be forced to reinvest your money in a very low-interest-rate environment.

Reinvestment risk is a big factor for investors when they pick long-term investments. When the country is in a period of high interest rates, as it was in the early 1980s, and you think that rates are about to peak and start to fall, you would be smart to choose the longest-term fixed rate you could get. For example, in 1982, it was possible to lock in a 14 percent fixed rate on a bank certificate of deposit. Smart investors picked the longest-term CD they could find.

fund's yield and share value may be affected by changes in the relative strength of foreign currencies and the U.S. dollar, or by political or financial developments in foreign countries.''

You get the picture. If you are overwhelmed by the complexity of the language, you may have already figured out that this could be a risky investment. There is a lot to consider in this prospectus. That doesn't mean the fund is a bad investment. But it does mean its performance is dependent on a great many different things. If you bought the blue-chip stock fund described above, you would expose yourself to the risk that the U.S. stock market would not do well. But if you choose a fund that invests in bonds all over the world, you expose yourself to many different types of risk. As the types of risk multiply, so does the overall risk level of the fund.

There is another factor to be considered when you're weighing the risk/reward relationship: your time horizon, or how much time you have to invest your money before you need it for your retirement, a down payment on a home, or college tuition. Your time horizon is crucial because investments have up cycles and down cycles. If your investment goal is far off in the future, you can afford to take more risk because you can hold on through the down cycles. If your goal is only a few years away, you should consider a more stable, less risky investment. For investment purposes, a short time horizon means a minimum of three years. A long time horizon is ten years or more. There are also investments for intermediate-term goals that fall in between. But if you are only six months away from your goal, you can't really be an investor. Instead, you must simply *save* your money.

An investor should go through this risk/reward exercise before selecting any mutual fund. But the best way to balance your risks is through diversification. Once you have decided to invest, you should select more than one mutual fund and spread your assets around. You may be comfortable with risk or you may be risk averse. Either way, don't put all your eggs in one basket.

Diversification is one of the chief reasons for investing in a mutual fund rather than buying stocks or bonds on your own. But no matter how modest the size of your investments or how diverse the mutual fund, you need more than one mutual fund. You should think in terms of a **portfolio.** Perhaps this sounds intimidating, but all it really means is that you're putting together a group of mutual funds that invest in

Portfolio   Collection of securities and other investments such as stocks, bonds, gold, art, and real estate.

YOU CAN'T ESCAPE IT BY NOT INVESTING: MICHAEL LIPPER ON RISK

"What little I know about life, I learned in two places," says Michael Lipper, president of Lipper Analytical Services, "the Marine Corps and the racetrack." What those two places taught him, he says, is that there are two kinds of people in the world: the gamblers and those who don't know that they're gamblers.

The way Lipper sees it, everyone is constantly at risk. "I can't avoid risk," he says. "What I can do is manage my affairs so that when something unexpected happens, I can isolate how bad it is." The number-one risk for most people is that they will lose their jobs. "The Fortune 500 companies have been a net contributor to unemployment in this country," according to Lipper. "If you do a balance sheet for most people, the biggest single investment they have is their job." The way to hedge that risk, he says, is to invest away from your job.

For example: "If I was an executive in an old industry like the steel industry in an old town, I would be investing in the Japanese steel industry or in companies that make facsimile machines because they would reduce the need for transportation. I would always be hedging my bets."

Further, Lipper says, everyone in this country has a dollar risk. If the dollar moves up or down against other currencies, your investments are worth more or less. For this reason, he believes that you must invest outside this country as well as in it.

Lipper, whose company tracks the performance of mutual funds, invests in mutual funds himself. He thinks an investor needs five funds to provide enough diversity: a short-term bond fund, a long-term bond fund, a middle-of-the-road equity fund, and two specialty funds. The specialty funds might be gold, international, sector funds, or a fund managed by a portfolio manager with a unique style.

different securities and in different markets in order to limit your risk. You're not betting on a single type of fund, on a single type of market, or on a single portfolio manager. Rather, you should realize that the economic picture and your own situation are going to change throughout your life and you are attempting to put together an investment portfolio that will hedge your bets, that will perform well in all types of situations.

Consider the case of two families, the Fowlers and the Kellers. The two couples married shortly after they finished college in 1970. Fortunately, both were thrifty and they immediately began saving money. By 1973, both couples bought their first homes. The Fowlers, happy with their real estate investment and with their discipline, were content

Certificate of deposit (CD)
Time deposit at a bank or savings and loan institution. When you buy a CD, you agree to leave your money in the bank for a specific period of time, which may range from 30 days to several years. In exchange, the bank guarantees you a specific interest rate, higher than that paid on a passbook account. If you take your money out early, you pay a penalty. Bank CDs are insured by the FDIC. You can also buy CDs from a stockbroker. The broker can canvass in the country and get you the best rate. However, you must pay a fee for the service.

NOW account Bank checking account that pays interest. These accounts were introduced in 1974 to help banks compete with money market mutual funds.

Cash management account
Brokerage account developed by Merrill Lynch in 1977. This type of account, which is now offered by many financial service companies, allows investors to buy and sell securities as well as to tap the account by writing checks or by using a credit card to make purchases. Idle cash is swept into a money market fund.

to let their nest egg build in a savings account. They were proud that they religiously put away $200 a month, $2,400 a year, come hell or high water.

The Kellers liked their house, too. And when inflation took off in the mid-1970s, they knew they had bought it at just the right time. Lynn Keller, an engineer, didn't consider herself a gambler and was content to sock away the same $2,400 a year as the Fowlers. But Bob Keller started reading about investing. He became very concerned that the same inflation that was boosting the value of their home was eating away at their nest egg. In 1974, inflation topped 12 percent. Their passbook savings account was paying 5.25 percent. Like thousands of other American families during the mid-1970s, the Kellers decided they needed to consider some investment opportunities in order to stay ahead.

They did some research and started conservatively, moving their money into bank **certificates of deposit**—a great investment in the late 1970s when interest rates were soaring. At the same time, they moved some of their regular monthly savings into a money market fund and they opened a **NOW account** at the bank to earn interest on the money they needed to pay the bills. By the time interest rates peaked in 1982, they were ready to diversify. The Kellers moved cautiously into mutual funds—one half of their accumulated investment of just over $40,000 went into a couple of stock mutual funds; the other half into bond mutual funds. They didn't pick spectacular performers. Their funds garnered only an average return. Still, they participated in the long bull market and suffered through the October 1987 market crash. By this time, the Kellers were getting comfortable with investing. They opened a **cash management account** at a brokerage company and consolidated their growing portfolio in one place. The Kellers had put away $36,000 over a 15-year period. Even after the crash, they had an investment portfolio of $88,357. The Fowlers, who saved the same $36,000, had accumulated $55,497 in their passbook account. They'd been too cautious even to move to a **money market deposit account** at the bank. (These calculations do not reflect taxes.)

Clearly most people would prefer to have the Kellers' nest egg rather than the Fowlers'. So why don't they go after it? Some are complacent, others are timid or just undisciplined. Probably many simply have no idea how to begin.

Understanding what mutual funds are and how they can work for you is the first step. Understanding risk and the importance of diversification is the next step. And confronting your own unique attitudes toward money, investing, and risk-taking is the final step before actually choosing a fund and investing.

Money market deposit account *Insured bank account that pays a market rate of interest. Offered by banks beginning in December 1982. Interest is recalculated monthly.*

POINTS TO REMEMBER

• When you look at investment risk, you might ask yourself first What is the risk to my principal, the amount I invested? Your second question should be: What is the return likely to be on my investment?

• Risk and reward go hand in hand. As the potential return of an investment increases, so does the risk.

• There is no investment that can promise high returns with no risk.

• Mutual funds are required to spell out in their sales literature the investment risks they will take.

• Even though you're buying a diversified mutual fund, you should try to build a portfolio with more than one fund, investing in more than one financial market.

Chapter 3

Zeroing In on Your Investment Personality

The relationship between a person and his money is one of the most mystical, intimate, and primitive marriages in our modern society. Your feelings about your money—how much you have, how you spend it or save it—probably have less to do with whether you're rich or poor than with the way you weigh security and opportunity in all aspects of your life.

Consider this story: Two professional women commuted to work together in Minneapolis every day for ten years. Gloria felt comfortable with her money. If she saw something she felt she couldn't live without, she bought it. If it were particularly expensive, she scrimped somewhere else. She also made some prudent investments. The point is, though, that she enjoyed the things she did with the money she earned. Her friend, Esther, resented every dime she was forced to spend. And she resented Gloria's wardrobe, her investments, and her contentment.

Then Esther came into some money, about a half million dollars, from a buyout of the company where her husband worked. Now Esther had much, much more money than Gloria. But having it didn't change her attitude toward her money; it didn't make her comfortable spending it. She bought a dark, cramped apartment on the second floor of a building on a noisy street in downtown Minneapolis. She took the bus wherever she went. And when she went to lunch with Gloria, even though they ordered almost the same thing, she always pulled out her pocket calculator when the check arrived to make certain she wasn't getting ripped off. Although she had plenty of money for the things she wanted to buy, she didn't enjoy spending it. Or saving it. Or investing it.

Compare Esther's cautious—almost adversarial—approach to her money with that of Sue Beyrau, an accounting manager for a St. Louis printing company. Sue has fun with her money, whether she invests it or uses it to splurge on something she wants. Sue knew nothing about investing when she opened an **Individual Retirement Account** in 1982. But she had no time for wimpy investments like certificates of deposit either. "I had never even dabbled in the market before," Sue says, "so I just jumped right off the cliff." For her first IRA, she picked American Capital Pace, a moderately aggressive stock mutual fund.

The second year, deciding that her first investment was a bit speculative, she opted for a bond fund—IDS Extra Income Fund—to balance her investment portfolio. The third year, as she gained knowledge about investing, Sue split her $2,000 IRA investment between shares of a utility stock and options, a highly speculative investment. When her options doubled in value within two months, she backed off a bit. But then she dived back in, buying more options that "absolutely went down the tubes." Did that cause her to run for shelter? Hardly. A few months later she had invested all her IRA money in warrants, a longer-term option to buy stock at a specified price and another highly speculative investment.

Sue, 43, may have moved from novice to high roller in record time. But her basic attitude about money probably didn't change. She was no doubt always a high-risk person at heart. Her IRA was simply the catalyst that brought her into the market. And once she started investing, she was hooked. For her it became a hobby; she spent a lot of time learning and a lot of time trading. In 1982, the year IRAs became tax deductible for most Americans, Sue and her husband, Jerry, had about $20,000 in savings—all of it in the bank. By 1988, they had a $125,000 portfolio, and none of it was in the bank. What they considered their liquid cash—about $20,000—was deposited in a tax-free fund that invested in high-risk municipal bonds.

Sue spends a great deal of time reading about investing and the

Individual Retirement Account (IRA)   Personal account for retirement. Employees who have no company pension plan or who earn less than $25,000 a year ($40,000 as a married couple) can contribute $2,000 a year and deduct it from income for tax purposes. A partial deduction is allowed for single taxpayers who earn up to $35,000 a year and for married taxpayers up to $50,000. Earnings on IRA investments accumulate tax-free until the account holder takes them out at retirement.

markets, although she claims three hours on the weekends and a half hour each morning over the newspaper would suffice. Her free-wheeling attitude about money stretches to parts of her life that have nothing to do with investing as well. This woman is no coupon clipper. For their twenty-fifth wedding anniversary in 1988, Sue and her husband planned to buy themselves a classic 1973 Corvette. Although the October 1987 market crash canceled those plans, it made them no more timid about money. A week after the crash, they started buying stock again. "If Macy's gave a sale, customers would be knocking down the doors," Sue said. "Now all of America's on sale and nobody shows up."

Sue is probably not a typical investor. For one thing, she's extremely active. She calls her **discount broker** hourly for stock quotes. She made about 65 trades in her personal account in 1987 and, despite the crash, she ended the year almost even. But she does know herself well. And, unlike Esther, she's comfortable with the money decisions she makes and they usually bring her pleasure. (A bad investment can cause a little pain, but she steps right back up to bat.)

Investment advice books discuss risk tolerance because it's important to match an investment to your appetite for risk. Sue's risk tolerance is high. But attitudes about money go deeper than risk tolerance. Some people, like Gloria and Sue Beyrau, have healthy attitudes toward their money. Before you can choose the kind of investments that are right for you, you need to do a little soul-searching. And maybe you need to decide if you're comfortable with money as well as whether you're comfortable with risk.

Perhaps you might even want to change your relationship with money a bit. Let's say you only feel comfortable investing where you know your money is "guaranteed." Six years ago, Sue, too, had her money in the bank, where it was guaranteed by the Federal Deposit Insurance Corporation. Maybe with a little more knowledge about investments, you, too, might loosen up and feel comfortable going after moderate risk/moderate return investments. On the other hand, maybe your investing experiences haven't been positive because you've picked very speculative investments and they haven't done well. You might feel you need some discipline. Or perhaps you're just a diehard conservative who can't sleep at night if the status of your investment is in doubt. You simply must feel secure with an invest-

Discount broker *Brokerage house that executes orders to buy and sell securities at a price significantly lower than that charged by a full-service broker. To keep their costs down, discount brokers don't offer advice, recommendations, guidance, or other related services. Their employees are paid salaries rather than commissions, which also helps keep prices lower.*

ALVIN CLOTZMAN DECIDED IT WAS TIME TO RETHINK HIS INVESTMENT PERSONALITY

When he retired in 1982, Alvin Clotzman had no pension. Because he knew he would have to live off his savings, Clotzman "got conservative" with his investments, he says. To some retirees, getting conservative might mean putting their savings in the bank. To Clotzman it meant moving from trading individual stocks and bonds to mutual funds.

Clotzman, 70, of Springfield, Virginia, says he's always had a healthy appetite for risk that has been seasoned over the years by experience. An entrepreneur who built his own sporting goods business, he took the same kind of risks with his money as he did with his professional life. But he never made the same mistake twice.

For example, he put $15,000 into wheat futures the day before President Jimmy Carter declared an embargo on grain exports to the Soviet Union. The embargo sent the price of wheat plunging and Clotzman couldn't sell because there were no buyers. He lost the whole $15,000 and he never traded wheat futures again. "It was an expensive lesson and I learned it," Clotzman says. "No one else could have taught it to me. I had to learn it myself."

It didn't make him risk averse, though. Until a couple of years before he retired on August 1, 1982, Clotzman continued to trade stocks. Then he started moving his assets gradually into mutual funds. By the time he retired, he was entirely invested in mutual funds. But he acknowledges that what he considers a conservative portfolio might give other retirees a jolt. About 75 percent of his portfolio is in bonds. But that portion is concentrated in junk bonds, international bonds, and some intermediate-term bond funds. The remainder is invested in growth stock funds, mostly funds that invest in the stocks of small, emerging growth companies, and a small amount is in a foreign currencies fund. Clotzman considers the emphasis on bonds to be conservative.

On the day he retired, Clotzman instructed all the mutual fund companies to send the monthly income on his investments to him rather than reinvesting them in the fund. Six years later, he was proud to report that he had been living very comfortably off his earnings. It had not been necessary for him to touch his capital. In fact, his initial investment had increased by 10 percent over that time. "My lifestyle has not changed," he says. "I have my home. I still belong to my country club. We have vacations when we please. We don't live a San Tropez existence, but we are comfortable."

Clotzman says he spends about 20 percent of his time reading investment publications like *Money* and *Changing Times* and monitoring his mutual fund investments. He moved into mutual funds because "I felt they use big bucks to hire the brains that are more qualified to make investment judgments than I am." They also allow him to move his money quickly.

For example, in early 1988, he had 10,000 shares of an international bond fund that was trading at just under $12 a share when the price started slipping. "With 10,000 shares, every time the price goes down a penny, you're losing $100," Clotzman says. He bailed out when the share price was $11.60. "I feel I have a built-in shield against disaster because I am in mutual funds," he says. "I can pick up the telephone and Presto! I'm in another fund." That doesn't happen when you're in wheat futures.

ment. If you had any money invested in the stock market or in **equity** (stock) mutual funds during the October 1987 market crash, your reaction to that loss in value should give you some insight into how well you can deal with **volatility.**

Your attitude toward risk will also depend to a certain extent on your age and the purpose of your investment. If you're 30 years old and you're putting money away in a retirement fund, maybe you feel that you can take a lot of risk. Or perhaps you want to buy a Persian rug for your home. The one you have your eye on costs $5,000 and you know there's no guarantee that your investment will appreciate even 1 percent a year. But for you, the pleasure of seeing and using the rug in your home is worth the risk. On the other hand, if you are investing to build a college fund for your 16-year-old son, perhaps you're not interested in taking any risk at all.

But be sure you aren't confusing risk with ignorance. If you invest in a mutual fund that is tied to aggressive growth stocks or a hot industry sector and you panic when the price plummets, that may be a reflection of your lack of information rather than your inability to tolerate risk. Perhaps you didn't know enough about the fund before you bought it and now you don't know enough to know whether you made a mistake.

Compare that investment with a real estate investment. When you decide to buy a home, you probably do considerable research to find a solid structure in a desirable location with certain features that will make the house lastingly attractive. Maybe you choose one with an in-law suite or a space for a live-in housekeeper because you think that these will be increasingly valuable features. You have the property inspected by an engineer. You check out the neighborhood, the schools, and the zoning regulations before you buy. Two years later, the housing market hits the skids. Do you bail out and move to a rental apartment? No. Your reasons for buying are still valid. You know the real estate market has its ups and downs. You made a sound choice and you stick with it, confident that, over time, your investment will do well.

The same thing should be true for your mutual fund investments. They may not provide a roof over your head, but if you "inspected the foundation" of your mutual fund in the same way you did your house, you would be confident enough to ride out the ups and

Equity Ownership interest in a corporation, which distinguishes stockholders from bondholders; a term often used interchangeably with stock, as in "He's invested in equities (stocks)," or "the equity (stock) market."

Volatility Tendency of a security to rise or fall sharply in value.

downs. For most people, risk and knowledge go hand in hand. After you become knowledgeable, you'll be more comfortable with risk. There will still be some variations of risk tolerance, of course. But those can be addressed for what they *really* are and you can find the appropriate investments to match your investment personality.

There's also a psychological factor to consider. Some people can't feel comfortable with a financial decision even though they know it's sound because it doesn't "feel right." Perhaps your financial planner suggests a tax shelter arrangement. You trust his integrity as well as his financial acumen. But there's something about the investment that you just don't feel fits you. That's probably a good reason to pass it up, even though it may be perfectly sound. But, on the other hand, you shouldn't throw reason out the window.

For example, consider Hugh Whitney. He decides to have extra money withheld from his paycheck each month for taxes so that he will build what he considers a "savings account" at the Internal Revenue Service. He knows as well as the rest of us that it doesn't make sense to let Uncle Sam have the use of his money for free all year. But he feels he just can't save unless he's "forced to." And he can't face up to the possibility of owing additional taxes if he doesn't have enough withheld. It doesn't make good money sense, but he's not losing his shirt. Not yet. But then, when Hugh gets his $850 refund, he blows the whole thing on some new stereo equipment because he feels he deserves a treat for having the discipline to "save." This is the kind of so-called conservative approach to financial management that begs for reform.

Or, worse yet, consider Marian Matthai's philosophy: She feels resentful that a change in the tax rules eliminated her right to take a $2,000 deduction for money she placed in an Individual Retirement Account. Because she earns more than $35,000 and works at a company that offers a pension plan, she no longer gets a tax deduction for an IRA contribution. Marian's decision is to "get even" with the Internal Revenue Service. So she has an extra $2,000 withheld from her paycheck during the year, gets the refund, and puts it in an account that she has earmarked for her retirement, although it is not designated as an IRA. Unfortunately, she's not making any point with the IRS. And, she's made a ridiculous financial decision that is costing her money. She would be much better off putting the $2,000 into a **nondeductible IRA** and letting it earn interest tax-free until retirement.

These money decisions have nothing to do with being risk tolerant or risk averse. They have to do with quirkiness. So rich is the lore about people's money quirks and so fascinating are their tales that Kathleen Gurney published a book about them: *Your Money Personality: What It Is and How You Can Profit from It* (New York: Doubleday, 1988; $18.95). Gurney, a psychologist who counsels people about how to overcome the negative aspects of their relationship with money, writes that people associate money with security, freedom, love, respect, power, and happiness.

She has some compelling examples. One young man spends $2,500 a year sending long-stemmed roses to women he's never met and then, once he's impressed them with his largess, he calls and invites them to dinner. A husband and father of five who is on welfare spends $2,000 a year on lottery tickets. A woman with an $85,000 salary proudly reports that she saves $1,000 a year by clipping supermarket coupons. And a successful salesman, who always takes a six-pack of beer when he attends a party, puts it in a place where no one can see it. When he's ready to leave, he retrieves it and takes it back home with him. You no doubt have your own favorite stories about the money quirks—or irks—of your spouse, your friends, your coworkers, and perhaps yourself.

People who consider themselves "conservative" or "risk averse" when it comes to money management have all kinds of excuses for taking some of the biggest risks in life—like leaving the financing of their children's education or their retirement to chance. If you're doing something that foolish, you should take a look at your options. You need to consider all kinds of risk: The risk that you will be without an income, without a pension, without money for a vacation, or without money to take advantage of a great opportunity like starting your own business.

To help you discover how to approach investing, take the quiz which begins on the next page. Remember, the investment types don't necessarily break down by age. A woman of 28 who just received an inheritance might fall into the same category as an older man who has received a lump sum from his company to buy him out of the pension plan. The similarities are in how much money you have, how long before you need it, how much time you're willing to spend, and your attitude toward risk.

Nondeductible IRA
Individual retirement account that is not eligible for a tax deduction. It allows higher wage earners who participate in company pension plans to continue to put away $2,000 a year in an account where earnings accumulate tax-free until withdrawal.

TEST YOUR ATTITUDE TOWARD RISK

To learn something about your attitude toward risk, you need to look beyond your ideas about finance. The decisions you make about everyday problems reveal a lot about your appetite for risk.

Your scores on this quiz may reveal some surprising things about your attitude toward risk. If you make your financial decisions with a spouse or a partner, each of you should take it separately.

1. Six months ago you stretched your budget to the limit to buy a new car. Yesterday your spouse lost his (her) job. Today is your wedding anniversary. You:

a. Make reservations at the best restaurant in town. You both need a boost.

b. Cancel your dinner reservations and eat a home-cooked dinner by candlelight at home.

c. Buy your spouse an expensive gift on credit and put your worries off for another day.

d. Scale down your celebration plans. Skip the expensive restaurant and settle for a movie, Chinese food, and a bottle of champagne.

2. You've been invited to a party at the home of a new neighbor and you're not certain about the appropriate dress for the event. You:

a. Call a friend or two to check out what they will be wearing before you make your decision.

b. Plan an attractive outfit that will be appropriate but not attention-grabbing.

c. Throw something on at the last minute.

d. Choose something that is bound to turn heads when you walk in the door.

3. You're planning to buy a house. Which of the following best reflects your strategy?

a. Go for a monthly mortgage payment that will fit precisely into your current budget and make the biggest down payment you can afford.

b. Stretch a little to fit the mortgage payment into your current monthly budget or borrow a little extra for the down payment.

c. Go for the biggest mortgage you can possibly afford, confident that your income will go up and your investment will appreciate.

d. You've found a place you just can't live without, but the price is well beyond your budget. You go for broke, borrowing additional money.

4. It's time to plan your vacation. You:

a. Discover a small ad in the newspaper for a 50-percent-off charter flight to Hawaii. You mail in your deposit and delight in your good fortune.

b. Call a trusted travel agent to suggest two or three places that he can vouch for, then pick one that sounds as if it has promise.

c. Take off on a mystery tour where the destination isn't revealed until you're en route.

d. Usually go to the same spot in the country or at the beach because it's comfortable.

5. Your friend takes you to an early morning sale at a nearby clothing outlet. The prices are reported to be great. The catch: You can't try anything on and you can't return it. You:

a. Plunk down $250 for a fabulous suit that you saw in a major department store for $500. The price is too good to pass up and you are willing to bet that it will fit or you can have it altered to your satisfaction.

b. Spend your time browsing but make no purchase because you're put off by the no try on, no return policy of the place.

c. Buy a couple of low-priced items figuring that you'll have lost just a little if the items don't fit.

d. Buy a half-dozen outfits because the prices are so unbelievable.

6. You're 30 years away from retirement. You:

a. Can't see any reason to do anything about it now.

b. Calculate exactly how much you'll need to maintain an acceptable lifestyle and begin putting away a percentage of your income that you estimate will grow to that amount.

c. Live frugally, and sock away an extra measure of savings; the stories of elderly people living in poverty scare you to death.

d. Figure you can live pretty well now and in retirement if you make some aggressive investments. With so much time to ride out the market ups and downs, you'd rather take some chances than be forced to alter your lifestyle now.

7. You're on a television game show. The host gives you the following options. Which would you choose?

a. He'll give you $1,000 in cash and the game is over.

b. He'll give you $2,000 worth of merchandise for your home. It's behind the curtain, and you can't see what it is.

c. You can flip a coin. If you win, you take home $5,000. If you lose, you get nothing.

d. You can spin a wheel, and take the amount indicated when the spinner stops. There are ten possible amounts that range from $100 to $25,000.

8. The weather forecaster predicts a major snowstorm. It's 3:00 P.M., and as you look out your office window, you see that it has begun to snow lightly and many of your friends are getting ready to leave. You:

a. Ignore the weather report and look forward to your plans to have a drink with some friends after work.

b. Wait around for an hour and keep tabs on the situation.

c. Head out the door immediately. You don't want to get caught in traffic if conditions worsen rapidly.

d. Go back to your desk and resolve to let the worriers get a head start. You'll leave after the panic-stricken have cleared the streets. At worst, you can spend the night in a local hotel.

9. Your friend calls up on a Saturday afternoon and asks if you'd be willing to go out on a blind date that night. You:

a. Decline. You never consider blind dates.

b. Accept on the spot. Adventure appeals to you.

c. Ask some questions to determine whether the person is likely to be a good match and then make a decision.

10. You are starting to get restless in your job. You think you deserve a promotion, so you ask for one. Your boss says not just yet. You:

a. Plan to work even harder, keep careful records of your accomplishments, and try again at your next review.

b. Threaten to quit.

c. Ask for a firm commitment in terms of time, conditions to be met, and so forth that will assure your promotion. Make it clear that you expect to be promoted or you will be looking elsewhere.

d. Refresh his memory with a list of your accomplishments and ask for reconsideration.

11. You think your boss is brilliant, but with him in charge, you're never going to get anywhere. Then he decides to start his own business and invites you to come along as the number-two person. You:

a. Go with him for a higher salary but no equity in his company.

b. Go with him for a pay cut and a share of the company.

c. Stay where you are and hope for the promotion to his job.

12. You're at the blackjack table in Las Vegas with a hand that totals 16 points. Recognizing that coming as close to 21 points as possible without going over is the object of the game, you:

a. Stand pat.

b. Take another card.

13. You have a friend who opens a business. She does so well that her husband quits his job and joins the business. They are looking for a couple of private investors to finance an expansion into three new locations. Their research shows a promising market; you have confidence in their management skills; and you have a substantial savings account that you don't need for any near-term expenses (i.e., it's not your "emergency" fund). You:

a. Keep half your money in savings and invest half in the business.

b. Hold on to your savings.

c. Liquidate your savings and put the total proceeds into the business. This is exactly the kind of opportunity you've been seeking.

d. Liquidate your savings, put the total proceeds into the business, and borrow additional money to invest.

14. You put 10 percent of your investment portfolio in gold because you believe it is a good idea to have some portion of your money in gold. Gold prices climb steadily for six months, then fall 30 percent in a month. You:

a. Resolve to hang in there.

b. Sell out as quickly as possible.

c. Buy more.

d. Sell half of your holdings.

15. You inherit a diamond ring worth $5,000. You consider insuring it and decide to:

a. Insure the full appraised value.

b. Insure the appraised value minus a $500 deductible, thereby lowering your premium.

c. Not insure it at all.

Scoring

Now it's time to see what kind of risk-taker you are. Total your score, using the point system below for each answer you gave.

1. a.5/b.1/c.7/d.3   8. a.9/b.3/c.1/d.5
2. a.1/b.3/c.7/d.5   9. a.1/b.5/c.3
3. a.1/b.3/c.5/d.7   10. a.1/b.9/c.3/d.5
4. a.9/b.3/c.5/d.1   11. a.3/b.5/c.1
5. a.5/b.1/c.3/d.9   12. a.1/b.5
6. a.7/b.3/c.1/d.5   13. a.3/b.1/c.5/d.9
7. a.1/b.3/c.7/d.5   14. a.5/b.1/c.7/d.3
                       15. a.1/b.3/c.9

If You Scored . . .

15–31   You're a staunch conservative and you probably won't change. Accept it and consider investments to match.

32–58   You're willing to take prudent risks if you think they might pay off. Choose investments that balance both growth and income.

59–82   You feel comfortable taking risks in many areas of your life. Do your homework and select some aggressive investments as part of your portfolio.

Over 83   Be careful. You have a tendency to take enormous risks. If this carries over into your investing, you may be foolhardy. Consider the downside risk of some of your decisions and make certain you could live with the results.

INVESTOR PROFILE SCORECARD

Now that you have an idea of your general tolerance for risk, complete this investor profile scorecard. Tally your points at the end of the quiz and see whether your profile score and your risk tolerance score (from p. 52) are compatible. It is important to look at both scores to get a complete financial profile.

1. If your age is:

    a. Under 29, give yourself 5 points.

    b. Between 30 and 39, give yourself 4 points.

    c. Between 40 and 50, give yourself 3 points.

    d. Between 51 and 62, give yourself 2 points.

    e. Over 62, give yourself 1 point.

2. If your current investment assets are:

    a. Under $2,000, give yourself 1 point.

    b. Between $2,000 and $5,000, give yourself 2 points.

    c. Between $5,000 and $10,000, give yourself 3 points.

    d. Between $10,000 and $50,000, give yourself 4 points.

    e. More than $50,000, give yourself 5 points.

3. If your current income is:

    a. Under $25,000, give yourself 1 point.

    b. Between $25,000 and $35,000, give yourself 2 points.

    c. Between $35,000 and $50,000, give yourself 3 points.

    d. Between $50,000 and $100,000, give yourself 4 points.

    e. More than $100,000, give yourself 5 points.

4. Pick the statement below that best describes your future earning power and add the corresponding points to your tally.

    a. I am concerned that my future earnings will not keep pace with inflation. (You may be retired or approaching retirement or working in a profession in which the pay fails to keep up with inflation.) (1 point)

    b. I expect my future earnings to just keep pace with inflation. (2 points)

    c. I expect that future promotions and pay increases will keep me a couple of points ahead of inflation so that my income will grow steadily in real dollar terms. (3 points)

    d. I expect future earnings increases will far exceed the rate of inflation. (You may just be getting started in a well-paid profession or business enterprise.) (4 points)

    e. I expect to receive a large amount of money in inheritance or from a pension plan payout or some other source. (5 points)

5. My major financial goals are:

    a. Zero to two years away. (1 point)

    b. Two to five years away. (2 points)

    c. Five to ten years away, or a combination of a and e. (3 points)

    d. More then ten years away. (5 points)

6. Pick the statement below that best describes your current situation and add the corresponding points to your tally.

    a. I rarely, if ever, save or invest my money. (1 point)

    b. I try to put away a little money now and then, whenever I have money left over at the end of the month or I receive a bonus or a gift. (2 points)

    c. I save or invest fairly regularly, in an amount that is less than 5 percent of my gross income, including any bonuses or gifts. (3 points)

d. I save or invest fairly regularly, in an amount that exceeds 5 percent of my gross income, including any bonuses or gifts. (4 points)

e. I always discipline myself to save or invest at least 5 percent of my gross income, including any bonuses and gifts. (5 points)

7. Give yourself one point for each of the following that you do regularly.

a. Skim the financial pages of the newspaper now and then.

b. Read the financial pages of the daily newspaper.

c. Tune in to the daily stock market news on radio or TV.

d. Usually know how the market performed each day.

e. Subscribe to or read at least one general financial or investment publication in addition to the daily newspaper.

f. Subscribe to an investment newsletter.

g. Watch investment or financial programs on TV.

8. Pick the statement below that best describes your current knowledge of investing and add the corresponding points to your tally.

a. I know very little about investing. If someone asked me what a money market fund is, I wouldn't know how to reply. (1 point)

b. I know a few things about investing but not enough to feel comfortable explaining it to others. (2 points)

c. I understand most basic investment terms and the fundamentals of how the financial markets work, but I wouldn't go beyond the basics in discussing investments with others. (3 points)

d. I have enough knowledge to feel comfortable explaining different investments to others, but I wouldn't venture into a discussion on futures, options, or commodities. (4 points)

e. I consider myself a knowledgeable investor. I am comfortable explaining sophisticated investment concepts, such as futures, options, or commodities, to others. (5 points)

Total your score.

If you scored less than 17 points, you should exercise caution in your investment decisions. If you also scored in the conservative category on the first quiz, this quiz further confirms that a conservative strategy will serve you well. If, on the other hand, you scored in the aggressive category of the first quiz, you need to carefully rethink your investment strategy. Perhaps you lack the resources to invest aggressively or your age, discipline, or level of knowledge suggest that you should temper your aggressive instincts.

If your scored between 17 and 30, you are well-positioned to take some moderate risks. If your score on the first quiz also placed you in the mid-range, you should feel confident with investments that involve moderate risks.

If you scored more than 31 points, you are in a good position to make some aggressive investments. Your combination of knowledge, interest, and resources suggests a healthy tolerance for risk. Check to see if your score on the first quiz supports this strategy. If you scored high on this quiz, yet earned a conservative rating on the first quiz, you could consider more aggressive investments.

POINTS TO REMEMBER

- The way you feel about your money—how much you make, how much you own, how much you owe—depends on more than whether you're rich or poor. Feeling comfortable with your money is important to your sense of well-being.
- Life is full of risks. Every day you take the risk of losing your job, or of failing to put away enough money for the lifestyle you want, for your children's education, or for your retirement.
- Every investment book talks about risk tolerance. Actually, your appetite for risk has a lot more to do with your knowledge than with your genes. The more you know about an investment, the more comfortable you're likely to feel.
- Think of a mutual fund investment the same way you would an investment in a house or a car. Don't put your money down before you check the wares. Inspect the foundation. Kick the tires. Once you feel confident of your investment choice, you'll be prepared to weather a few storms.
- You can't ignore your psychological comfort zones when it comes to money. But you shouldn't let foolish money quirks rule your financial life either.
- Think through your spending and saving habits. Throw out those that are costing you too much. And vow to work to educate yourself so that you can feel comfortable with the rest of your financial and investment decisions.

PART II

Using Mutual Funds to Solve Your Investment Problems

Chapter 4

Just Starting Out—Building a Basic Mutual Fund Portfolio

L ouise Donovan collected her master's degree in journalism from Northwestern University two years ago. She'd been warned about how tough it is to get that first job in such a competitive field, but she had high hopes, lots of enthusiasm, and dogged determination. She vowed she would not give up until she got a spot at one of Chicago's two top newspapers. Eight months later, she admitted she'd have to lower her sights. Big metropolitan dailies just don't hire reporters without experience. And she wasn't really willing to relocate, because she had marriage plans. So she settled for an entry-level job at a Chicago trade publication, pulling in $15,000 a year.

The following year she married Joe Greco, three years out of graduate school in architecture. Like Louise, Joe has big dreams. He's planned to be an architect all his life. Perhaps he won't be another Frank Lloyd Wright, but he *knows* he's good. And he's confident that he'll make a mark in his field. He doesn't mind putting in 55- and 60-hour weeks, spending weekends hunched over his drafting table, forgoing vacations, and skipping holidays for the princely annual sum of $17,500.

The Grecos, both in their mid-20s, are long on idealism and short on cash, own no property, and have big college loans to pay off. They rent an apartment in a marginal neighborhood in Chicago that's furnished with some hand-me-downs from their parents. Still, they're proud of what they've accomplished with it. Joe redesigned and painted the living room. When Louise started bringing in a little freelance magazine work, he built a work space for her in front of a big north window. Now, when Joe works on the weekend, Louise can spend Saturday mornings in her home office working on the articles that she hopes will get her a job in mainstream journalism. She's doing all right, too. Last year her freelance work brought in $2,500.

Louise's mother is proud of the kids. But she's more a realist than an idealist. Although the Grecos have good prospects, Anne Donovan thinks they need to start now if they want to achieve their financial goals. In fact, she made the tedious suggestion that Louise use the money she earns freelancing to begin an investment program. Specifically, she suggested that Louise open an Individual Retirement Account or a Keogh account, which would provide some tax savings as well as give her an early start on a retirement nest egg. Louise pointed out that she and Joe have more interesting things to do with their spare change than put it into the bank for 50 years.

Her mother tried a new tack: Do they want to live in an apartment all their lives? Wouldn't they like to own their own home some day? That struck a chord. Joe would love a raw space that he could design in his own style. Naturally, Louise would like her own study. But the Grecos are artists, writers, dreamers. They're not financial planners. They have little money and no idea how to start. Neither has taken an economics course or even read the financial pages. They spend their reading time with *Architectural Digest* and *Vanity Fair,* not *Business Week*. But the idea of buying a house does motivate them. Louise sells a women's magazine on the idea of a story on how to set up an investment program. That way, she figures, she can use her research to make a little money, killing two birds with one stone.

You may see something of yourself in Louise and Joe. And you may share some of their problems as well as some of their needs. Do you:

- Have a low tolerance for risk?
- Dislike the idea of locking up your money for a long time?
- Have only a small amount of money—or no money at all—to start an investment program?

- Use the daily financial pages to wrap up the garbage?
- Excuse yourself to get another drink when people start discussing interest rates at a cocktail party?

No matter how old you are, you may be just starting out, too. Perhaps you don't have much money, don't know much about investing, and would like to build up some savings in a fairly short time, say four or five years, for a vacation, to start your own business, to make a down payment on a home, or for some other short-term goal. Or you might be just beginning to save for your retirement, even though it's only a few years away. Why not follow along with Louise as she does her research?

FUND FAMILIES

One of the first things Louise learns is that mutual funds are organized into families. Louise's mother, an experienced investor, points out that there are plenty of parallels in other industries. Every company that sells products to consumers does its best to capitalize on its reputation and good name to sell more goods. That's marketing. Maybe you buy all your suits at Brooks Brothers. You move from Fort Lauderdale to Portland, Oregon, and discover that you need a new raincoat. If Brooks Brothers has one, you'll probably buy it there rather than try a new store. The same kind of marketing synergy propels clothes designers like Ralph Lauren to put their names on sheets, towels, and perfume. If you like the look of the dress, why not try the bed linens? Any company that develops a successful consumer product will try to capitalize on its reputation and expand its customer base by appealing to different appetites.

Naturally, successful mutual fund companies want to do the same thing. But the law requires them to set things up a little differently. Every mutual fund is its own company; it has to stand on its own as a separate entity. But as early as 1932, the Keystone Company saw the wisdom of grouping several mutual funds under a larger umbrella. Keystone saw that Americans were reeling from the Depression's impact on the financial markets and that they weren't eager to invest their

SOME OF THE LARGEST MUTUAL FUND FAMILIES AND THEIR TOLL-FREE PHONE NUMBERS

The Boston Company Advisers
800-446-1013

Kemper Financial Services
800-621-1048

Dean Witter Reynolds Inc.
800-869-3863

Merrill Lynch Asset Management Inc.
800-637-3863

Dreyfus Corporation
800-645-6561

T. Rowe Price Associates
800-638-5660

Fidelity Investments
800-544-6666

Shearson Lehman Hutton
212-528-2744 (not toll-free)

Franklin Advisers Inc.
800-342-5236

Vanguard Group
800-662-7447

money, if indeed they had any. So the mutual fund company tried to entice reluctant investors with a family of eight funds, each with a different objective. The individual companies were all managed under the Keystone name and shared the Keystone reputation. Since the stock market was still in the doldrums, the emphasis was on bonds. The family included five bond funds, including the first speculative or "junk bond" fund. It was rounded out by a balanced stock and bond fund, a common stock fund, and a fund that specialized in low-priced stocks that might profit during economic recovery. This was the first "family of funds," with different members for different types of investors. The term wasn't coined back in 1932. In fact, it didn't show up in financial jargon until the early 1980s. But today groups that offer a range of funds and services have become known as mutual fund families.

Fund families, like human families, contain members with diverse personalities. Some are comfortable, conservative, homebody type funds. Like your grandmother, they might make you feel safe and secure. Some are racy, fickle, unpredictable funds, like a bachelor uncle who likes to paint the town red.

Funds benefit from being grouped in families much the way people do. Just as it's cheaper to live with a roommate because you split costs, two or more funds grouped together benefit from economies of scale. Once the necessary employees, computers, and other record-keeping are in place for one fund, they don't have to be duplicated for the next one. You benefit from dealing with fund families, too. It's convenient to be able to pick up the telephone and move between funds of the same family no matter what type of investment account you have.

Today there are over 350 families to choose from. A family might range in size from a small group of three or four sophisticated and highly specialized funds, like the G. T. Global group of international funds, to a group that offers 25 to 30 funds with a full range of investment objectives, like Dean Witter or T. Rowe Price, to families like Dreyfus and Fidelity with well over 50 funds. Because you, like Louise and Joe, are just starting out, you need a fund family rather than a single fund. With a fund family, you can start with one or two simple, straightforward investments. As you gain experience and your confidence grows, you can move to some of the more exciting relatives.

Because Louise and Joe don't know yet what investment choices they'll need several years from now, Mrs. Donovan suggests they take the time to choose a fund group carefully for their first investment. As they look over the fund families, their research breaks down into these categories: performance of funds, type and variety of funds, investing costs, and available services. They want a group of funds that offers a broad range of investment options—a variety of stock and bond funds, money market funds, international funds, gold and precious metals funds, and some specialty funds such as those that invest in particular industry sectors.

You can learn quite a lot yourself by calling the toll-free numbers and asking for basic information on the funds. Are the service reps helpful? Do they answer your basic questions so that you can understand them?

Obviously, performance is a major consideration. When you're judging how the fund company stacks up:

• Look first at the stock funds. This is where you will find the greatest differences in performance. Even if you're not interested in a stock fund right now, chances are you will be at some point. You want a family that offers well-managed stock funds. (For information on how to monitor performance, see Chapter 13.)

• Examine the variety of bond funds offered by the family. Check to see if it offers taxable as well as tax-free bonds, short-term as well as long-term. Different maturities are important for different market environments. A fund group with a good variety is what you want.

• Now look at money market funds. Does the group offer the full range—general purpose, tax-free, and those that invest in government securities only?

• Finally, check to see what specialty funds the family offers. OK, so you're just a beginning investor. Maybe you still don't know a stock from a bond. Now is the time to see what kind of variety this group offers beyond the plain vanilla stock and bond funds. As your knowledge about investing grows along with the size of your portfolio, you'll need to diversify. Does it have a gold or precious metals fund? Global funds? One-industry or one-country funds?

Once you've found some families that meet your performance requirements and offer the variety you want, consider services and costs.

Load Fee or commission paid by the investor when he buys mutual fund shares. Also called a front-end load, it can be as high as 8.5 percent. Loads between 1 percent and 3 percent are called low-loads.

• How much does it cost to buy and sell the funds? Charges you pay when you invest in a fund are often referred to as **loads.** But you need to check for fees that are charged to sell the funds as well as to buy them. Some companies charge both, some neither. Some funds charge only a redemption fee, a fee when you sell the fund, and yet call themselves **no-load**. This practice has been curtailed recently by the SEC.

No-load Mutual fund that charges no fee or commission to buy or sell back its shares. As mutual funds have adopted a variety of new types of fees, there are increasingly fewer funds that do not charge the investor in some way for their marketing and distribution costs.

• What are the funds' management and administrative fees? These are separate from selling costs. All fund managers take certain expenses out of the assets of the fund before income is paid to shareholders. (For more detailed information on fees and charges, see Chapter 12.)

• Can you move your money between funds in the group by telephone? Is there a charge? Is there a limit to the number of times you can do it each year? Do you pay a sales fee each time you move from one fund to another? Do you pay an exit fee as well?

WHEN YOUR INVESTMENT PRODUCES INCOME . . .

You have two choices about what to do with the income generated by your mutual fund investment. You can either have it reinvested in the mutual fund, which means your income buys more shares, or you can take the money out and spend it.

Reinvestment is the wisest course if you want your investment to grow. But some investors, like retirees, need the income. These investors typically choose a bond fund because the income is higher and more predictable.

Interest from a bond fund is income that is earned by your capital. You are not eating into the capital itself. If you wish, you can receive these income payments monthly, quarterly, twice a year, or annually. This is considered ordinary income and you must pay tax on it.

You can also choose to receive the capital gains distributions—or the money made by the portfolio manager from trading securities—in cash. But this is not the same as receiving income. These distributions are considered a return of capital because they reduce the amount of your investment. Once these distributions have been made, the net asset value of your mutual fund declines by the amount that is paid out.

The rule of thumb in investing is that you should avoid spending your capital, if at all possible. If you want to follow that advice but need income, choose a bond fund, which generates interest income without reducing the amount of your capital.

If you're interested in a particular type of account or service, of course you'll want to make sure the fund group offers it. Do you plan to set up an Individual Retirement Account? A Keogh account? A college account for your kids? What fee does the fund company charge for these accounts? What's the minimum initial investment? Some investors like to receive the income they earn in a fund in monthly checks. It's possible. Many investors prefer to have all the money earned in the fund reinvested to buy more shares. Some funds even allow you to use the dividends from one fund to buy shares in a different fund in the family.

Since Joe and Louise are starting out small, Mrs. Donovan suggests they find a family that offers an **accumulation plan.** What this means is that the group waives the minimum investment in the fund if you

Accumulation plan
Method of buying mutual fund shares through small, regular, voluntary purchases.

agree to put money in regularly. With an accumulation plan, there is no fixed dollar goal and regular contributions are not mandatory. But the idea is to discipline yourself to save, to make investing a part of your budget. There are several different methods you can use. With some fund groups you may start out with as little as $100 in a fund and then agree to make regular investments of as little as $25 or $50 a month.

One convenient way to set up an accumulation plan is to use either a payroll deduction or a direct deposit from your bank. You may be able to make arrangements with your employer to deduct a certain amount from your paycheck at regular intervals and send it directly to the fund company. Or you can have your bank do the same thing. Many fund companies allow you to split your investment between two different funds so that you can begin to build a diversified portfolio.

FUND OPTIONS

Louise understands the idea of fund families, but the types of funds sound like Greek to her. Her mother decides she needs a short primer on investing before she's ready to make a choice. All investments are split broadly into two categories: those that provide investment income and those that provide the potential for investment growth. Consider these examples. A bank passbook account or a bank certificate of deposit (CD) are income investments. If you put $1,000 in a one-year bank certificate of deposit that pays 8 percent, your $1,000 will earn income of $80 in a year. But your principal amount—the $1,000—will still be the same. Your principal will also be totally safe during the year. Assuming you used a bank insured by the FDIC, the federal government guarantees it. Guaranteed income and low risk are the hallmarks of conservative investing.

On the other hand, a real estate investment in your home provides you with no income, but it might provide spectacular growth. Let's say you make a down payment of $20,000 to buy a $100,000 home. The $20,000 is your investment. We'll assume you've chosen wisely and luck is on your side. In five years, you sell the house for $150,000, or a $50,000 profit. Ignoring after-tax interest costs on your mortgage, your $20,000 principal investment has provided you with a 250 percent return. That's growth! But you had no guarantee that your home would appreciate at all. You could have paid too much for it and been forced to sell it at a loss. Perhaps you have bad taste. Maybe you bought a white elephant and you can't unload it at any price. *Growth investments* provide no guarantees. They offer the potential of a higher return than *income investments*, but also the risk of a loss.

Most investments aren't quite so straightforward. But they mix the same elements: income versus growth; low risk versus high risk. As a general rule, stocks are considered growth investments and bonds are income investments. It follows that stock funds are growth-oriented and bond funds are income-oriented.

But mutual funds move along a spectrum from the most conservative, low-risk—a money market fund, which provides income much like a bank certificate of deposit—to an aggressive growth stock fund, which provides very little income but the potential, although not the promise, of high growth, like the real estate investment in your house. Whichever fund group you choose and whichever types of funds you plan to use in your portfolio, there's one mutual fund that you really can't be without, the money market fund.

Growth investment An investment that has as its primary goal long-term appreciation or increase of principal. Common stock and mutual funds that invest primarily in common stock are growth investments.

Income investment An investment that has as its primary goal the generation of income, in the form of interest or dividends, as opposed to growth or capital appreciation. Preferred stock, bonds, money market instruments and mutual funds that invest primarily in these securities are income investments.

MONEY MARKET FUNDS

The most basic, conservative mutual fund investment, and the linchpin of most mutual fund groups or families, is the money market fund. As a beginning investor, it will be one of your most important tools. The advantages and uses of these accounts are numerous.

• Even a diehard conservative would be hard put to find any fault with their safety. Although they are not insured like bank accounts, no investor in a money market account has lost his money because of a default.

• They pay a competitive, short-term interest rate.

• They are highly liquid, which means you can get your money out easily and quickly. Because most accounts offer check-writing privi-

NINE QUESTIONS TO ASK ABOUT A MONEY MARKET MUTUAL FUND

• What is the minimum required to open the account? What is the minimum to keep it active?

• Is the account part of a family of funds that includes other funds that suit your needs?

• Is check writing permitted? What is the minimum amount for each check? Is there a maximum number of checks permitted each month?

• How long does it take to clear the deposits you make into the account?

• Does the fund allow you to transfer money by wire? What is the minimum amount? (This comes in handy if you need to move money quickly into your bank account.)

• Can you switch your money from the money fund to another mutual fund in the same family by telephone? Is there a fee?

• How does the company report on activity in your account? Are your canceled checks returned? Can you get them if you need them? Is there a fee for this service?

• Is the interest rate competitive with other money market funds?

• Does the fund charge a fee for check writing and other transactions?

---

leges, you can earn interest on money even if you need it to pay next month's rent. Some money market funds, like those at the big brokerage houses, can even be tapped with plastic cards that can be used in a bank automatic teller machine to get cash, at an electronics store to buy a VCR, or at a French restaurant to buy dinner. And many offer wire transfers, which means you can move your money to where you need it by this afternoon or tomorrow morning.

• When the account is one in a family of funds, you can use it as a parking place for money you decide to move out of the stock or bond markets. Or you can use it as a depository for money that you want to be able to move quickly into the market.

But what *is* a money market fund, Louise wants to know. How does it work? Money market mutual funds don't buy or sell money. The fund manager uses the money you invest to buy short-term debt certificates, sometimes called **short-term paper,** issued by the U.S. Treasury, state and local governments, banks, or large corporations. The money invested is a loan to the government, bank, or corporation,

Short-term paper
Short-term loans to corporations or government that can range from overnight to 90 days. Interest rates fluctuate to reflect current market conditions. Short-term paper is one of the basic investments of money market funds.

whose term might range from overnight to one week or 90 days. These debt certificates are called "money market instruments" because they can be converted into cash so quickly that they are considered the equivalent of cash.

Here's how they work: Because the investments made by a money market fund are so stable, the funds can offer a fixed share price instead of one that fluctuates from day to day. Each share is valued at one dollar. That means that for every dollar you invest, you own one share of the money market mutual fund. In other words, money market funds preserve your *principal*. So how do you earn money? Although the share price remains stable, the *interest rate* is adjusted daily to reflect changing market conditions. This interest is credited to your account. Back in 1981, money market accounts were earning nearly 17 percent. In 1988, they were averaging just under 7 percent. In early 1989, some were paying 11 percent. Obviously, 17 percent is much more attractive than 7 percent. If you understand that the yield fluctuates based on current interest rates, you will be able to decide how much of your money to keep in a money market fund.

There are factors other than interest rates that should influence your decision, though. No matter what your investment needs, risk tolerance, or time horizon, a money fund should make up some part of your portfolio. It is suitable for the most risk-averse investor. It is suitable for the high roller who needs to park cash somewhere for the short term. And it's suitable even if you only have a three- or six-month time horizon before you need your money.

But clearly, there are times when you will want to have more of your portfolio in a money account, other times when you want less in a money account (or cash) and more in growth and higher-income investments. For example, if you expect to use a chunk of your investment in the near future to make a down payment on a home, to take a spectacular vacation, or to start your own business, you should be accumulating it in a money market fund rather than in the more volatile stock and bond markets. Likewise, if you see signs that the economy or the markets are deteriorating and you want to safeguard the profits you've made in more aggressive mutual funds, you also may want to switch money into cash (or a money market fund) and wait on the sidelines for a while.

Louise learned that for years, rates of the highest- and lowest-paying funds didn't differ much and shopping for the highest interest rate was a waste of time. But when interest rates headed up in early 1989, some fund companies spotted an opportunity to differentiate themselves by offering higher rates. For example, with the average fund paying about 9.5 percent in April 1989, one new money fund, Dreyfus Worldwide Dollar, was paying over 11 percent. The fund was able to do it by investing in foreign debt, lower-grade securities, and securities with maturities of up to one year and by temporarily waiving all management fees and administrative expenses.

This aggressive management strategy didn't significantly increase the investment risk, though. The SEC tightly regulates money market funds. They can invest only in the top two credit-quality grades of debt, as rated by one of the major rating agencies. They must keep their average portfolio maturity at 120 days or less. And they cannot buy any security with a maturity of more than one year. Dreyfus Worldwide was able to achieve its higher return by investing in dollar-denominated securities in the Euromarket. These securities, which might include CDs from big Japanese banks, are no less safe than those issued in the United States, but they pay higher rates because of differences in market regulation.

Because the SEC mandates that funds invest only in high-quality loans, the risk of default on one of the loans in a money fund is very low. There is some risk, though, in buying loans with a longer maturity, which is that the fund will be more vulnerable to rising interest rates. If long-term rates rise, the loans or "paper" the fund is holding could decline in value. That still doesn't mean you'll lose money. There is one case in money fund lore that sometimes surfaces as an example of a fund that could not maintain the one-dollar share price. In 1979, the First Multi Fund for Daily Income slipped to a share price of 94 cents. But as William E. Donoghue, newsletter publisher and money market guru, points out, this fund was not really a money market fund according to SEC standards. Its average maturity of 650 days made it, instead, a short-term bond fund.

No money fund has ever "broken the buck," the industry jargon for failing to hold the one-dollar share price. But one money market fund that stretched its maturity after the October 1987 stock market crash got caught with longer-term loans as interest rates started to rise. No investors lost money. But in order to preserve the one-dollar share price, the fund company dropped the yield by 1.24 percent to 4.63 percent.

This was a rare occurrence. If you stick with a fund from a reputable company with a return somewhere in the middle of the pack, you'll do just fine. If you decide to go for one of the newer, more aggressive funds like Dreyfus Worldwide, you'll get a higher return for only a hint more risk. Experts suggest that you choose a fund with at least $100 million in assets and that you stick with an average portfolio maturity of 40 to 60 days. You can get this information by calling the fund's toll-free number. If you're a real fretter, do some extra homework on the fund's safety. There are two recognized resources on money market funds: *Income and Safety*, a monthly newsletter published by Norman Fosback in Fort Lauderdale, and *Donoghue's Money Fund Report*. Both rank funds by yield as well as by average maturity. And they provide information on the funds' asset size. Most public libraries subscribe to one or both.

Perhaps you don't like even a hint of uncertainty. Then consider those funds that invest only in securities backed by the U.S. government. They pay a slightly lower rate of interest, but they are as safe as a mutual fund investment can be (see Chapter 5). Or, if you are in a high income tax bracket, you may want to consider money funds that are free of federal, state, and local taxes (see Chapter 9).

Checking to see what fees the company charges to the account and what services and conveniences it offers is important, too. Management fees usually range from .2 percent to .5 percent (or 20 to 50 **basis points**). But some funds now carry a fee that is authorized under **Rule 12 (b) 1** that allows them to deduct an additional amount—perhaps another tenth of one percent or 10 basis points—for marketing purposes. You'll want to find out the total amount of the fees that will be deducted from the assets of the account before interest is credited to accountholders. A study by the Donoghue Organization, Inc., showed that expenses can range from less than .5 percent to more than 1.5 percent. This could make a big difference in your income.

Louise figures she could write a book just on money market funds. She's willing to drop her research here. After all, she and Joe don't have much money to invest anyway. And, with all these positive attributes, why not just stop with a money market fund? Why look any further for investments? Because, Mrs. Donovan points out, a money

Basis point *One one-hundredth of one percent. Basis points are used to express such things as expenses and yields that are less than 1 percent; 1 percent equals 100 basis points.*

Rule 12 (b) 1 *Rule introduced in 1980 by the Securities and Exchange Commission that allows mutual funds to add an annual charge for marketing and distribution. This charge, which ranges from .1 percent of the fund's assets to 1.25 percent, can be used for advertising or to pay additional compensation to brokers who sell the funds.*

market fund provides no opportunity for growth of your investment. It simply pays income at current market rates. Even a novice investor needs to combine investments that provide income with those that provide the opportunity for growth of principal. That means they need to look at bond funds, which provide a higher and more predictable income than stocks, and at stock funds for growth potential.

Investing in the stock and bond markets also diversifies your investment portfolio in another important way. Over time, stocks and bonds tend to perform well in different environments. By investing in both, you cushion yourself even if one of the two markets performs poorly. For example, in early 1987, the bond market hit the skids while the stock market soared. Bonds continued to bounce along through the year until October when the stock market crashed. Then bonds rallied. For the fourth quarter of 1987, the stock market, as measured by the **Standard & Poor's 500** stock index, dropped 22.5 percent. But the bond market, as measured by both the Shearson Lehman Government/ Corporate Bond Index and the Salomon Brothers Broad Investment Grade Index, gained 5.8 percent.

Standard & Poor's 500 Index (S & P 500) *Index of 500 widely held stocks that is often used as a proxy for the stock market. Included are the stocks of 400 industrial companies, 40 financial companies, 40 public utilities, and 20 transportation companies.*

GROWTH AND INCOME FUNDS

There are several ways for a small investor to diversify. Mrs. Donovan suggests a growth and income fund as a conservative choice that will help the Grecos learn about diversification as they move into mutual fund investing. These funds do invest in both the stock and bond markets. But few mutual funds can be neatly pigeonholed. Instead, they stretch along a continuum from those requiring you to take the greatest risk for the greatest potential reward (such as the most aggressive growth stock funds) to those, like the money market funds, that are far more stable but promise less. Of those mutual funds that invest in the stock market, growth and income funds fall in the middle of the pack. They attempt to offer a steady income without giving up the opportunity for your investment to appreciate or grow in value. Because they aim for both above-average yields and some capital appreciation, these funds are one type of a group sometimes called **"total return"** funds. The goal is to offer a solid overall return with limited

Total return *Return on an investment that includes both the income it produces and the change in the value of the principal.*

risk. To achieve this, most of these funds invest in the stocks of blue-chip companies that pay dependable dividends.

On average these funds offer less spectacular returns during a roaring bull market but suffer less than more aggressive funds in a bear market. Many offer a steady, conservative return. But, like any fund group, growth and income funds are managed by men and women who embrace a wide range of management styles. Some portfolio managers adhere closely to the low-risk line. Others go bargain hunting for cheap or even very speculative stocks that they think have a good chance of appreciating. There are some excellent all-purpose funds in this group. As with most types of funds, you need to learn how the portfolio manager sees his responsibility of providing growth and income before you can decide whether this is the particular fund for you.

ASSET ALLOCATION FUNDS

What, Louise wonders, about those investors who have done enough research and just want to bail out now and have a glass of wine? Is there something for those of us who feel we can't stand to learn any more about investing than we already know? Yes. Even if you're a novice, asset allocation funds could work for you. Rather than choosing different funds to diversify your portfolio, you choose one fund that does it all. The asset allocation fund manager takes the responsibility for spreading your investment dollars over four or five different investments to provide you with a safety net if one type of security does poorly. A typical asset allocation fund might include investments in gold and precious metals, stocks, bonds, cash, and international securities.

These funds are set up in two basic ways. One type is considered a "passive" fund because there is no active management of the assets. The money that comes into the fund is simply split into five pots. For example, 20 percent of the assets might go into each one. The idea here is that you have a diversified portfolio simply by spreading your investment over these various options. This type of fund would give you instant diversification.

The second type of asset allocation fund lets the portfolio manager

PURSUING ABOVE-AVERAGE YIELDS: GROWTH AND INCOME FUND MANAGERS CHART DIFFERENT COURSES

All growth and income funds have the same goal: to buy stocks with above-average yields that still have the potential for capital gains, or growth of your capital. But the way portfolio managers pursue this goal varies a lot.

Consider the Washington Mutual Investors Fund managed by Capital Research. This company operates very conservatively, splitting each portfolio between three or four different fund managers. Each manager operates entirely independently, buying and selling as he sees fit. They confer regularly. If one wants to buy a stock and another wants to sell it, they make a deal.

James K. Dunton, the lead manager for Washington Mutual Investors, sees it like this: "No one does a good job every year. They might have three or four good years and then they give a year back. It's no different from the sports world where you see someone go into a slump. It's a natural phenomenon. You can't keep up the edge indefinitely."

By splitting up the fund's assets, the company reasons, it will blunt the swings. If one of the three managers has a bad year, the other two will probably offset him. The goal is consistency. "We are moderating the amplitude of the swing," Dunton says. The fund rarely has a terrible year. Chances of a spectacular year are equally remote. "Trying to come up with a consistent performance is better than trying to hit the ball over the fence every time," Dunton says. This conservative approach has made the fund one of a handful that have beaten the market averages in every ten-year period for the past 30 years.

Now consider the approach of Michael Price, who manages the Mutual Shares fund. Price goes bargain hunting, looking for companies that are bankrupt or in reorganization; stocks that he can buy cheaply with a good potential for appreciation. Although most investors would not consider bankrupt companies a conservative investment, Price obviously knows how to pick them. His fund, too, is a top performer. In 1988, it was up 30.92 percent.

Does it matter how a portfolio manager gets good results? Michael Lipper, president of Lipper Analytical Services, which ranks the performance of mutual funds, thinks not. "It's like when you get into a taxi," Lipper says. "What you're interested in is that you get to the right point in the quickest possible way. You may not know the quickest way yourself. And you probably don't know what's underneath the hood. What you want is an accomplishment. How it's achieved is not important."

decide how to allocate your assets. He may have total flexibility to put the money wherever he wants and he may be able to use any type of financial instruments he chooses. He could be 100 percent in bonds, 100 percent in gold, or any mix in between. A good example of this type of fund is the Dreyfus Capital Value Fund, which was converted to an asset allocation fund on May 1, 1987, when Stanley Salvigsen took over as manager. Salvigsen, who is an investment strategist, makes all the investment decisions. He can put all of the money in stocks, in bonds, in cash, in international securities, or in whatever he feels is warranted based on his outlook for the economy. He can also use options and futures and make use of sophisticated trading and hedging techniques.

As it happens, Salvigsen got off to a good start. The week of the October 1987 market crash, his fund was up slightly. For 1987, the fund was up a healthy 34.45 percent, even though Salvigsen had managed it for only the final eight months. This return is very attractive. But you must remember that other fund managers have tried the same techniques over the years. What they are trying to do amounts to market timing—getting into the right sector at the right time and getting out before it collapses. One new twist on this is that some portfolio managers now use computers to tell them when to switch sectors. Still, more people fail than succeed with **market timing** techniques. If you choose this type of fund, you must remember that you are picking a particular talent as well as the idea of spreading your assets around. You are choosing someone to make your investment decisions for you.

Market timing The use of economic and technical financial information to guide your decision on when to buy and sell securities.

Even if you choose to let the portfolio manager do your work, you have to keep tabs on his performance—and his health. When you buy the fund, find out who the portfolio manager is and how long he's been in the job. Many of the publications that rate mutual funds provide this information, as do various publications that are available in the library. (For details on where to get information to track mutual funds, see Chapter 13.) If you buy the fund through a broker or financial planner, he will be able to get information on the fund manager. Or you can call the fund's toll-free number and ask the company. If the service representative doesn't know, ask him to call you back with the information. As a group, asset allocation funds have not been great performers. And they are certainly not low-risk funds. You should have a good reason if you're picking one.

DIVERSIFICATION

Maybe, like Louise, you want to put all your money in conservative, low-risk securities. If you don't have a long time horizon, you don't want your money in something volatile that may be in the doldrums just when you find the perfect house and you need to pull out your cash to make a down payment. But even if you have a short time horizon, it still pays to diversify your portfolio. No matter how small your investment, you will achieve more stability and balance in your investment portfolio and your money will grow larger over time if you put it in more than one type of security, if you combine income and growth, and if you bet on more than one mutual fund manager. Even as a beginner, you should aim to split the money you have available among a minimum of three different funds.

THE GRECOS' CHOICES

• Louise does the necessary research to pick a mutual fund family that offers both the options that they need now and those they might want in the future. Because they've decided to use a growth and income fund, she checks to make sure the fund family has a good performer in that category.

• To get around the minimum amount required to open a regular mutual fund account—which ranges from $1,000 to $3,000 and up at most mutual fund companies—the Grecos sign up for an accumulation plan. After depositing an initial lump sum of $100, they can make regular deposits of $50. These will be deducted from Joe's monthly paycheck and sent to the fund company. This money goes into a money market account.

• Louise deposits $100 of her freelance money in a growth and income fund and promises to invest half of what she earns from her extra writing in regular $50 lumps.

• The Grecos know they need to add at least one more fund to their

The Grecos' Portfolio

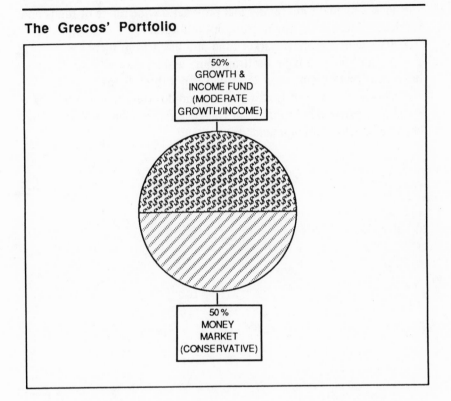

portfolio for balance. But they just don't have the cash to invest right now. Still, they've made a start: 50 percent in a conservative, liquid money market account and 50 percent in a fund that provides both growth and income.

POINTS TO REMEMBER

If you are just starting out, you might want to consider the Grecos' choices, or you may find funds in another chapter that meet your investment goals. But, you should keep these rules in mind:

• No matter how little money you have, discipline yourself to make regular investments.

- Pick a mutual fund family that provides a wide range of funds and services. Your needs might grow in the future.
- Start with a money market fund and build from there.
- As soon as you have built up some assets, diversify so that you have your investments in at least two if not three funds.
- Choose the type of fund you want and do some research to pick a consistent performer in that fund category rather than picking a fund because someone recommended it to you.

Chapter 5

Penny-Wise and Cautious—Conservative Strategies for Wealth Building

S usan Schwartz is thrifty. When she buys a winter coat, she waits until after Christmas—or better yet, until the Presidents' Day sale. She clips coupons and she watches for ads in the Thursday food section before she does her grocery shopping. When she goes to a movie, she hits the Saturday "twilight hour" special where she can get a discounted ticket. And she never makes a major purchase without studying *Consumer Reports* and shopping several different stores.

Susan, 33, has always been proud to consider herself a saver rather than a spender—someone who goes for the guaranteed return. She tucks away a hefty 15 percent of her $35,000-a-year salary in a bank passbook account, where she earns the standard 5.5 percent. She likes to see the balance mounting up and she even goes into the bank to get her interest posted so she can see how much she's earning on her savings. To date, she has over $20,000 in a passbook account.

When friends tried to talk Susan into switching her money to a bank certificate of deposit to get a higher interest rate, she balked. She understands savings and checking accounts and she wants to stick with what she knows. Her boyfriend, Jim, told her how foolish she is to let her day-to-day money sit in a checking account when she could be earning interest on it if she moved it into a bank money market or NOW account. Susan wants none of it. She smugly reminds Jim that although her earnings may seem meager to him, at least she still has her money, while he lost 25 percent of his in the 1987 stock market crash. Susan insists on being in total control of her money and her financial future.

But in 1987 something unexpected happened to Susan, too, something beyond her control. Her employer switched to a new benefits program, dropping the pension plan in which she was already vested and putting in place a 401 (k) plan instead. This sounds like alphabet soup to Susan. Yet she realizes she must learn about it. Her future security depends on it. First she demystifies it by learning that 401 (k) refers to the section of the Internal Revenue Service code that permits companies to offer these retirement plans. It allows employees to set aside a portion of their salaries before tax in a special retirement account. For every dollar she puts away up to the first 4 percent of her salary, her employer matches her.

If she doesn't participate, Susan will be left without a retirement plan. Furthermore, as a friend points out, the employer match will add $1,400 to her salary. This actually amounts to an increase in pay that she'll miss out on if she doesn't contribute to the plan. And she learns that the possible returns on her money are much higher than the 5.5 percent she earns on her passbook account. She knows she must do it. But she's afraid. It means that she can't continue to put as much money into her passbook account, which is her security blanket. Susan decides to be open-minded; to try to loosen up a bit and consider her options. But she's just not ready to leap off the high board. She wants to move gradually. And she wants to be absolutely certain that she's made the right choice before she makes a move.

Perhaps you see something of yourself in Susan's cautiousness. Maybe you'd like to be able to increase your investment return a little, but only if you can understand your options; if you can be certain you're not taking unacceptable risks. Do you:

- Always ''go for the guarantee''?
- Have considerable income or money to invest?

- Have plenty of time before you need your money?
- Need to make investment choices for your company 401 (k) plan?
- Feel a bit timid with your money?
- Flip the channel when a business program comes on the tube?

You also may be penny-wise and cautious, even if you don't have a 401 (k) plan. If you have a considerable amount of money sitting in

BEFORE YOU SIGN UP FOR A 401 (K) . . .

If your company offers a 401 (k) plan, sign up! These salary reduction plans are one of the few attractive tax shelters left. The money you contribute is automatically deducted from your income for tax purposes. Here are the things to check for.

- Maximum employee contribution was set at $7,000 in 1987. The limit moves up with the Consumer Price Index—to $7,627 in 1989. But some employers impose lower limits on employees. Check your limit.

- Most employers "match" part or all of your contribution. They may kick in 25 cents for every dollar you sock away or they may match you dollar for dollar up to a certain percentage of your salary. If the employer matches you dollar for dollar up to a certain percentage of your salary, aim to put in at least that much. It's like getting a salary increase.

- Check on the investment options your plan offers and on how often you are allowed to alter your investments. You want to build a diversified portfolio. In most cases, you can split your contribution among two or more options. Do it.

- In 1989 the IRS tightened the requirements for withdrawing money before age 59½. With-drawal means that you take the money out and don't pay it back. You are allowed to do that only for a handful of reasons—to buy a primary residence, to pay for college tuition, to pay medical or funeral expenses, or to avoid eviction or mortgage foreclosure. Even then you must prove that you have exhausted every other means of getting the money. You must pay tax on it plus a 10 percent penalty and you are prevented from making new contributions for at least one year.

- Loans are a different matter. Most companies allow you to borrow money from your plan. Although the law requires that loans be repaid in five years, your employer can stretch that to 10 or 15 years if you buy a principal residence. When you take out a loan, the interest you pay goes into your own account.

- If you leave your company, your 401 (k) plan goes with you. The money belongs to you. But it's intended for your retirement. Don't spend it. Roll it over into an Individual Retirement Account.

- If you work for a nonprofit group, your employer may sponsor the same type of plan. These plans are called 403 (b) plans.

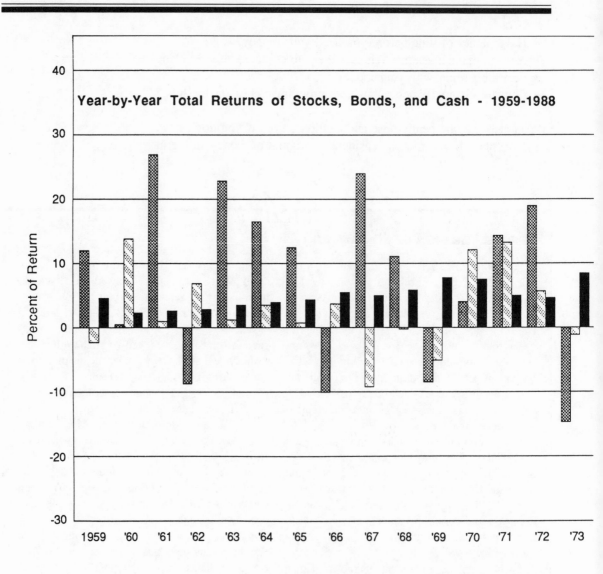

Year-by-Year Total Returns of Stocks, Bonds, and Cash - 1959-1988

a place where it's not bringing you much of a return and you don't need to save for short-term goals, you should be concentrating on building your wealth, on your retirement, on making your money work harder for you. But if you are risk averse and know nothing about investing, perhaps you're too reluctant to go after the higher but less predictable returns. If you consider keeping your nose to the grindstone and your

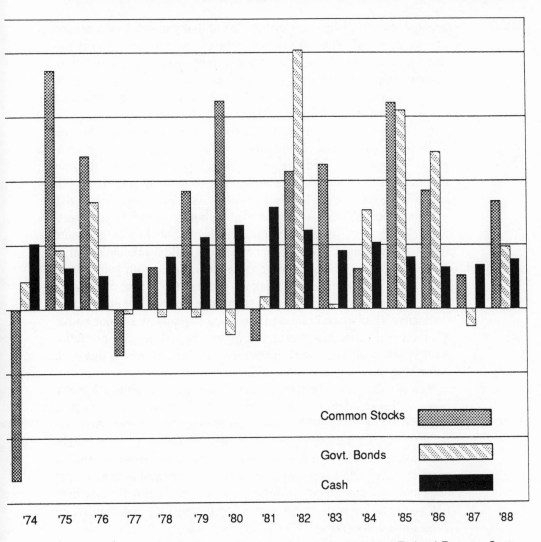

Common Stocks

Govt. Bonds

Cash

'74 '75 '76 '77 '78 '79 '80 '81 '82 '83 '84 '85 '86 '87 '88

Source: Ibbotson Associates, Inc., and Federal Reserve System

eyes on the weekly grocery ads to be a safe and conservative approach to life, you need to rethink your attitudes. Even if you're a very conservative investor, you can find investments that you can feel comfortable with that earn a better return than a passbook account.

First, you must broaden your concepts of risk. Susan thinks she isn't taking any risks because she keeps all her money in an insured bank account. But risk is not simply the chance that you will lose a portion of your principal. You must consider the effect of inflation on savings that earn low rates of interest. If your earnings don't outpace inflation, you risk being without money for your retirement. In fact, you need to see your entire life in terms of the risks you are taking and then consider what you are doing to hedge your bets.

Look at your job. Is it secure? Is it in a growth industry? Do your skills make you a valuable contributor to the industry? To your company? Do you have good prospects? Even if you are thrifty with your money, you might be taking a big gamble on your income. Diversification is the best way to hedge your chief risks. Your number-one risk is losing your job. Consider your earning power as part of your portfolio. Think first of hedging your bets here. Should you get more training or education? Does it make sense to build a sideline career in another industry? There are some things you can do with your investments, too. For example, don't put all your money in your employer's stock so that your job and your investments are dependent on the same company. Your second-biggest investment is probably in your home. That's a real estate investment and it, too, is part of your portfolio. Real estate is an aggressive investment and you should hedge with something more conservative.

You get the idea. Hiding under the bed with your money is not a conservative strategy. It's dangerous. You need to take charge of your financial future. You need to move from saver to investor. And you need to set up a portfolio, even if it's very conservative, that hedges your chief risks through diversification. When you take a big risk in your life—like setting up your own business—you need to think of that as part of your investment portfolio. Perhaps you should offset the high risk you're taking with your livelihood by putting other assets in something more conservative.

Even if you want to be cautious with your investable assets, you can still earn a very good return on your investment with conservative mutual funds as long as you can afford to stash your money away for some time. The first step is to do a little research. If you know little about the markets, perhaps all you remember is the bad news, like the stock market crash in October 1987. You probably need to see evidence that over the long haul the stock market outperforms other investments.

Don't invest any money until you're convinced that, over a long period, the investment you've chosen will return your principal plus significant earnings. There are many investments that, although they are not guaranteed, have a proven track record over 10, 20, or even 30 years. If you are patient and you can afford to leave your investment alone during periods of market volatility, you can be certain that it will grow over time. If you've never trusted anything but a federally insured bank, maybe the first step for you is to move some of your savings to a mutual fund designed especially for the cautious.

GOVERNMENT SECURITIES FUNDS

The safest mutual fund investment is a money market mutual fund that invests only in the IOUs of the U.S. government. Governments, as they are sometimes called, are split into two categories: securities issued by the U.S. government itself and those issued by its agencies.

U.S. Treasury securities, or **treasuries,** are the most creditworthy of all IOUs. They are issued by the U.S. Treasury. Repayment of principal and interest are guaranteed by the full faith and credit of the U.S. government. Those securities issued by government agencies, such as the Government National Mortgage Association, the Federal Home Loan Bank, the Federal National Mortgage Association, or Federal Home Loan Mortgage Corporation, are guaranteed by the federal agency. You can find a money fund that invests only in treasury securities, one that invests only in agency securities, or one that invests in both. (Money market funds are described in detail in Chapter 4.)

Like any money market fund, government securities money market funds pay current market rates of interest. The price of each share is always one dollar. The interest rate is not guaranteed. Instead it is adjusted daily to reflect market conditions. All money market funds are considered safe. But if you're a real fretter, you may worry that the corporation that issues an IOU might file for bankruptcy and default on its obligations. No money market fund has ever lost its investors' money. But those money market funds that invest only in the short-term securities of the government and its agencies are even more secure. You can be certain that the borrower will not default unless the

Treasuries Debt of the U.S. government. When the government needs to borrow money, it may issue TREASURY BILLS (*T-Bills*), which range in maturity from 91 days to one year. Two other types of debt instruments issued by the U.S. Treasury are TREASURY NOTES, intermediate securities that range from one year to ten years, and TREASURY BONDS, which range from ten years to 30 years.

government collapses, in which case your money market fund could be the least of your worries.

Money funds that invest in governments offer all the convenience of a regular money market account, including check writing, wire transfers, instant liquidity. Why, then, doesn't every investor choose the extra safety of a government securities money market fund? If you've learned the lesson about risk and reward, you've already guessed the answer. Because these funds invest in higher-quality loans—those with the guarantee of the U.S. government or its agencies—the yield is lower than a regular money market fund, perhaps .2 percent or 20 basis points lower.

For example, if the yield on a regular money market fund is 6.2 percent, a government securities fund might pay 6 percent. So, if you invested $10,000 in a regular money market fund for a year, you would earn $620. The government securities fund would pay $600. This is a good example of how you give up some potential for gain if you decide to play safe. It's very straightforward. You decide whether you prefer the extra .2 percent income or if you like the extra safety. (Since most money market investors reinvest the income, the dollar amount is actually a little higher due to the effect of compounding.)

GOVERNMENT BOND FUNDS

Although it's not government *insured,* Susan feels comfortable with a government *guarantee.* She understands how the government guarantee reduces both the risk and the reward in a money market fund. The same concept works with bond funds. Bonds are simply longer-term IOUs. When a corporation or a U.S. government agency—or the U.S. Treasury itself—needs to borrow money for a longer period of time, it might issue bonds. There are two risks to consider when investing in bonds: credit risk, or the risk that the bond holder will default on his debt; and interest rate risk, or the risk that a change in rates will affect the value of your bonds. If you stick to U.S. Treasury bonds, you eliminate credit risk. But you cannot eliminate interest rate risk.

Unlike the short-term debt in a money market fund that has a constantly fluctuating interest rate to reflect market conditions, bonds offer an interest rate that is guaranteed until the bond matures. Here's how bonds work: The face value of each bond is generally $1,000, which is referred to as **par.** When the government issues a bond, it promises to repay the face value at some set time in the future, which might be as early as next year or as much as 30 years from now. The 30-year U.S. Treasury bond is the bellwether of the bond market. It is referred to as a **long bond.** Stories about the bond market in the financial pages of the daily newspaper refer to what happened to the long bond in the previous day's trading.

The issuer also agrees to pay the bondholder a specified rate of interest or a **coupon.** Let's say you bought a five-year U.S. Treasury bond in 1988. You paid $1,000 and the government agreed to pay you an 8 percent coupon interest. You can be certain that you will receive your $80 in interest each year, paid in two $40 installments. And, in 1993, you can be certain that you will get your $1,000 back. So in five years, you will earn $400 on your $1,000 investment. Of course, you can also reinvest your interest payments and make more money. So far, it's nearly as straightforward as a money market fund.

Because of this predictability, bonds were long considered an extremely safe albeit somewhat boring investment. They were recommended for conservative investors—like retirees or widows—who needed certain, regular income. From the late 1930s until the late 1970s, the interest rates, or coupons, on bonds fluctuated only 3 percent to 5 percent per decade. Not only was the income predictable, but it was also quite low. One study showed that from 1941 until 1980 inflation-adjusted yields on five-year treasury bonds never beat 4 percent. In only 10 of those 40 years did inflation-adjusted yields exceed 2 percent. Bonds were an investment for the timid—and perhaps the most conservative and *penny-wise* of investors.

But, like many investments, bonds were whipsawed by the wild inflation brought on by skyrocketing oil prices in the 1970s. Double-digit inflation rewrote the investing rules. In a sense, holding a bond with a fixed interest rate and a fixed term when inflation soared into the double digits was like being a banker who had made a 30-year mortgage at 5 percent. Both were in terrible shape. But the homeowners who borrowed the money and the government agencies and corporations that issued the bonds were sitting pretty. They had locked in a cheap, long-term interest rate for the money they needed to borrow.

Par *Face value of a security. For bonds, par is typically $1,000. The bond is issued for $1,000 and it is redeemed for $1,000 at maturity. In between, it may sell at par; less than par, which is called "selling at a discount"; or above par, which is called "selling at a premium."*

Long bond *Generally, any bond with maturity of over ten years. However, when bond traders talk about what "the long bond" did in recent trading, they are referring to the 30-year Treasury bond, the bellwether of the bond market.*

Coupon *Interest rate on a bond, based on the face value of the bond when it is issued and set until maturity. Coupon refers to the detachable coupons that were once part of the bond. Every six months the bond-holder removed a coupon and presented it to the issuer to receive his interest. Although few bonds today have these coupons, the interest rate is still referred to as the coupon.*

Like bank mortgage holders, bondholders knew their interest rates would stay the same until maturity. And, if they held U.S. government bonds, the government guaranteed that they would get their regular coupon interest payments each year and that they would get their principal back at maturity. But the 5 percent interest they were earning did not look very attractive when there were other investments available that paid 18 percent. So what happened if the bondholder wanted to sell his bond before maturity so he could invest his money in a higher-yielding investment? Because the interest rate was fixed, the *price* of the bond had to change to reflect the change in its market value.

Say you pay $1,000 for a 30-year treasury bond that yields 8 percent. Consider this extreme example: The following year, interest rates skyrocket to 16 percent. Because your interest rate is locked in at

Short-term bond. *Maturity of two years or less.* Intermediate-term bond. *Maturity of three to ten years.* Long-term bond. *Maturity of more than ten years.*

WHEN BONDS WORK WELL: LACY H. HUNT AND BOND CYCLES

Lacy H. Hunt, one of the most respected bond market economists, says, "Bonds can be excellent sources of investment for certain periods," as long as investors understand that "no one investment is good for the entire business cycle."

Hunt breaks up the economic cycle into five distinct stages. The first is economic revival after a downturn, second is acceleration, third is maturation of economic growth, fourth is an easing off, and fifth is an economic plunge. Bonds are the choice of the smart investor in only two stages, the plunge and the revival.

What this means is that bonds work well in periods of recession and even in the beginning of an expansion, according to Hunt. Such periods are characterized by low inflation and, therefore, relatively low interest rates. But when the econ-omy starts to accelerate, the smart investor reduces the portion of his portfolio that is in bonds. "When the economy begins to expand and inflation and interest rates pick up, bond prices go down," Hunt says.

Investors should then move quickly into investments such as money market funds that take advantage of high interest rates. Bonds are hurt by these rising rates. But it's difficult for most investors to understand this, Hunt says. They argue that the bond yield is still 8.5 or 9 percent, while money market funds might only be yielding 6 percent. "But the thing they don't understand is that there is a much larger price risk," Hunt says. The share price of a bond mutual fund is very volatile in this period of economic expansion.

8 percent and an investor could buy a new issue at 16 percent, he will not be willing to pay you $1,000, or par, for your 8 percent bond. Your bond must fall in price so that it will offer a return equal to 16 percent. So if interest rates double, you may only be able to sell your bond for about $500. If you wait until the bond matures, you'll still receive the full $1,000. But you'll have lost the opportunity of switching to another investment that provides a higher rate of return. It's highly unlikely that interest rates will double overnight and that your bond will lose half its value, of course. But you must remember that interest rates drive the bond market; even tiny movements in interest rates affect the value of your investment.

That doesn't mean bonds don't have a place in your portfolio. But perhaps you don't want to buy an individual bond and put all your eggs in one basket. If you prefer to diversify your investment in the bond market, all types of bonds are available in bond mutual funds. Remember that a rise in interest rates will result in a decrease in the net asset value of your bond fund. Likewise, a drop in interest rates will cause the value of your bond fund to increase. For example, as interest rates fell over the five-year period ending December 31, 1986, the bond market experienced one of its longest rallies. The average U.S. bond mutual fund returned 117 percent over that period. In 1985 alone, many bond funds delivered a total return—interest plus appreciation in principal—of over 20 percent, some more than 30 percent.

Is there anything you can do to reduce your exposure to interest rate risk? Under normal conditions, the longer the time until maturity, the higher the interest rate. That's because you're shouldering interest rate risk for a long period. Therefore, intermediate-term treasury bonds normally pay a lower rate of interest than long-term bonds. But these shorter-maturity issues are also less volatile. So you can pick a bond fund with a shorter maturity, knowing that the net asset value will be less volatile, less affected by interest rate risk.

Maturities on bonds run from three months to 30 years. The most conservative bond fund is a short-term government bond fund. After the market crash of 1987, when many investors were leery of any type of mutual fund, fund companies introduced these limited-term funds with average maturities of just two or three years. They are a relatively safe, liquid investment. They pay higher interest than a money fund, yet the price fluctuates much less than that of a longer-term government bond fund. They make sense for a beginning investor who is looking for a higher yield than a money fund.

The second way to deal with interest rate risk is to buy a long-term bond fund when you expect interest rates to fall. Needless to say, this isn't easy. But bonds are generally considered good investments for sluggish economic periods. In a time of low economic activity, when businesses aren't doing well, they're not looking for money to expand. Because there's no demand for credit, interest rates remain low and bond prices remain high. So bonds are a wise investment for periods of recession or when fears of recession surface. For example, during the second quarter of 1989, as Americans worried about recession, interest rates fell and bonds rallied. But when the economy takes off, loan demand picks up and interest rates rise, so bond prices fall. So if you think the economy is slowing down, you may want to move into bond funds.

Your third choice as an investor is to pick a bond fund manager who will adjust the maturity of the fund depending on changes in the economy and in interest rates. If you decide to let the manager do the work for you, you should do a little research on how he's done in past bull and bear markets. Because bond funds have become such a popular investment in the eighties, most major business publications now rank their performance just as they do with stock funds. (Chapter 13 talks about where you can go for more information on funds.)

INDEX FUNDS

So far, Susan feels she might be able to learn to trust a U.S. Treasury money market fund. From there, perhaps, she could take a small step up the risk/reward curve to a short-term government bond fund. But, her boyfriend tells her, no matter how conservative she is, she shouldn't put all her money in money market and bond funds, both of which are income investments. Even conservative investors, he insists, need to have some portion of their assets in investments with potential for growth.

Stocks are the most popular growth investments. Stock investments provide you with ownership in the company and the potential to participate directly in its earnings growth. And stock mutual funds offer a variety of choices, from funds that invest in conservative blue-chip

BUYING "THE AVERAGE" WITH INDEX FUNDS: JOHN BOGLE'S BRAINCHILD

Most investments promise to beat the averages, to help you do better than the next guy. The idea behind an index fund is that it's smarter and cheaper to simply buy the average. Because few investors want to be simply average, index funds were initially a hard sell.

When John C. Bogle, chairman of the Vanguard Group, introduced the first index fund for individual investors, the Vanguard Index Trust, in 1976, indexing was considered "downright un-American," he says. Bogle says he "used up the leather in three pairs of shoes trying to get an underwriter that would do the deal." Dean Witter Reynolds did it in August 1976 and the index fund started with $12 million.

Back in 1975, when Bogle started developing the fund, indexing was in its infancy. Big institutions were beginning to adopt it and Paul Samuelson, the Nobel laureate economist, had started a lively intellectual debate about what he saw as the obvious advantages of indexing.

Samuelson argued that although all stock pickers and mutual fund managers try to beat the market average, few, alas, succeed. In fact, the performance of two thirds to three quarters of all mutual funds lags behind the market average, as measured by the Standard & Poor's index of 500 stocks. There are some good reasons for this, Samuelson discovered. The costs of trading, administration, and other fees mean that fund managers must beat the market by 2 percent if they are to come out even after expenses.

The idea behind indexing was to minimize trading, eliminate management fees, and reduce the other costs of doing business by simply putting together a basket of the same stocks that make up the overall market index. An investor who bought into this mutual fund would get performance that matched the market at a very low cost. Wells Fargo was an early developer of these funds for institutional money, or that money invested for big institutions, and money managers quickly saw the advantages.

The concept caught on more slowly with individual investors, although the Vanguard fund did its job of tracking the market and cutting expenses. When Vanguard brought out the fund, the expense ratio was 45 basis points, or less than .5 percent of assets under management. By 1988, it had dropped to 26 basis points, or .26 percent of assets under management. That compares to an average equity fund expense ratio of 1.1 percent. To put it another way, on an investment of $10,000, the annual management fee would be $26 for the Vanguard fund compared to $110 for the average stock fund.

In 1986, Vanguard brought out the first bond index fund. And the next year, the company took the idea one step further. It introduced the Extended Market Portfolio, which buys stocks in the Wilshire 5000 index. This is an index of all stocks traded, except for the S&P 500. Now an investor can buy the entire market by putting together a combination of the two indexes. "We think we'll move from the idea of index matching to market matching," Bogle says. "If you buy 70 percent of the S&P and 30 percent of the Extended Market Portfolio, then you'll match the overall market."

companies, like IBM, to the speculative stocks of small biotechnology companies that have not yet produced a single product. Within this range of choices, there are many that might be suitable for a cautious investor who is just learning the ropes. Still, Susan lacks the knowledge to evaluate a stock fund. But there is a stock fund that lets her off the hook. This is a fund that is designed to hedge the bets; it allows you to bet on all the horses in the race, so to speak. It is called an index fund.

The goal of an index fund is to track the performance of the stock market. When the overall market advances, a good index fund follows right behind. When the market declines, so does the fund. The fund gets its name because it follows a broad index of the market. Rather than using a portfolio manager to pick stocks that he thinks will outperform the market, an index fund uses investors' money to purchase a group of stocks that are weighted in the same way as a broad market index. For example, a typical stock index fund contains the same stocks as the Standard & Poor's 500 stock index, a broad gauge of the market.

You could think of indexing as akin to gardening. If you're a gardener, chances are you plant a variety of seeds, knowing that some will harvest better than others. You probably don't place all your money on tomatoes or on squash. You pick a little of this and a little of that. You don't know exactly what you'll harvest. But your chances of getting something are pretty good. If you plant only lettuce and the rabbits eat it, you're out of luck.

Likewise, an index fund contains a little of this and a little of that—all the stocks that represent what we think of as the overall market. It holds roughly the same securities in the same relative amounts all the time, so there's no need for a manager. Instead, these funds are "passively managed." That simply means that the securities are bought and held. They are rarely traded. Some active mutual fund managers move out of the market and into a cash position when they think the market is weak. But an index fund is always fully invested in the securities of the index it tracks.

An index fund offers advantages and disadvantages. Obviously, you are better off simply "owning the market" with an index fund than investing in a mutual fund that underperforms the market. And the truth is that the majority of money managers do underperform the

An Index Fund Should Track the Index It Follows

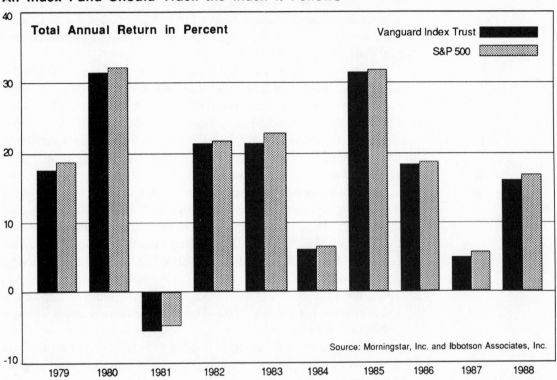

Total Annual Return in Percent

Vanguard Index Trust

S&P 500

Source: Morningstar, Inc. and Ibbotson Associates, Inc.

market averages. An index fund will *never* outperform the market, but neither should it underperform by much. A good index fund will closely track the movement of the index it follows, falling slightly shy of the market's performance because of administrative fees. Secondly, because index funds are not actively managed or traded, there is no management fee. Finally, an index fund saves you from the chore of picking a money manager and monitoring his performance. If you believe that the stock market is a good bet over time but you don't want to bother with these details, an index fund is a good choice for you.

As you know by now, the really influential investors are the institutional investors who invest billions of dollars for pension funds, insurance companies, and mutual funds. Because they invest in such large quantities, they pay less in fees, commissions, and expenses than individual investors. This resembles the wholesale and retail business in any product area. For example, a restaurateur buys his fish in the wholesale market, where he pays far less per pound for tuna steak because of the quantity he buys than you pay in the retail market when you visit your local fish store.

Because of their low cost and their ability to track the market, index funds have long appealed to institutional investors. Costs to these big-money managers are extremely low, much less than an individual investor pays. For example, a typical fee for an actively managed institutional fund is .5 percent of the assets under management (or 50 basis points). But for an index fund, that fee is 10 basis points, or .1 percent of assets under management.

Individual investors must pay more for index funds than institutions do. And many mutual fund companies have been reluctant to offer them at all. The oldest index fund available to individual investors is the Vanguard Index Trust. This no-load fund that tracks the Standard & Poor's 500 stock index was introduced in 1976. And it's done a good job of tracking the average. From August 1976 through August 1987, the fund earned a 407.7 percent rate of return, compared to 435.0 percent for the S&P 500. The expense ratio is about 28 basis points or 2.8 cents on $10.

Even if you're a conservative investor, an index fund can work for a portion of your money. Your investment is almost certain to grow much more quickly than it would in any guaranteed bank account. Your biggest risk is that you might need the money at a time when the market is in the doldrums. For that reason, it's always prudent to put only a part of your portfolio in stocks. If you want to buy an index fund, first check the performance of the index that the fund purports to mimic. Next, check to see how close the fund has come to tracking the index. And check the expense ratio. A true index fund should have low costs and it should demonstrate good success in following the index.

BOND INDEX FUNDS

What's good for stocks can also be good for bonds. Like a stock index fund, a bond index fund doesn't require any fancy fund picking. It aims to match, rather than outperform, a broad bond market index.

These funds were developed to provide a low-cost way to participate in the overall bond market without picking particular sectors or maturities. You make two decisions: that you want to invest part of your portfolio in bonds, and that you'll be happy to do as well as the overall bond market.

The Vanguard Group of funds developed the first bond index fund in December 1986. It is designed to track the **Salomon Brothers Broad Investment Grade Bond Index.** This index outperformed 65 percent of professionally managed bond funds in the period from 1980 to 1986. Historically, bonds have not produced returns as high as those in the stock market. But diversification in a portfolio is important. If you want to put part of your portfolio in bonds, but you're mystified by the workings of this market, an index fund will diversify your portfolio and should match the performance of the bond market as a whole.

Salomon Brothers Bond Index   Broad index that measures the movement of the bond market.

WHEN AN INDEX FUND REALLY ISN'T

You should be aware that not all index funds follow the same principle of tracking the overall market with an unmanaged fund that charges low fees. When index funds began to catch on, many fund companies introduced funds that follow various indexes. For example, the Gateway Option Income fund is a no-load fund that follows the Standard & Poor's 100 stock index. It uses options and futures in an attempt to add income. The Bench Blue Chip Portfolio fund attempts to track the Dow Jones Industrial Average (although Dow Jones will not allow it to use their name). The Rushmore OTC Index Plus fund tracks the NASDAQ 100 index of over-the-counter stocks. And the Colonial International Equity Index follows the European–Australian–Far Eastern Index. Many of these funds differ from the "passively managed" index funds. The indexes are not representative of the broad market, for one thing. Because many charge a sales commission, they are not low cost. And the securities are actively traded by managers who try to outperform the index rather than match it.

That means that they more closely resemble **sector funds**—funds that invest in only one sector of the market, rather than the market as a whole. (See the discussion of sector funds in Chapter 10.) That

Sector fund   Mutual fund that invests in one segment of the market. The idea of most mutual funds is to diversify investment dollars over a broad spectrum of securities. Sector funds concentrate in one particular market segment, such as energy, transportation, gold, small stocks, or international stocks.

doesn't mean they're poor investments, but they're not conservative investments. On the contrary, they can be very volatile. And an investment in them needs close tending. If what you want is a true index fund, look for these characteristics: no sales charge; low expense ratio; fully invested in a broad market index like the S&P 500; passively managed.

401 (K) PLANS

Salary reduction plan
Employer-sponsored plan that allows employees to set aside pre-tax dollars for certain health and retirement needs. Salary reduction plans used for retirement are named for sections of the IRS code that established them: 401 (k) plans *for employees of for-profit companies;* 403(b) plans *for employees of nonprofit organizations, for example, school systems, universities, and nonprofit hospitals;* 457 plans *for employees of the federal government and its agencies.*

Susan's most immediate need is to figure out what to do about her company's 401 (k) plan. Even if you do not share the conservative investment goals of this chapter, you, too, may be befuddled about these **salary reduction plans** designed to help you invest for your retirement. If your employer offers a salary reduction plan and you have not invested in it or you have not thought through how to integrate this plan into the rest of your investment portfolio, it's time to do it. Like Susan's boyfriend, Jim, you may be willing to take a few more risks with your plan.

These plans, named for the section of the Internal Revenue Service Code that authorized them, were approved in 1978, but the original rule was murky. It was not until November 1981 that the IRS made it clear that employees could put away pretax dollars of their own into the investment plans. The idea immediately took off. In 1982, just 2 percent of the Fortune 100 companies offered 401 (k) plans. By 1986, nearly 90 percent of the largest companies offered them.

No matter what your investment type, if you have the opportunity to participate in one of these plans, you can't afford to pass it up. They are one of the few tax shelters to survive the Tax Reform Act of 1986. These plans offer the opportunity to sock away pretax dollars—up to 25 percent of your income, minus the 401(k) contribution, or a maximum of $7,627 in 1989 (the cap moves up each year with the Consumer Price Index). Some employers may actually set the percentage limit lower to ensure compliance with other IRS requirements that apply to the plan as a whole. Let's say you earn $45,000 a year. If you put $7,000 into a 401 (k) plan, that reduces your taxable income to $38,000. If you pay tax at the 28 percent rate, that would save you

$1,960 in federal taxes. You would probably be able to save additional money in state and local taxes depending on state and local tax laws.

Better yet, most of these plans give you a salary increase that you would otherwise miss out on. That's because most employers match at least part of your contribution. For example, many companies kick in 50 cents on the dollar or even match dollar for dollar the contributions you make up to a certain percentage of your salary. Let's say you make $60,000. Your employer may match your contribution dollar for dollar up to 4 percent of your salary. That means that if you join the plan, your employer will pay you $2,400 extra, bringing your income up to $62,400.

The IRS recently tightened the rules on premature withdrawals from these plans. In most cases, you must pay taxes as well as a 10 percent penalty if you withdraw the money before age 59½. But you can borrow money from your plan and pay yourself interest. Although you can't deduct the interest for tax purposes, you can tap the fund to borrow money for your child's education or a down payment on a home, for example. And, finally, you control your retirement account. You make the investment decisions. And if you leave your job, your 401 (k) money goes with you. (But you must roll it into an Individual Retirement Account or another retirement plan to avoid paying taxes on it.)

Like Susan, you probably know you should contribute. If you don't, you may not have a retirement plan. But what can you do with your contribution? How do you fit it into your overall investment portfolio? It's not as if you can pick from the entire universe of investments for this retirement money. Your employers have already picked the plan. They've also picked the investment manager. You have no control over that. But there are still questions you can ask.

Most companies offer three to five different investment options. Some employers allow you to choose between two different money management firms. Typically these are the same companies that offer mutual fund and insurance investment products. Often the funds that you can buy with your 401 (k) money are the same ones you might select as a regular investor. In some cases, you might even have the opportunity to buy a popular fund that has been closed to the public. For example, the Windsor Fund, managed by John Neff of Wellington Management, closes to new investments from time to time. It would accept only those investor contributions that came through 401 (k) plans or Keoghs or IRAs. If your company offers such an option, it could allow you to buy into a fund to which you have no other means of access.

Chances are, though, that you have a typical range of mutual fund options plus a **guaranteed investment contract** (GIC), which is an insurance company product that guarantees your principal and offers you a fixed rate of return. You might also be able to choose stock in your own company. And your mutual fund choices might include a government bond fund, a growth stock fund, and a balanced fund. Most companies allow employees to split their contributions in any way they choose. They also generally permit you to switch your investment quarterly. This means that you can't count on leaping out of the stock market on the spur of the moment if you think it's heading down the tubes. You certainly can't be a market timer with this money, switching from one market to the other to pick up short-term gains. You should consider your 401 (k) as a long-term portfolio. And, as with any portfolio, you should diversify. You should also consider it part of your overall portfolio, which includes your home, your children's college money, and your other investments.

GICs are the most popular choice for 401 (k) plans, with 40 percent of the money going into this investment in 1987. If you're very conservative, you'll probably want to put part of your investment here. These insurance company instruments are the equivalent of a bank certificate of deposit. You will get your principal back, with a specified amount of interest. The interest rate can vary, so you must check to see what your company's offering pays. Company stock is also a popular investment. But, if you remember the rule of thinking about everything in your life as a risk, you may not want to bet your livelihood and your retirement account on the same company. In most cases, it makes sense to diversify by investing in a general equity mutual fund instead.

What about the mutual fund options in the 401 (k) plan? First find out about the fund company and managers available to you. Some mutual fund companies have portfolio managers with great records as stock pickers. If you're an aggressive investor like Jim and you're interested in a speculative growth fund, the manager's record is all-important. Some perform spectacularly, some dismally. Since you

Guaranteed investment contract Contract between an investor and an insurance company that guarantees return of premium and that pays a set rate of interest. A popular investment for 401 (k) plans.

probably have only one aggressive choice in the plan, you need to check that fund's records. Look in the annual mutual fund rankings that appear in *Money* magazine, *Barron's, Forbes,* and *Business Week.* Check the ten-year performance records of the various funds they offer. Even if the fund is offered only for 401 (k) plans, you can find out the name of the fund manager and check his record with other funds he manages. Some funds are managed by insurance companies and the performance won't show up in published lists. In that case, you can ask your benefits department to provide the information.

If you're an aggressive investor and the fund manager of your plan offers a fund with a truly spectacular track record, you'll probably want to put a chunk of your money there—perhaps 40 to 50 percent. The rest should be split among one or two other investment choices. If you discover that the management company you're saddled with doesn't have a great stock-picking record, don't put your money in its stock fund. In that case, look into the performance of its bond funds. What about its "middle-of-the-road" funds, like a balanced or growth and income fund? If you pick more conservative, income investments for your 401 (k) money because you feel they're the best of your options, take a look at the rest of your portfolio. Maybe you want to be more aggressive with your other investments to balance your more conservative 401 (k) choices.

SUSAN SCHWARTZ'S CHOICES

It would be an exaggeration to call Susan a conservative investor. Until now she hasn't been an investor; she's simply been a saver. But she's ready to dip her toe into the water. Her company offers three stock mutual funds, two bond funds, and a guaranteed investment contract.

• She puts $4,000, or 11 percent of her salary, into the 401 (k). With her employer's contribution, it will bring her annual total to $5,400. She chooses a stock index fund for 20 percent of her money, an intermediate-term government bond fund for another 20 percent, and a GIC for 60 percent.

• She picks a mutual fund family and moves $5,000 from her pass-

Susan Schwartz's Portfolio

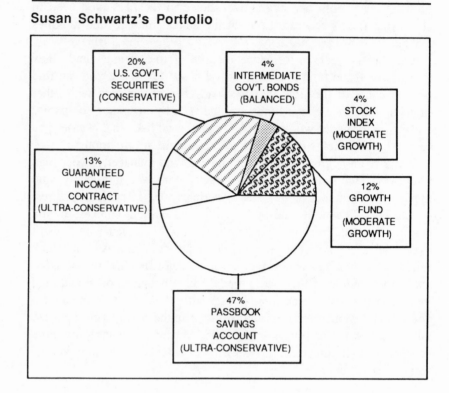

book account into a U.S. government securities money market fund. In six months, she promises to check her investments. Her goal is to move 20 percent of this money into a growth investment.

• Susan is moving cautiously. But she's moving. When she grows comfortable with her new investments, she plans to move more of the money from her passbook account into the government securities money market fund, and from there into other investments. Her goal is to gradually move 20 percent of her overall assets into growth investments—not a lot, but enough to give her portfolio a little kick. And she'd like to move toward 50 percent in income investments like money market and bond funds. But she'll always want to have a chunk of her money—about 30 percent—in guaranteed-return investments like bank accounts and guaranteed investment contracts (GICs).

POINTS TO REMEMBER

As you try to adjust your portfolio to take on a little more risk, remember:

- If you think that risk simply means that you might lose the dollar you have in your hand, you need to broaden your thinking. You risk losing your job, losing new opportunities, losing your chance for a better life.

- The safest money market funds are those that invest exclusively in IOUs of the U.S. Treasury, backed by the full faith and credit of the U.S. government.

- It's true that risk and reward go hand in hand. But the gradations of risk can be very subtle. You can choose a slightly less risky investment that returns only pennies less than its less secure cousin.

- The volatile interest rates of the past decade have made bonds, once a conservative income investment, a far more unpredictable investment, driven by changes in the direction of interest rates as well as the creditworthiness of the issuer.

- One conservative stock market investment is an index fund, a basket of stocks that tracks the performance of the overall market.

- Employer-sponsored retirement plans such as 401 (k) plans are excellent tax shelters. Everyone who's eligible should take advantage of them. But as with any portfolio, investments in these retirement plans should be diversified.

Chapter 6

Going Nowhere—When Discipline Is the Issue

J ack Carpenter has always been proud that he came of age in the sixties—an exciting time to be alive, to learn, to experience new things. Like many of his peers, he valued experiences over possessions. Sure, it was nice to have a cold beer and a decent pair of jeans. But the most expensive thing he really had a yen for was some good stereo equipment. It would be nice to relax with some good music at the end of the day. Yet it wasn't worth putting on a three-piece suit every day.

Jack went to Berkeley. He marched for civil rights and demonstrated against the Vietnam war, environmental pollution, and nuclear armaments. He spent several years with the Peace Corps, did some traveling in South America, and spent lots of time working for things he considered important, such as politicians who he thought might change the things that were wrong with society.

When sixties hippies evolved into preppies during the "Me Decade," Jack didn't make the transition. He never started jogging and he didn't cook gourmet food. Then, when preppies became yuppies, Jack stayed far behind in the 1960s. His idea of relaxing was still hanging out, drinking a few beers, reading *Rolling Stone,* and listening to some good music. Fortunately, he could afford a decent stereo now. But he shunned VCRs, microwaves, Akita dogs, and BMWs. Maybe the lifestyle of the protest era was only a memory for most people, but he didn't think that meant he had to be a glutton. Still, he did notice that there were fewer and fewer old friends to hang around with. And he began to get restless.

Now Jack is 40. A couple of years ago he could still laugh at his peers who devoured *Money* magazine and chatted with their stockbrokers several times a day. But no more. He decided it was time to settle down. Fortunately, he had gone to a good school and hung around long enough to get a master's degree. And he is talented enough to get a decent job in advertising. He pulls in $40,000 a year at a Denver agency. His wife also is planning to go back to work. But they have little—or no—money tucked away. And, because Jack has always considered ''money'' something of a dirty word, he knows nothing about investing.

Furthermore, they've never set goals. They still rent an apartment; they don't have much furniture; no art, rugs, collectibles. The money Jack brings in just sort of dribbles away on the fantasy of the moment— a trip to San Francisco, a new compact disc player. When they see something they like, they buy it. If they overspend, then they do without. On the plus side, Jack and Beth have plenty of time. Once Beth lands a job, they should be making good money—maybe $60,000 a year. They can tuck away money a little at a time, work at building their net worth, saving for retirement, and accumulating assets to improve their way of life. Besides, Beth is intrigued by the idea of investing. Because Jack has shown such contempt for it in the past, she hasn't wanted to let him know that she sees some romance in it. The Carpenters know they need to do something. They need to set goals; they need to discipline themselves to save and invest; they need to make progress toward building a better life for themselves. They don't know how to start. But Beth is willing to do a little research to find out.

Whether or not you share their politics, you may see something of the Carpenters in yourself. Do you:

- Have little discipline when it comes to saving or investing?
- Wish you had set some financial goals?
- Have little money put away for investments?
- Feel uncertain of your tolerance for risk—perhaps because you've never even thought about it?

- Prefer to spend your free time listening to music, reading novels, going to movies or hockey games—anything but reviewing the latest financial news?
- Have plenty of time to tuck away small amounts of money before you need it for some major life event?

You, too, may be going nowhere if you haven't paid much attention to your overall financial needs, if you've just left to chance such things as financial planning, retirement needs, college education, wealth building. If you subscribe to the catch-as-catch-can theory of finance, figuring that you'll always be able to pay your bills, because you always have, you may find that you're not really getting anywhere. If you're the type who does a year-end review of your general progress in the game of life, maybe you find that there hasn't been much to note on the financial side; that your net worth never really seems to change.

Few people can achieve what they want without some type of financial plan, without some goals and some method for investing money so that it will grow and outpace inflation. It's true, you may get a big inheritance. You may win the lottery. Or you may invent something that becomes a runaway success. But, for most of us, the only real way to achieve what we want is with a steady, regular plan of putting money away. For those of us like the Carpenters, who have always spent as much as we've had, discipline can be a problem. Fortunately, there are some answers.

DISCIPLINE, DISCIPLINE

The problem many investors have—particularly novices like Jack—is that they believe they must figure out how to "buy low and sell high" in order to invest. But, because they know little about how the markets operate, they're befuddled as to how to go about it. It seems too complicated. But there is a method of investing that allows you to avoid this difficulty. Rather than trying to guess whether the markets are heading up or down, you simply invest the same amount every month over a long period. Perhaps this method sounds too simple to be called a strategy, but there's beauty to this simplicity.

First of all, most fund companies allow you to start small. Many waive the normal initial minimum deposit on a fund if you agree that you will make regular deposits. It's also convenient. You can have the money deducted from your paycheck or from your bank account, if you like. Or you can simply send in a regular check. Many fund companies will accept deposits of as little as $50 a month. And, if you want to diversify your portfolio, you can deposit $100—$50 in each of two different funds.

There's something more than convenience behind this idea, though. Studies show that over a long period, investors who make regular investments tend to pay less per share for their mutual fund shares than those who purchase them for a lump sum. Because you are investing the same amount every month, your investment buys more shares when the market is down and fewer when it is up. This is just the opposite of what many investors tend to do on their own. When the market turns down, they sit on the sidelines. For example, after the **October 1987 market crash,** many investors moved out of the stock market and into money market funds or bond funds. But the stock market quickly moved up from its postcrash low. On top of that, during the final quarter of 1987 and the first quarter of 1988, the average stock mutual fund easily outperformed the market. In fact, nine out of ten of the U.S. stock fund categories measured by **Lipper Analytical Services** outperformed the index average in the first quarter of 1988, with the average stock fund gaining 7.43 percent while the S&P 500 stock index rose 5.69 percent. So this was a good time to be in stock mutual funds.

But many investors who had experienced the October plunge missed the subsequent rise. Some investors wait until they feel certain that the stock market is on a strong upward course again before they start buying shares. By then they pay inflated prices. The regular, disciplined method of investing, which financial people call **dollar cost averaging,** is designed to help you avoid this investing pattern. It also allows you to spread your risk, because you are paying varying prices for shares of the same fund.

October 1987 market crash
Drastic drop in stock markets around the world on October 19, 1987. In the United States, the Dow Jones Industrial Average dropped 508.32 points—22.6 percent — to 1,738.42. The 1987 crash far exceeded the drop of 12.8 percent on October 28, 1929, which ushered in the Great Depression.

Lipper Analytical Services
Wall Street research company that tracks the investment performance of mutual funds. Lipper sells its mutual fund research to institutions. But the quarterly fund rankings are available to consumers in Barron's. *Other magazines, like* Money *and* Forbes, *also publish rankings based on Lipper's results.*

HOW DOLLAR COST AVERAGING WORKS

Consider an extreme example. Let's say you decide in January to invest $100 each month in the Rowland Fund. The fund is selling at $25 a share and your $100 buys 4 shares. But over the next two months, the market nosedives. In February, Rowland Fund drops to $20 a share. Your $100 that month buys 5 shares. In March, the price sinks to $12.50 and your $100 buys 8 shares. In three months, you have purchased 17 shares of Rowland Fund. Had you, instead, put $300 into the fund in January, you would have had only 12 shares. So at the end of March your investment is worth $212.50 (17 shares times $12.50 a share) rather than $150 (12 shares times $12.50 a share).

Over the course of the next seven months, the market drops further before climbing back to where it began in January. At the end of ten months, shares of Rowland Fund have risen back to $25. And your advantage has increased, too. Your $1,000, invested in $100 increments each month, has purchased 78 shares, which are now worth $1,950.

Consider the result if you had invested the entire $1,000 back in January. You would have purchased 40 shares, and ten months later, your 40 shares would have been worth the same $1,000. And that assumes that you didn't panic and sell when the price hit $8—always a temptation—and that you didn't then regret your impulsive decision and buy back in (gulp!) when the price hit $25 again, netting you a miserable loss.

Of course, the market usually doesn't fluctuate quite so dramatically in ten months. And this method of investing is not designed for short-term profit taking. In fact, it's only useful on a long-term basis. It shouldn't be used for emergency money. But what it does provide is the discipline of regular purchases no matter what happens to the market. In his book *Life Cycle Investing,* Donald R. Nichols sums up this investment strategy by saying, "The disciplined, elegant simplicity of this method helps investors shun two emotional mistakes: avoiding investment when prices are depressed and investing more when prices are rising."

Dollar cost averaging
Method of buying stock or mutual fund shares by investing the same amount of money on a regular schedule regardless of the market price. Dollar cost averaging allows investors to avoid guessing whether the market is going up or down. The advantage of this method is that your dollars buy more shares when the price is down, fewer when the price is up. Studies show that investors who use dollar cost averaging tend to pay less per share over time than those who purchase shares in a lump sum.

Using Dollar Cost Averaging in a Fluctuating Market

Period	Amount Invested	Market Price Paid	Shares Purchased
Jan.	100	25	4
Feb.	100	20	5
March	100	12.50	8
April	100	10	10
May	100	8	12.50
June	100	8	12.50
July	100	10	10
Aug.	100	12.50	8
Sept.	100	25	4
Oct.	100	25	4
	$1,000		78

Your average cost per share ($1,000/78 shares): $12.82
Average market price per share (Total of market price = $156.00/10): $15.60
With dollar cost averaging, $1,000 buys 78 shares over 10 months
At the average market price, $1,000 buys 64.1 shares
$1,000 invested in January buys 40 shares

The only real homework you need to do is in the beginning when you select the fund or funds you will purchase. From there the technique is very simple: You commit yourself to investing a certain amount of money at regular intervals—monthly, quarterly, or even weekly—over a long period. You put the money in faithfully whether the market goes up or down. This is not a legal promise. It's a voluntary plan. But it only works if you live up to it. And that requires two things: first, that you stick to your plan and, second, that you ignore the ups and downs of the market. The more you can resist the temptation to tinker with your formula when your perception of the market changes, the better it will work. Discipline and objectivity are the keys to this method of investing.

What kind of fund works best? No matter what type you choose, your cost should be less than the average price per share over a long period. But some experts argue that the more volatile the fund, the better you will do. That's because, when the price falls, your dollars will buy more shares. Although this is true, you must consider how you will feel if the value of your investment sinks like a stone. Say you kick in your monthly $100 and buy three shares at $33.33 each. The next week the market crashes and the shares you own are worth $20 apiece. Your $100 investment is now worth $60. If you're in it for the long term, believe that over time the method will work, and have the stomach for it, pick an aggressive fund. But you do need to consider your psychological reaction to market swings. And the method will also work with a more conservative fund. If that's more your style, go for that instead.

Ten years is considered a minimum time horizon for dollar cost averaging. Fifteen is better. But the investment is not risk free. As with all investments in stocks, its success depends on the fundamental assumption that the value of the mutual funds will grow over time because of growth in earnings and dividends of corporations these funds are buying. The stock market has proven to be superior to any other investment over time. But your plan can come a cropper if the end of your time horizon—the day you need your money—happens to coincide with a severe bear market.

Dollar cost averaging is a disciplined way of buying mutual funds. But it doesn't address the question of selling at all. As you approach the time when you need your money, you should reevaluate what you're doing. It might make sense to continue the discipline, but to start moving your investment into a more defensive kind of fund. For example, if you accumulated assets for 15 or 20 years for retirement, as you approach retirement, you should be moving from the accumulation phase to the preservation phase. One option would be to move into an income fund or even a money market fund when it's to your advantage, when the price of your shares is up during a bull market.

CONTRACTUAL PLANS

Perhaps you like the *idea* of investing, but let's face it, like Jack Carpenter, you're a hard-core spender. Unless the kids need shoes, you'll blow your last few bucks on a new suede jacket, a bunch of fresh

Contractual plan A mutual fund investment plan that requires an investor to sign a contract agreeing to invest a predetermined amount of money periodically over a certain number of years to reach a set investment goal. The plans have been criticized for their high up-front sales commissions and have fallen off in popularity. Nonetheless some investors still choose them because they offer the discipline that enables them to invest.

daisies, theater tickets, or dinner out. You know yourself well enough to know that you won't tuck away even ten dollars on an infrequent basis. Don't despair. There's something for you, too. **Contractual plans,** which were at the height of their popularity in the 1950s and 1960s, are designed for people with no self-discipline. If money burns a hole in your pocket; if you are counting on a winning lottery ticket to finance your retirement; if you've never even been able to discipline yourself to put money in the bank, perhaps you want to take a look at these plans. But they're by no means an ideal investment. They carry hefty up-front fees. They are designed for those of us who must be *forced* to invest.

A contractual plan is a contract between you and the mutual fund company. Unlike the accumulation plans discussed in Chapter 4, these plans represent a legal contract. You will be penalized if you fail to live up to the terms. You decide how much money you want to invest and you pick the term of the contract. For example, you may say that you want to invest $10,000 over a 15-year period. The mutual fund company then draws up the contract and tells you how much money you must invest each month to reach the goal of $10,000 at the end of 15 years. This does not mean that you will *have* $10,000 at the end of the period. You are investing your money in a common stock mutual fund, so there are no guarantees. But your hope is that you will have much more than the $10,000 you invested. Your contract specifies the term of the investment, the total amount you put in, and how much you contribute each month; it says nothing about how much you will actually have at the end of the period.

First, look at the advantages. You have become an instant convert from spendthrift to thrifty. You've made investing a part of your monthly budget, just like your mortgage payment and your car insurance. And, because you are making regular, monthly payments, you are taking advantage of dollar cost averaging. The consistent influx of new money is a big plus for the portfolio manager as well. Because he knows just how much new money is coming in every month, he can plan his stock purchases accordingly. This normally helps his performance and, therefore, the performance of the fund. One of the big difficulties many fund managers have, particularly in a sliding stock market, is that lots of shareholders redeem their shares at the same time and the manager has to sell stock into a falling market to raise cash for the redemptions. This is not a problem for the manager of the contractual plan because the money comes in, month after month. For this reason, many of these funds perform very well.

One of the better-known contractual plans is offered by Fidelity Investments. Two funds, Destiny I and Destiny II, are available under the plan. Both have performed extremely well—so well that other investors would like to have a chance to invest in them. But they are available only through a contractual plan. Fidelity provides this example: If you invested $300 a month for 15 years from January 1, 1974, to January 1, 1989, your total investment would equal $54,000. If you had all your dividends reinvested in the fund, your investment would be worth $271,258 at the end of the 15-year period. That's a gain of over 402.3 percent on your principal. Not bad for a reluctant investor!

Now let's look at the downside. Like insurance policies, contractual plans are not bought, they're sold. What that means is that salesmen have to work hard to persuade confirmed spenders to invest their money. These people are a tough sell. And when they succeed the salesmen are highly rewarded with a hefty **commission.** You, the reluctant investor, are paying it. For example, Destiny I and Destiny II carry a **sales charge** that totals 8.96 percent of the full amount of your investment. Most of the charges are deducted in the first year of the plan. That means two things: much of the money you contribute in the first year doesn't go to work for you and, if you change your mind, you will lose money because of the sales fees.

You do have some protection. For example, by law no more than 50 percent of the first year's installments can go for sales charges. You also can get a complete refund if you change your mind during the first 45 days after the investor's certificate is mailed to you. At that point you would get the sales charges and fees back as well. Further, if you sign a contract that requires you to pay 50 percent of the first year's installments as fees and other charges, you have the right to change your mind for up to 18 months. However, you will still have to pay part of the sales charges. And, if you opt to get out of the plan, you will receive the value of the account at that time rather than the amount of your initial investment.

The plans do allow you some flexibility. For example, the Destiny fund allows you to pay in advance or to skip a payment and catch up later. If you get in a real jam, you can keep your account active by

Commission   Portion of the purchase price that is paid to a salesperson or middleman. You pay a commission to a real estate agent when you sell your house. You pay an insurance salesman a commission when you buy a policy. And you pay a commission to a stockbroker when you ask him to buy or sell securities for you.

Sales charge   Charge to invest in a mutual fund, which goes directly to the company. It differs from a commission, which is paid to the salesperson.

INVESTING IN A CONTRACTUAL PLAN:
CONSIDER THE EXAMPLE OF FIDELITY DESTINY FUND
If you had invested $15,000 in monthly increments of $125 (an initial payment of $250) in Fidelity Destiny Fund, for the 10-year period of 12/31/78 to 12/31/88, your investment would have been worth $35,556.19 at the end of the ten-year period. You would have paid these fees: monthly sales charges of $62.50 deducted from 1st 13 monthly payments and $4.50 deducted from each subsequent payment, and custodian fees of $3.00 deducted from the initial payment and $1.50 deducted from subsequent payments.

INVESTMENTS			DEDUCTIONS		END OF PERIOD	
PAYMENTS ($125/MO)	DIVIDENDS INVESTED IN SHARES	CAPITAL GAINS INVESTED IN SHARES	COMMISSION	CUSTODIAN FEE	TOTAL VALUE OF SHARES	TOTAL NUMBER OF SHARES
$15,000.00	$3,829.61	$17,526.88	$1,294.00	$180.00	$35,556.19	2,982.902

Fidelity offers this note of caution: The period from 1979 to 1988 was one of generally fluctuating security prices. The results shown should not be considered as a representation of the dividend income or capital gain or loss which may be realized from an investment in the fund today. Periodic investment plans cannot assure a profit or protect against depreciation in declining markets.

And also this note: No adjustment has been made for income taxes payable by shareholders on income dividends or capital gain distributions.

simply making one payment in a 12-month period. You can also borrow as much as 90 percent of the value of your account once a year. And, of course, you can simply break your contract. But the incentive to keep going is that you have paid all those up-front fees. These plans are really for the hard core who plan to stick with it for the long term. Don't consider one unless you know you won't invest regularly any other way.

SOCIALLY RESPONSIBLE FUNDS

Socially Responsible Mutual Funds Worth Considering

Perhaps, like Jack Carpenter, you're not only a reluctant investor, but also one with a strong social conscience. In that case, you'll be interested to know about a small group of mutual funds—perhaps ten or twelve—that limit their investments to companies that they consider ethical or socially responsible. Some of these funds, like the Dreyfus Third Century Fund, have been around since the early 1970s. The number of funds in this category doesn't seem to shrink or grow. But ethical investing has come into the limelight recently, as concerns about nuclear armaments, apartheid in South Africa, tobacco, alcohol, industrial pollution, and discrimination against minorities have grown. Just as many states, cities, and universities were selling their stock in companies that continued to do business in South Africa in the mid-1980s, some mutual fund managers put together portfolios of the stocks of companies that adhered to strict "socially responsible" standards.

These are funds for people who want to put their money where their values are; who don't want to help companies that they feel are destroying the world, or simply making it less pleasant. Critics of these funds say that it's foolish to restrict your investments in any way, that doing so only limits your potential return. They also argue that by eliminating companies that manufacture cigarettes or make weapons, for example, the portfolio manager will have to screen out many large, multinational, multi-industry blue-chip companies that have steady earnings growth. The companies that meet the ethical criteria are likely to be smaller and their stock more volatile. For that reason, these funds often perform like small-company funds, doing well when the stocks of small, emerging growth companies are in favor and poorly when they're not. (For a discussion of small-company funds, see Chapter 9.)

During the five-year bull market of the 1980s, small companies underperformed the market averages and so did these funds. "Ethical funds" took a real beating in the October 1987 market crash. But then, in 1988, when small-company stocks started to recover, the socially responsible funds did well, too. For the first six months of 1988, seven of these funds attracted investor attention when they beat both the market average and the average gain for equity mutual funds. For example, in 1988, the Parnassus Fund gained 42.44 percent and Ariel Growth, another socially responsible fund, was up 39.97 percent.

Overall, performance figures for the mutual funds that adhere to these "socially responsible" standards do not appear to be much different from those of the average mutual fund. The socially responsible funds do not all have the same investment objectives. Some are growth funds, some are balanced, some are industry or sector funds specializing in one particular sector. For that reason, they are not ranked by

Calvert Ariel Growth

Calvert Social Investment Fund: Managed Growth Portfolio and Money Market Portfolio
800-368-2748

Dreyfus Third Century
800-645-6561

New Alternatives
516-466-0808
(not a toll-free number)

Parnassus Fund
800-999-3505

Pax World
603-431-8022 (not a toll-free number)

Pioneer Fund

Pioneer II

Pioneer III
800-622-0181

Working Assets Money Market
415-989-3200
(not a toll-free number)

For a longer list of socially responsible investments and more information on the subject, including names of organizations and newsletters that specialize in socially responsible investments, try your local library or bookstore for Ethical Investing *by Domini and Kinder (Addison-Wesley, 1986).*

the rating services in a single group. If you feel strongly that you don't want your investment dollars going to assist something you abhor, you can probably do all right in these funds. If you don't feel *too* strongly about it, you can do better elsewhere. If you do decide to pick a socially responsible fund, you still must decide what investment objective you're after and check to see if there's a fund that suits both your conscience and your investment needs.

BALANCED FUNDS

Assets   Property with value. Your personal assets include your home, car, furnishings, jewelry, clothing, and investments. When money managers talk about assets, they mean the amount of money they're managing, which they refer to as "assets under management."

Another way for a beginner like Jack to diversify is *within* the same fund. One way to do that is with a balanced fund, which combines stocks and bonds in more or less equal parts in the same portfolio. The original idea of these funds, which have been around since the late 1920s, was to provide the investor diversification within a single fund by spreading the investment dollars over both of the major markets. At least one early fund manager, who moved his **assets** out of stocks and into bonds throughout 1929, was able to save shareholders from much of the fallout of the 1929 crash. Like other managers in other general fund categories, those who manage balanced funds have different approaches. Some may tilt the fund more toward securities that have the potential to appreciate; others may opt for income. Either way, a balanced fund is a conservative, middle-of-the-road investment that gives you diversification within a single investment choice.

In a troubled investment environment, for example, when the stock market is choppy but bonds are doing well, the balance should keep the net asset value of your fund fairly steady. In unusual times, like the bull markets in both bonds and stocks that lasted for the first half of the decade of the 1980s, the performance of balanced funds is top-notch, outperforming most other kinds of mutual funds. If both the stock and bond markets are doing poorly, though, you can expect shares of a balanced fund to reflect that as well.

But these versatile funds can be right for just about any investment environment. If you are a conservative investor or even if you are a more aggressive investor who needs some ballast in your portfolio of high flyers, a balanced fund can be for you.

CUSHIONING INVESTORS FROM EXTREMES: WALTER MORGAN ON BALANCED FUNDS

When Walter L. Morgan, an ambitious young Philadelphia CPA, set up one of the early mutual funds at the height of the 1920s stock market frenzy, he opted for caution. It was not a trendy position. From a low of 65 in 1921, the Dow Jones Industrial Average had risen to 300 by the end of 1928. It seemed that the sky was the limit. Why not jump on board?

Morgan, who had made some wildly speculative and unsuccessful investments of his own earlier in his life, was nervous about the toppy market and refused to be caught up in the frenzy. "Many stocks were selling at 50 to 100 times earnings and the wild market was approaching the edge of unreality," he said.

Looking for "an anchor to windward," he decided on a large position in fixed-income securities and preferred stocks when he created Industrial and Power Securities Company. It was one of the first of what were to become known as "balanced funds," because they invested in both stocks and bonds in order to protect the portfolio from sharp turns in one market or the other. (Scudder, Stevens & Clark introduced its Balanced Fund the same year.)

The objective of Morgan's fund was "to provide more protection (through larger cash and bond reserves) if markets appeared high and to attempt to build up profits through a larger common stock position if stocks appeared undervalued." Although, as Morgan says, he didn't expect "to bat 1,000," he did think he could turn in a better record than the average investor could earn for himself.

The fund, which Morgan later renamed Wellington for one of his heroes—the Iron Duke— started operations with $100,000 in assets on July 1, 1929. Balance was an immediate problem because most investors contributed stocks rather than cash. These Morgan sold rapidly to buy bonds. By the end of the summer, he had reduced the portion of his portfolio in common stocks to 75 percent.

As the stock market surged wildly, Morgan continued to dump stocks. By September, when the Dow Jones reached a record peak of 381, Morgan had 40 percent of the portfolio in common stock and 60 percent in fixed income. When the market crashed in October, Morgan's caution served him well. The fund's net asset value lost only a few pennies, dropping from $12.84 to $12.36. But after the market break, the fund managers moved back into stocks, thinking they were fairly valued. Meanwhile the market continued to sink like a stone until the middle of 1932. The fund's NAV fell as well—to its lowest point of $5.62 in 1933.

Nonetheless, the theory of balance between different types of securities that perform well in different types of markets has served Wellington and its investors well over the years. Although the returns have not been spectacular, neither have investors lost their shirts. From 1929 through 1987, the fund chalked up an average 7.7 percent annual return. That's lower than the 9.7 percent total return for the S&P 500; it's higher than the 4.9 percent return for the Salomon High Grade Corporate Bond Index. In other words, Wellington has done what Morgan intended from the beginning—cushioned investors from the extremes.

GROWTH FUNDS

That you haven't set investment goals until this point in your life doesn't necessarily mean that you're risk averse. You might simply lack knowledge about investing. Even if you're just getting your feet wet as an investor, if you're not too timid and you have some time to let your money grow, a growth fund could be a good choice. The line between growth funds and aggressive growth funds is a fine one. Aggressive growth funds (which are discussed in Chapter 11) go after the big returns. They offer the greatest potential reward and exact the greatest risk. A growth fund is just one step below an aggressive fund.

But honest men often disagree about which category a particular fund belongs in. To see the shadings of difference between the two types of funds, consider the funds managed by Harry Hutzler. Hutzler has managed two small, top-performing mutual funds for several years. Most of the services that rank the performance of mutual funds put both funds in the aggressive growth category. Hutzler, who manages the funds for AIM Management, gets heated about this. To him, the funds are totally different.

The Weingarten fund, which he has managed since 1969, is a growth fund, Hutzler says. For this portfolio he seeks the stocks of well-established companies that have consistent growth over the last ten years at a rate much faster than the economy as a whole. To qualify, a company must have earnings growth of at least 16 percent for a number of years. The strategy has served him well. The fund was up 616 percent for the ten years that ended on December 31, 1988, or 21.8 percent compounded annually. His second fund, the Constellation Fund, sports a portfolio of smaller, less-established companies that Hutzler believes have the potential for spectacular growth. This fund, which gained 510 percent, or 19.8 percent a year, over the same period, is an aggressive growth fund, according to Hutzler.

Although his reasoning is sound, it is easy to see how investors become confused by fund categories. Yet, if you consider the way

REWARDING OVER TIME, BUT THE RIDE CAN BE ROUGH: HENRY HUTZLER ON GROWTH FUND INVESTING

Harry Hutzler has beaten the stock market by at least two to one—sometimes three to one—for every ten-year period since 1969. One of the mutual funds he manages gained 616 percent, or 21.8 percent compounded annually, in the ten years that ended in December 1988. The other was up 510.3 percent, or an average of 19.8 percent.

Hutzler's secret? He doesn't believe in studying the economy; he ignores changes in interest rates, the trade deficit, the value of the dollar; he shuns market timing and refuses to try to pick the hot industries.

Instead, he picks growth stocks based on their fundamentals and stays fully invested in the market at all times. When the market goes down, so do his funds. But that doesn't worry him. He knows that as long as "I stay in there with both feet, I'll come back quickly."

Like all stock growth funds, the two funds Hutzler manages—Weingarten Equity Fund is a growth fund, Constellation is an aggressive growth fund—are considered aggressive investments. Just as they outperform the market over time, they also sink lower during a downturn. For example, Constellation, which invests in small growth companies, fell 43 percent from the market peak in August 1987 to the crash in October 1987, compared to a 33 percent drop for the overall market, as measured by the Standard & Poor's 500 stock index. But the fund also rebounded more quickly. From the crash through late February 1988, it was up 35 percent, compared to 18 percent for the S&P.

What does this mean for you as an individual investor? Even if you're not interested in using such a time-consuming method of analyzing stocks yourself, you can see from this record that a well-managed growth stock portfolio will perform well over the long term. If you decide that you want to put part of your money in growth or aggressive growth stocks, though, two things are crucial: You must examine the portfolio manager's performance record very carefully and you must diversify. Over a long period, your investment should do well. But you need some of your portfolio in income investments or cash to balance your investment.

Hutzler differentiates his funds, you will see what should be the dividing line between a growth and an aggressive growth fund. The former aims for growth of your investment but attempts to achieve it with established companies. Aggressive growth fund managers have much more latitude in deciding how to go about achieving their results. One way they do that is by investing early in new, promising companies in the hope of spectacular returns.

REAL ESTATE FUNDS

Real estate limited partnership *Real estate investment unit that consists of a general partner and limited partners. The general partner organizes the deal and is responsible for managing it. The limited partners, or investors, have liability only up to the amount of their investment. They hope to receive income and capital gains from the deal. Because there is not a liquid market for reselling these investments, they are generally considered a long-term investment, usually at least five to ten years.*

Jack Carpenter is conservative. But he and Beth do need to diversify. And, unlike many of us, the Carpenters don't have a real estate investment in their home. Real estate is a good balance to a portfolio of stock, money market, and bond funds. Although the stock market and bond market do not necessarily move in tandem, many of the same economic factors influence both types of securities. But, over time, real estate has been more stable than stocks and bonds and—more important in terms of diversification—real estate returns show little correlation with those of stocks and bonds. That means real estate investments do well in periods when stocks and bonds do poorly, such as times of high inflation. Although a portfolio of stocks would no doubt outperform a portfolio of stocks, bonds, and real estate over a ten-year period, the diversified portfolio would show more consistent returns, because real estate would balance the other two.

Investors have long realized this, of course. And many investors have a real estate investment in their home. Wealthy investors have the opportunity to invest in **real estate limited partnerships.** In order to make partnership investments, investors generally have to prove that they have substantial investment assets, excluding the investment in their homes. More recently, though, mutual fund companies have made real estate investments available to small investors as well. Some of these investments are real estate mutual funds. Because mutual funds must invest in securities, these mutual funds invest in real estate management and development companies and in the stocks of companies that will do well when the real estate market does well, such as paper and lumber companies, building supply companies, and railroads.

Other mutual fund companies offer a way to invest in the real estate market through what amounts to a no-load real estate partnership that invests in the properties themselves. If you're considering one of these investments, it's important to remember that this is *not* a mutual fund. One of the most important distinctions of a mutual fund is that the portfolio is marked to market every day and you can buy or sell at the net asset value. A limited partnership does not offer this advantage. If you want to diversify your portfolio by making a real estate investment, be certain that you know whether you are choosing a mutual fund that invests in real estate securities or a limited partnership.

THE CARPENTERS' CHOICES

The Carpenters have studied the options for solving their investment problems and getting started on a long-term investment program. Beth doesn't feel that they need the discipline of a contractual plan. Yet they don't feel they know enough to decide when to get into the market and when to get out. Here's what they've decided:

• They can scrape together the $1,000 to open a money market account, which Beth has learned is the linchpin of a beginning investment program.

• They plan to use the regular investment technique of dollar cost averaging. Slow and steady appeals to them. They will start with $250 a month.

• They choose a mutual fund family with a good record for stock growth funds. Maybe they're not aggressive investors yet. Still, they plan to let their money grow for a long time. They will put 40 percent of their money, or $100 each month, into a growth fund.

• They know they need to diversify, but they know nothing about the bond market. Another 40 percent, or $100, goes into a balanced fund. Even if the stock market heads south, this fund's investment in bonds should hold them on course. (A short-term bond fund would work to balance their portfolio, too.)

• The other 20 percent, or $50, goes into the money market fund.

POINTS TO REMEMBER

You may not make the same choices as the Carpenters. Still, you can learn something from the options they chose and the ones they discarded. And you should be able to get started on your own investment program. Remember:

The Carpenters' Portfolio

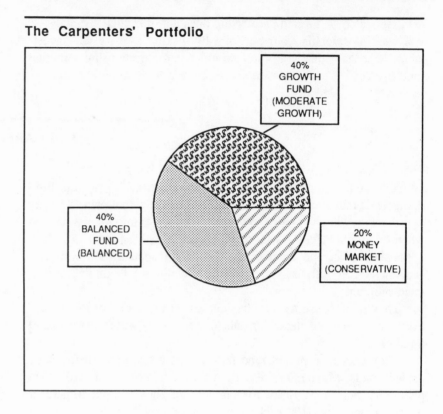

- It's never too late to set goals, start an investment program and begin building your wealth. There are even some special mutual fund programs to help you.
- Dollar cost averaging allows you to start small and helps you to discipline yourself to become a regular investor no matter how the markets perform. Over time, investments using this method outperform lump sum investments.
- If you're a hopeless spendthrift, there's something for you. For a stiff fee, a contractual plan will force you to invest.
- A small group of socially responsible funds allow you to put your money where your values are.

• Even if you're starting small and you don't know much about the markets, you can diversify your portfolio. Balanced funds spread your money over stocks and bonds within a single fund.

• If you're slow to start, but adventuresome nonetheless, you might try a growth fund or even a mutual fund that invests in real estate.

Chapter 7

Gotta Get There Fast—Strategies That Work When Your Goals Are Short-Term

E dward and Nancy Shapiro earn a good income. Because they have no children, they can afford the "good life" in southern California. They have a comfortable home, two cars, and wonderful vacations. But they're not spendthrifts. Unlike many of their friends, they've resisted the temptation to overspend by running up big credit card debts. In fact, they feel well pleased that they're able to keep their spending and saving in line. They invest a good chunk of their income and they both enjoy doing it.

As a lawyer who works in the mergers and acquisitions department of a major West Coast law firm, Ed spends a lot of time dealing with Wall Street issues. He must read *The Wall Street Journal,* the *Los Angeles Times,* and *The New York Times* to learn what's happening in the world of takeovers. And because he's good at what he does, Ed figures he knows quite a lot about the investment game as well.

Although Nancy isn't so directly involved in wheeling and dealing, she's a principal in a public relations firm whose clients are mainly in financial services. So she, too, must keep abreast of financial news. In addition to the dailies, she reads many trade publications and financial newsletters.

Between the two of them, the Shapiros figure they've got the financial services world covered. They don't mind the work because they like their jobs and they enjoy keeping up to date on investments. Because they feel very knowledgeable, they're never afraid to try something new. When they hear an investment tip at a cocktail party, chances are they'll put their money on it the next day.

In fact, the Shapiros consider themselves trendsetters of sorts. Not for them the dull middle-of-the-road investments. They want to be on the cutting edge. Nancy spends a lot of time culling magazines and financial newspapers looking for new types of investments. And they're usually the first among their friends to take a chance on a brand-new product.

Lately, though, Nancy's been concerned about their investment record. They've had financial setbacks—some major, some minor. For example, when they took a gamble on currency funds, they picked the wrong currency. And when one mutual fund company introduced short selling for mutual funds, they decided to try it—just before the market took off. They also got into a one-country fund at the wrong time. And, even in those cases where they've made good picks, their frequent buying and selling has had some costly tax consequences.

Nancy would like to set up her own public relations firm within the next couple of years—as soon as she feels they have a little nest egg to carry her over the startup phase while she's signing up clients. Ed figures the best way to do this is to take the $15,000 they have in the stock market now and put it into something with potential for real growth. He's all for going for broke. He figures they may be able to double their money in three or four years if they're lucky.

Nancy's not so sure. After all, it's her business. She points out that if they put all their capital at risk, they could lose it all and there goes her business. But, Ed counters, if they put the whole thing in a money market fund, they won't lose it but they'll never reach their goal either.

You don't have to live in California to get carried away with trendy investments. Many investors all over the country find, at least occasionally, that they have bought into something without really assessing its merits, and that their investment programs are suffering because of it. You, too, might have something in common with the Shapiros. Do you:

- Have a healthy appetite for risk and like the idea of being "in the market," buying and selling frequently to earn a better return?
- Spend a lot of time reading personal finance advice, chiefly looking for "hot tips"?
- Sometimes feel that the more time you put in, the worse off you are?
- Often get unpleasant surprises at tax time as a result of your investment decisions?
- Have only a modest amount of money to invest and can't afford to lose what you have?
- Need your money for a short-term goal?
- Feel that you're just not making any progress as an investor, no matter how hard you try?

You, too, may have a high risk tolerance, a small amount of money, and a short time horizon that requires very high performance by your investments to achieve it. If you expect too much; if you are unrealistic about returns; and if you are concerned about the rocky performance of your investing history, you may need to slow down. Even if you're knowledgeable about investing and spend a lot of time reading financial journals, you may be easy prey for a hot new investment that can send you to the poorhouse if you expect more from your investments than they can give you. Investors who are unrealistic about returns often choose those vehicles that are advertised as having a big potential reward. But they don't read the fine print. They also often trade impulsively without considering the tax implications and without ever sitting down to figure out how much they're really gaining—or losing.

If you're an investor who will try anything, you need to consider the dangers of trendy investments. You need to learn to separate the trendy from what is simply new. You need to learn to discipline yourself and educate yourself as you set reasonable goals. If you have short-term goals, be realistic. Consider this: If you earn 7 percent, you can double your money in ten years. That's certainly a realistic goal and you should be able to find any number of investments that will help you reach it. But if you've only got two years until your financial objective, you'd be wise to lower your sights. Not many investments will double your money in two years, and those that might are likely to be very risky.

You also need to consider the heavy record-keeping needs of frequent trading and the possible tax consequences. Whenever you trade mutual fund shares, it is a taxable event. You must keep records and, if you have made money, you must pay taxes. Beginning in 1987, capital gains from your investments lost their favored tax status. They are now taxed at the same rate as your earned income.

If you sell shares for more than you paid for them, that is a capital gain and it is taxable. If you sell them for less than you paid, it is a capital loss. For tax purposes, you subtract the losses from the gains and pay tax on the difference. If you're doing a lot of short-term trading, you have to remember that whatever gains you're enjoying will be reduced by federal, as well as state and local, taxes. You need to take a look at what you've gained on an after-tax basis rather than just the difference between your original investment and the price you got when you sold your fund shares. If you've identified yourself as a "trendy investor," you also need to take a hard look at those investments that seem so irresistible to see what the downside might be.

None of this means that you should simply park your money in a money market fund or a bank CD. Nor does it mean you should avoid the investments in this chapter. An argument can be made for nearly any investment for the right person under the right circumstances. But you should look carefully at these investments—at all investments—before you plunk your money down. Particularly if your goals are short-term, you must have a realistic return in mind before you start looking for investments to meet your goals. You also need to diversify your portfolio. If your goals are short-term, make a bet with a small part of your money, but put a big chunk in something safer with a more steady return.

GINNIE MAE FUNDS

Ginnie Mae funds probably don't seem a trendy investment to most people. Since the U.S. government guarantees the repayment of principal and interest on the mortgages that are purchased by the fund, and they yield more than U.S. Treasury bonds, many view them as a solid income investment. After their introduction in 1984, these U.S. government bond funds, which invest in **mortgage-backed securities**, practically became a household name. By 1986, Americans were pumping $5 billion a month into these funds to capture the high yields—up to 14 percent—that they offered. Now that was a trend!

Many of these investors really didn't understand how the funds worked. When both their net asset value and the interest rate started dropping in 1987, many shareholders began looking more carefully at their Ginnie Mae investments. Ginnie Mae bonds are backed by home mortgages. When you go to your bank to get a mortgage, the bank grants you the loan, but it doesn't keep the mortgage on its own books. Instead, it sells the loan into the **secondary mortgage market.** This market is made up of both government agencies and private issuers and packagers of individual residential mortgages. Like the other players in this market, Ginnie Mae, or the **Government National Mortgage Association,** to use its actual name, collects a large group of home mortgages, puts them into a pool, stamps the entire pool with its government guarantee, and then slices the pool up into chunks to be sold as bonds. These securities are called **mortgage passthroughs**, because principal and interest are passed through to the bondholders every month. And the government guarantees the timely payment of principal and interest.

But the government does not guarantee that the yield will remain the same. Neither does it promise that the price of the bond or the net asset value of a bond mutual fund will not decline. Like most bonds, Ginnie Maes are affected by changes in interest rates. But they can be negatively affected whether rates go up or down. If interest rates rise, the per share price of a Ginnie Mae fund will decline, just like any other bond. But if interest rates drop significantly, homeowners may refinance their mortgages, paying off the old, higher-rate loans and obtaining loans at the new lower rates. When this happens, the portfolio manager of the Ginnie Mae fund is left with more money to reinvest but with less attractive options. Chances are he will be forced to reinvest it at a lower rate.

This is not to say that no one should invest in Ginnie Maes. They carry a yield that is higher than U.S. treasuries—about 1 percent or 2 percent higher. And the government guarantee of repayment of the

Mortgage-backed securities Securities that are backed by individual home mortgages.

Secondary mortgage market Market in which individual home mortgages are packaged together and resold. The primary mortgage market is your local bank or savings and loan. Years ago, bankers were limited in the number of mortgage loans they could make because they kept all their mortgage loans on their own books. Today they can package their mortgage loans and resell them to a government agency or to private investment bankers who will then slice them up and resell them as bonds. These bonds, which are backed by mortgages like yours, can be bought and sold in this secondary market.

Government National Mortgage Association Agency of the Department of Housing and Urban Development, known as Ginnie Mae.

Mortgage passthrough securities Bonds that "pass through" the principal and interest payments on mortgages from the mortgage borrowers to the bond buyers.

GINNIE MAE—SWEETHEART OF THE MORTGAGE MARKET

By 1983, Americans expected sky-high inflation—and interest rates—to go on forever. For an entire decade, since the Arab oil embargo, the price of everything—gasoline, groceries, synthetic clothing—had been soaring.

The only good news was that many investors had figured out a way to get the same double-digit return on their money by depositing it in money market funds or locking it up in a bank certificate of deposit.

Then suddenly interest rates dropped sharply from their peak of nearly 16 percent in 1981. Investors who had put their money in a bank CD at an interest rate in the double digits found that when the time came to roll it over, the bank was offering 9 percent in 1983. Those returns were no longer satisfactory. Investors demanded something new.

By this time, many investors were growing comfortable with the idea of mutual funds. Perhaps the only mutual fund they owned was a money market fund. But they felt secure about its safety and they liked the idea of being able to earn a higher return than they could get in a bank. As they looked around for higher-yielding investments, many settled on government bond funds, which were paying 10 to 11 percent interest.

In 1984, the Franklin Group of Funds in San Mateo, California, figured out a way to give investors even higher rates—those 14 percent rates they'd grown accustomed to. To do this, Franklin converted its government bond fund into a U.S. government bond fund that invested in Government National Mortgage Association securities, or Ginnie Maes. These bonds are created by pooling a group of residential mortgages and then slicing them up into individual securities. The bonds are backed by this U.S. government agency.

Ginnie Mae quickly became America's sweetheart. The lure was irresistible. Not only did the bonds pay one of the highest yields available, but the principal and interest were backed by Uncle Sam. At the time Franklin converted its government bond fund, it had $10 million in assets. Once it became a Ginnie Mae fund, investors began pumping as much as $50 million to $60 million a day into the fund. Other mutual fund companies quickly opened their own Ginnie Mae funds. And by 1986, $5 billion a month was pouring into these funds.

principal and interest on the underlying securities means a higher degree of safety for the investor. Furthermore, the yields on Ginnie Maes may fall more slowly than those on other bonds because it takes some time to refinance a mortgage. For this reason, the funds can still offer a more attractive yield than many other bond fund options. So they may be a good choice for many investors. But they are not comparable to a bank CD, because the interest rate is not guaranteed, nor to a money market fund, because the net asset value of the fund is not fixed.

GOLD AND PRECIOUS METALS FUNDS

Gold is hardly a recent trend either. It has fascinated people for centuries: piles of gold coins, fine gold jewelry, maybe even a gold throne or the gold bathroom fixtures in the palace of Ferdinand and Imelda Marcos. Certainly everyone equates gold with wealth and luxury. But is it a good investment? If you're looking for something to provide a real kick for a portion of your portfolio, gold *is* an option. But if you invest at the wrong time, gold can decimate your portfolio.

From 1934 to 1971, the U.S. government fixed the price of gold at $35 an ounce. Individuals were prohibited from owning it. When the fixed price was lifted in 1971, the price of gold shot up, tripling by 1973. At the end of 1974, the ban against private ownership of gold was suspended and individuals were allowed to own gold. During 1974, speculation about a "gold rush" drove the price of gold up to $200 an ounce. But once ownership became legal, the gold boom didn't materialize and the price fell back to under $170. The price of gold didn't really take off until the roaring inflation in the late 1970s. When investors saw the value of their other investments eroded by inflation, they turned to gold. The price of gold started moving up in 1978 and skyrocketed in 1979. On January 21, 1980, gold peaked at $875 an ounce. Once inflation cooled, investors again moved away from gold and back into other investments and the price slipped back to the $300 to $500 range.

Unlike other securities investments that fall in and out of favor, gold has a legion of fervent followers who believe that it is the only true source of value. These "goldbugs" argue that world currencies may rise and fall just as securities of corporations do, but that gold has an inherent value; that you can never go wrong if you buy gold. Other investors believe that gold is a good investment only for times of inflation when the value of paper money is eroded. There have been many such times during the past century, when the value of currencies

Gold Funds Don't Always Track the Price of Gold

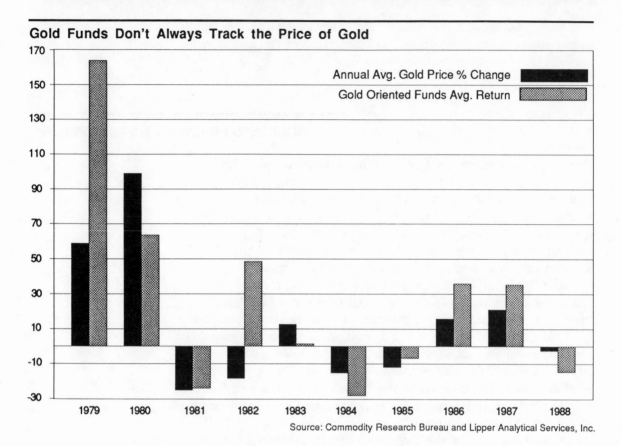

Source: Commodity Research Bureau and Lipper Analytical Services, Inc.

plummeted and those people who had their money in gold were well served.

It is difficult to be objective about the future value of gold. If you look at it strictly on the basis of supply and demand, as you might do with oil, for example, gold would not be particularly attractive. Although it does have commercial uses, there are many ready substitutes that could be used if the price got too high. Yet there is no way of estimating the value of its mystique. If people around the world suddenly decided that gold was tacky and unattractive, that to own it was foolish, its price would, of course, plummet. But that's unlikely to happen. Instead, gold prices will no doubt continue to soar during times of inflation or fears of inflation and fall during times when the world economies are in the pink of health.

What does this mean for you as an investor? One advantage of gold is that it tends to perform well in economic environments that don't favor stocks and bonds. Investors seeking to diversify their portfolios find this trait attractive. On the downside, gold is extremely volatile. And its price moves are hard to predict. It is not, for that reason, a particularly suitable investment for market timing. Rather, it might work well for a small portion of a well-diversified portfolio. Like any volatile investment, it should not be used for the mortgage money or your emergency fund. Instead, it should be part of a long-range investment program.

Perhaps the least suitable way to invest in gold is by buying bullion. If you don't take possession of the gold, you'll have to pay for storage. If you do take possession, you'll have to pay state sales tax. You will also probably have to pay additional fees when you get ready to sell it in order to have it checked to make sure you didn't tamper with it. And you can expect to pay for shipping and insurance costs as well.

Perhaps the easiest way to buy gold is in a mutual fund. Many mutual funds specialize in gold and precious metals. Typically, only a small part of the fund is invested in the actual commodities. Much is invested in stocks of gold and other precious metal mining companies. Yet many of the funds do track the price changes in gold itself. These funds are now available from most major mutual fund companies. They were spectacular performers in 1987, when the stock and bond markets nosedived. The top-performing gold fund, the Oppenheimer Gold & Special Minerals fund, was up 71 percent for 1987. The average gold fund was up 35.66 percent.

Many gold funds are "managed." That means that the portfolio manager can use his discretion in deciding when to move in and out of investments in gold. For example, the Oppenheimer Fund, as well as the IDS Precious Metals Fund, another spectacular performer in 1987, with a return of 54 percent, can move 100 percent into cash or even bonds if the portfolio managers think the environment warrants it. Kenneth Oberman, Oppenheimer's manager, believes that investors want to be protected from gold's extreme volatility. When he doesn't like the outlook for gold, he moves the fund's assets into other precious metals as well as nonprecious metals. If you choose this type of gold fund, you are, once again, relying on a particular portfolio manager's talents.

You do have another choice. You can pick a fund that is required to keep its assets in gold. For example, Benham Capital Management Group introduced a gold index fund in 1988. This fund will attempt to mirror the performance of the gold industry as a whole by investing in the stock of 30 U.S. and Canadian gold mining companies. (It will not invest in South Africa.) Like a true stock or bond index fund, it will not attempt to time the market or speculate on individual stocks, so transaction costs will be low. It will do well when gold rises in value, and decline when gold declines, by approximately the same percentage. This type of fund is designed for investors who want to diversify a portion of their assets into gold and do not want a portfolio manager to make decisions about when to get in and out of precious metals.

On the surface, gold funds seem to be appropriate investments for high flyers, because in some years they produce such spectacular results. However, in other years, the gold market can be uneventful.

There are two smart ways to use gold funds. You can attempt to time the market by moving in and capturing gains when the price of gold soars. Or, you can diversify a small portion of a large portfolio into gold.

OPTION INCOME FUNDS

Option   *Security that gives the owner the right to buy or sell the underlying instrument for a specific price during a specific period.*

Covered call option   *Option that is sold on a security held by the option seller. Differs from a naked option, which is a call option written by someone who does not own the stock.*

Ed Shapiro invested in an option income fund because it was a trendy investment. Now he realizes that he might have just thought it was trendy because it was so complicated. In fact, although they are billed as a safe, stable, conservative investment, as Ed found out to his regret, these funds have some real drawbacks in choppy markets.

Option income funds invest in the stocks of large, established companies that pay regular dividends. The strategy used by the manager is to write **covered call options** on the stocks in the portfolio to increase the fund's income. Here's how that works: A call option is the right to buy a stock at a specific price for some defined period in the future. The investor who buys the option pays what is called a *premium* for this right. For example, let's say a stock is selling at $100 a share. An investor might pay a premium of $5 a share for the right to buy the stock at $110. He's hoping, of course, that the stock will go above that price and he will still be able to buy it for $110. The portfolio manager

UPSIDE LIFT WITH A DOWNSIDE CUSHION: SUMNER ABRAMSON AND OPTION INCOME FUNDS

It was a very dry period for mutual funds, Sumner Abramson recalls of 1977. Fund assets were declining. Investor interest was nonexistent. Like many other people, he was looking for new products.

Abramson, who was with Colonial Management at the time, found something interesting in the Tax Reform Act of 1976. The tax act clarified the tax treatment of options trading for mutual funds. Options are a financial instrument that give the holder the right to buy or sell the underlying instrument if it reaches a certain price within a certain period. For this right, he pays a premium. For example, if a stock is trading at $25, you might buy an option to buy that stock at $27.50 in the hope that the stock would go even higher. For that right, you might pay $2.50. If it doesn't reach the price within a specified period, the option expires worthless and you lose your $2.50 per share. If the stock goes to $30 a share, you can buy it for $27.50.

Because an options buyer ends up with nothing if the stock doesn't reach the exercise price, options are a speculative investment. But there's a very conservative way to use them as well. You can *sell* them to add to the income on the stock you already own. That's what Abramson chose to do.

He put together a portfolio of stocks. Then he *sold* options on all of the stocks, collecting the premium from the buyer. If the stocks in his portfolio reached the *strike* price, the option holder had the right to buy them at that price. If they didn't, Abramson simply pocketed the option premium. So he was selling the right to participate in a strong market rally. But if the market went down, the income he made from the options would offset some of the decline in his stocks. He gained a little on the upside and got a little cushion on the downside.

When he introduced the first option income fund in 1977, stock funds were very much out of favor. Investors—if there were any at the time—were looking for income. Abramson knew that the way he marketed the fund was critical. And trading options was a pretty arcane concept to explain to unenthusiastic investors. He left for the beach for inspiration to write the prospectus.

"I would write a page and then I would show it to my wife," he recalls. "She's not in the business. If she understood what I wrote, then I knew it was OK." The fund was marketed as an income fund. "It was designed to produce a high current level of income—higher than bonds," Abramson says.

The idea caught on. When the fund was introduced in April 1977, it brought in $60 million in shareholder dollars, the largest mutual fund launching since the Manhattan fund in 1966. "I think shareholders were more interested in the fact that we got the income rather than how we did it," Abramson says.

who sold him the option pockets the premiums and adds them to his fund's income.

This extra income should make the net asset value more stable, because if the market goes down, income from the options should offset some of the loss in the value of the stocks. If the market stays flat, the fund should outperform other stock funds because of the additional income from selling options. But if the market soars, the fund will underperform, because the investors who bought options on the stocks will use them to call away the stocks from the portfolio manager.

Those who favor the funds claim that this is a very conservative way to wring extra income from a portfolio of safe, solid stocks. In a flat market, that's true. But in a volatile market, the strategy doesn't work so well. First of all, the portfolio manager gives up the upside potential in his stocks for a small additional amount of income. If all the stocks in the portfolio shoot up through the exercise price of the options, the portfolio manager must give up the stocks to the holder of the options and the fund doesn't enjoy the gain in the share price.

On the other hand, if the stocks plunge through the floor, the fund manager has a different problem. He still has a small amount of income from the premiums, which he can use to bolster his returns. But he does so at great cost because the premiums are considered a gain for tax purposes. And he doesn't have any loss to offset it against unless he sells the stock. If he sells the stock and offsets the loss against the premium gain, the fund doesn't perform so well. If, on the other hand, he hangs on to the stock to make his portfolio look better, he will be left with a lot of dogs. Either way, if the stock prices plummet, the option income will not be enough to offset the loss.

The developer of option income funds, Sumner Abramson, acknowledges that they are not designed to do well in a market crash. If the stock market crashes, you're better off to be out of it. But in a flat market, option income funds can provide a high level of current income. For example, in early 1988, they were paying income of 13 or 14 percent, higher than bond funds. In many market environments, they provide higher current income than bond funds. Still, the funds have some real negatives including the possibility of big tax bills. This is another type of fund that you should consider carefully before you plunk your money down.

MARGIN BUYING

What interests Ed Shapiro more than trendiness is investments and strategies that have the potential for a big payoff from a small up-front investment—like buying on margin, which is just borrowing money from a broker to buy securities. If you've ever made an investment in a home or any other piece of real estate, you understand the idea of leverage. It means you are using borrowed money to lever your investment. For example, you might buy a $150,000 house with only $15,000 as a down payment. You have leveraged your $15,000 to make a $150,000 investment. If your house increases in value to $200,000, your leveraged $15,000 investment has increased by $50,000, or 333 percent.

Leverage works the same way when you invest in securities. You put up only part of the price of the securities you plan to buy. But you are committed to paying the full purchase price at some time in the future. You might compare it to ordering a piece of custom furniture. You make a down payment when you place your order. Then, when your rocking chair is delivered, you pay the balance. Buying stock on margin makes sense when you think a particular stock or mutual fund is going to increase rapidly in value. You buy the securities on margin, making a small down payment, and then hope to sell them when the price goes up, paying back the broker and pocketing your gains. But once you buy stocks on margin, you own them, even though you have not paid the full price yet. When you sell them, you must repay your broker at the price agreed on when you bought them—even if you sell at a lower price.

Let's say you think a mutual fund is going to do very well. You want to put $10,000 into the fund, but you don't have that much. You can buy the fund "on margin," putting in $5,000 and borrowing the remainder from the broker. If things go as you expect and the value of your investment grows to $15,000, you owe the $5,000 you borrowed, plus interest. But you have doubled your money, interest aside. However, if you are wrong, and the value of your investment sinks to $7,000, you still owe the $5,000 plus interest. Now you've lost $3,000.

To buy on margin, you must set up a **margin account.** You can use

Margin account Brokerage account that allows the investor to borrow money to buy stocks and bonds or "buy on margin." An investor who has a margin account can buy a security by posting only a portion of the purchase amount in cash and collateral. The brokerage firm lends him the rest.

either cash or securities in the account as collateral. During the stock market crash of 1929 many investors had highly leveraged accounts. In those days they were able to buy stock by depositing as little as 10 percent of the equity value in their account. When prices plunged in the crash and they had to ante up the money they owed to brokers, many investors were ruined. Today the rules on margin accounts are much stricter. Most brokers require you to post 50 percent of the value of your purchase into the margin account. If the value of the mutual fund you purchased on margin goes down to 30 percent of the amount you deposited, you will then get a **margin call** and must put up more money.

Margin call   Notification to an investor to post more cash or securities in his margin account.

SHORT SELLING

If you think a stock or mutual fund will rise in price, you may buy on margin. If you think it will fall, you may sell short. The short seller borrows securities and sells them at the current price. If he is right and the price declines, he can buy them at the new, lower price, paying back the lender and collecting a profit. If he is wrong and the price rises, he still has to buy the shares and pay them back, even though it means taking a loss.

Consider this example: The stock of Capital Corporation is trading at $20 a share. An investor tells his broker to sell short 100 shares of Capital. The stock drops to $15 a share. The investor buys 100 shares of Capital at $15, for $1,500, pays back the securities to the broker, and collects a $500 profit (less interest on her loan)—the difference between the price at the time of the **short sale** and the price he paid for it later on the open market.

Short sale   Stock trading technique whereby the investor borrows stock and sells it, hoping that its price will fall so that he can buy it back at a lower price and repay his loan, pocketing the difference as his profit.

An investor must also maintain a margin account in order to sell short. If an investor buys stock on margin, he is borrowing to buy the shares. If the price of the stock he buys declines, he must increase the collateral in his margin account. If he is selling short, the margin account is flipped upside down. He must maintain the money in his margin account to make certain that he can buy the shares to repay those he borrowed. Therefore, if the price of the shares *increases*, he must add to his margin account.

Fidelity Investments introduced short selling on its sector mutual funds in 1987. The principle is the same as that for short sales of individual stocks. The investor must open a margin account in which he puts cash or securities worth 50 percent of the value of the shares he's borrowing. And, as the price of the shares changes, he must keep a balance equal to at least 30 percent of their value in the account. As with an individual stock, the idea of short selling industry sector funds is that a mutual fund investor can make a bet *against* an industry sector. For example, if he expects energy stocks to decline, he can short the energy portfolio.

Short selling gives investors yet another way to use mutual funds. For example, if you believed, in September 1987, that the stock market was too high in general and that financial services, in particular, were trading in the stratosphere, you could have shorted the financial services sector. Then, when the market crashed in October, you would have done very nicely.

But this is a technique only for the knowledgeable. Many people argued throughout 1985 and 1986 that the market was moving too high and that nearly everything was overvalued. Investors who placed their bets then probably lost a lot of money. In selling short, as in buying on margin, timing is critical. And few things are harder than timing the market.

COMMODITY FUNDS

Ed and Nancy Shapiro have also dabbled in the **commodities** markets. They're not big enough investors to trade themselves. Commodity futures are a fast-paced and highly speculative investment—a game for the big guys. But they have gotten a taste of it by using commodity funds, which are designed to blunt some of the risks by pooling the money of several investors and putting it under the control of a professional trader. If you have an appetite for risk and are looking for something that can do well when stocks and bonds do poorly, take a look at commodity funds.

Commodity funds are really limited partnerships rather than mutual funds. They are sold in units, typically of $5,000 each, or $2,000 for

Commodities Bulk goods such as metals, oil, grain, and livestock traded on a commodities exchange. Funds that invest in commodities or commodities futures are highly volatile. But some of them have turned in spectacular returns.

an IRA. A general partner sets up the fund, collects the money, and assigns a trading manager to trade commodity futures—at a profit, he hopes. The trader may speculate in 15 to 30 different commodities including livestock, grain, oil, metals, and financial futures such as Treasury bills or stock market indexes.

Many investors are attracted to these funds because they've heard reports of fantastic potential returns. *Managed Accounts Reports,* which monitors and reports on the approximately 125 funds available, compares their returns with those of mutual funds. In 1987, when the best-performing mutual fund, Oppenheimer 90-10, gained 93.6 percent, the Tudor Futures Fund was up a remarkable 201.1 percent. In all, eight different futures funds gained over 100 percent for that year. Not a single mutual fund gained that much. Public commodity funds returned an average of 40.02 percent for the year. That compared with a measly 2.29 percent for equity funds and 1.99 percent for bond funds.

Furthermore, some studies indicate that futures have a negative correlation with stocks and bonds. What that means is that when one does well, the other does poorly and vice versa. An investor who wants to put together a diversified portfolio that will do well in all markets is naturally interested in investments that perform well in different market environments.

Of course, there's a downside. Although there are indications that commodities perform well when stocks and bonds do poorly, the studies are controversial and some experts argue that this hasn't been proven. More important, though, is to consider the difference between the commodities funds and open-ended mutual funds. The commodities funds are not a short-term, liquid investment. Although they do post a net asset value daily, there is no secondary market for them. In other words, you buy your units from the general partner. If you want to sell, you must sell them back to the general partner. You can't sell them on the open market. Again, they are not mutual funds.

Some funds impose a 10 percent penalty if you want to get out of the investment within six months or less. And, in order to liquidate your investment, you typically have to give written notice and wait either until the end of the month or until the end of the quarter before receiving your money. The funds also charge much higher fees than a mutual fund. For example, a typical futures fund pays the trading

Performance of Commodity Funds, Equity Funds and U.S. Government Bond Funds

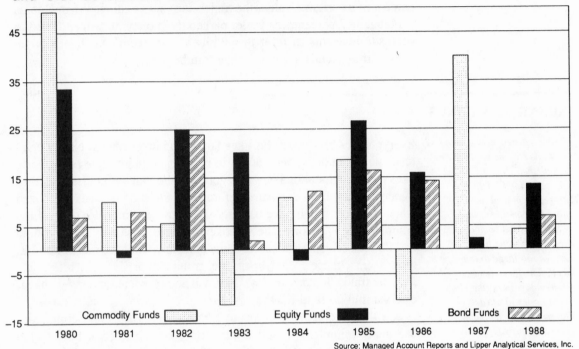

Source: Managed Account Reports and Lipper Analytical Services, Inc.

manager .5 percent of the assets every month, or 6 percent a year. In addition, the manager receives a performance or incentive fee if the fund does well. And the fund is charged for commissions on all the trades made. That brings the total cost of these funds to between 18 and 20 percent, considerably higher than the .5 percent to 2 percent expenses charged for a typical mutual fund. Because the cost is so high, the trader must work pretty hard to generate a good return. For example, to cover the cost and return 25 percent to investors, he must earn around 45 percent.

And the funds have extreme volatility over the short term. One of the most successful of the commodities traders, Richard J. Dennis of Chicago, had a tough time in early 1988. For the first quarter of the year, the average fund was off 8 percent, according to *Managed Account Reports*. But Dennis did a lot worse. Although his Dennis I fund lost only 4 percent, Dennis II dropped 43 percent. Typically these funds have a cutoff point. For example, when the fund drops to 50 percent of its original value, the trader must stop trading. When Dennis II plunged 43 percent, the trader parked the money in cash and tried to persuade investors to reset that limit to 32 percent. As this example shows, these funds are not for the fainthearted.

BRAND-NEW FUNDS

Clone   A new mutual fund that takes its name from an established "parent" fund in the same fund family. A large, successful mutual fund is sometimes cloned when the fund company decides that the fund has grown too large to manage well. The large fund closes to new investors; the clone fund hopes to attract investors through name recognition, which may create a favorable association with the original fund.

Fund Assets. Does size matter? Some investors believe that small funds can't be managed effectively and very big funds can't outperform the market averages. There is no consistent evidence that this holds true. Still, a major shift in asset size is

Everyone has his quirks. Ed likes fast-paced investments. Nancy can't resist plopping her money down in brand-new funds. She particularly likes the excitement of a new category of fund that has not been offered by any mutual fund company before. And she's sometimes tantalized when a successful fund closes its doors to new money. If the fund company opens a **clone**, she's hooked. She reasons that if the first fund hadn't been such a great success, the company wouldn't have closed it. Now's her chance to get in on the ground floor. Ed will bite if his favorite fund company or a well-known and respected money manager offers a mutual fund for the first time.

Are these good reasons to buy? Not necessarily. Fund companies use many gimmicks to sell funds. It's your job to look beyond the smoke and see what you're buying. Although all funds are obligated to point out that their past record does not predict future performance, at least a past record is something you can evaluate. With a new fund, you're flying blind.

Some fund companies close a fund when they feel the fund has gotten too big to achieve its objective with the best possible performance. If the fund has been very successful and has a well-known name, it makes good marketing sense to use it again. But if you're considering a clone fund because you can't buy into its "parent," the first thing you'll want to check is whether the new fund has the same manager and the same investment guidelines. For example, when Vanguard closed the highly successful Windsor Fund to new money in 1985, it opened Windsor II. Although the new fund has the same investment approach, it is not managed by the legendary John Neff, who's guided Windsor for 25 years. As it happens, the new fund only slightly underperformed Windsor during its first three years and was outperforming Windsor in 1989. But you couldn't have known that in 1985.

What if a well-established money manager opens a fund for individual investors? If you're knowledgeable about investing and have followed the manager's record, this might make some sense. Here you could, indeed, get in on the ground floor. Likewise, if you see that a fund company is setting up a fund to invest in a country where investing was previously not available to U.S. funds and you know a lot about that country, you might spot a good opportunity.

The only real answer to the question about new funds is that you should not make an uneducated investment in a new fund simply because you read an ad in the newspaper announcing that it is open for business. Investing in new funds requires more care than putting your money in established funds.

worth noting. If an unusual number of investors are leaving a fund that's caught your interest—or putting new money in—you'll want to find out why.

THE SHAPIROS' CHOICES

The Shapiros compromise. They decide they must slow down a bit to reach their goal. But they still need to put a portion of their money into something with the potential for a real kick. They will take a large portion of their money and put it in a high-yielding income fund where they should get good yields without enormous risks. The rest goes into sexier, higher-risk investments. But they can't pick just one. The riskier the investment, the more important it is to diversify. If they do well and the markets are with them, they'll reach their short-term goal. If everything goes against them, they will lose. But this may be the only way to get that big chunk of money that they want in a short time.

• They put $7,500—half of their money—into a Ginnie Mae fund for income.

• Another $2,500 goes into a commodity fund.

• Another 16 percent—or $2,500—goes into a brand-new stock fund managed by a money manager whose reputation Ed has been following for five years.

• Ed will put the final $2,500 into a margin account where he hopes to win big by making some bets on the direction of the market.

• The Shapiros promise to resist the temptation to tinker constantly with these choices.

The Shapiros' Portfolio

16.7%
MARGIN
ACCOUNT
(SPECULATIVE)

16.7%
AGGRESSIVE
GROWTH
FUND
(AGGRESSIVE)

16.7%
GOLD
(SPECULATIVE)

50%
GINNIE MAE
FUND
(BALANCED)

POINTS TO REMEMBER

The Shapiros have made some very aggressive investments with their money. But they do have a balanced portfolio, with an income anchor in the Ginnie Maes. And they do have the potential for big gains. You may not make the same choices. But you need to consider the same things.

• If you set unrealistic goals, you're easy prey for investments that make unrealistic promises. Slow down. Study the options.

• If you're making many trades but don't seem to be getting anywhere, sit down and figure out how you've done in the past year. How much investment income did you report on your taxes? How much time did it take you to compile the records? Did you come out ahead?

• Ginnie Mae funds and other mortgage-backed security funds offer you safety of principal and interest. But these government agencies do not guarantee that the NAV of your fund will not plunge. These funds are very sensitive to changes in interest rates.

• Gold can be a fickle investment. Predicting its future price is nearly impossible. Consider it as an investment to diversify a portfolio that is heavy on the stock and bond markets. Don't lose your objectivity.

• Borrowing money to buy mutual funds in the hope of a rise in the price or borrowing mutual fund shares to sell short in the hope of a drop in prices are sophisticated trading techniques. Don't get involved unless you know the ropes. And don't stake your whole future on this kind of trading.

• Funds that invest and trade in commodity futures are not mutual funds. They are organized as limited partnerships. Although they sometimes show spectacular returns, they are highly volatile. And, like other limited partnership investments, they don't offer liquidity.

• Brand-new funds require extra diligence on your part before you plunk down your money. Novelty alone is not a good reason to invest.

Chapter 8

A Fistful of Dollars and No Time to Lose—Sensible Investing Under Pressure

Al Nikaloski considers himself a run-of-the-mill guy. Maybe slightly above average. He had never set his sights on the top executive suite. He'd always been content to be cautious and comfortable. He was well brought up, well educated, and well paid. Why not simply do a good job and then enjoy life?

Like a lot of people in Detroit, Al went to work for one of the Big Three automakers. At that time, in the 1950s, people in America's heartland believed that what was good for the Big Three was good for America, that you couldn't go far wrong by casting your lot with an industry that was driving the U.S. economy. Al spent most of his life at the automaker, working his way up to a respectable job as a midlevel executive. He liked his work, he liked his company, and he liked his leisure.

Although Al was pulling in a more-than-decent $45,000 a year, he never gave much thought to investing. No kids. No college to pay for. Good company benefits. And a top-notch pension plan. That, after all, was one of Al's motives in joining a big corporation. If he had wanted to take responsibility for his own financial needs, he would have gone into business for himself. That's the way he figured it. It was a trade-off. He toed the company line and he got the company benefits.

Then, at age 51, Al was "outplaced," that is, laid off. However you choose to put it, it wasn't part of Al's plan. He had expected to work until age 65 and retire comfortably on a combination of a full pension and Social Security benefits. Not only was he out of work, he was also out of the company pension plan. Like many companies, Al's employer gave him a choice of either receiving regular monthly benefits after retirement or receiving a lump sum on termination. In addition to his two years' severance pay, Al has the option of taking a lump sum of $150,000, which represents the company's contributions to the pension plan on his behalf. If he does, then he's on his own.

Al's not simply depressed; he's in a panic. He hopes to find a new job or at least some part-time work. In the meantime, which choice should he make about his pension? Either way, the money he's put away for retirement has stopped growing. If he takes the cash, what should he do with it? How can he make it stretch to cover his retirement? Does he have to pay taxes on it as if it were ordinary income? His friend, Lou, a financial planner, tells him that the Tax Reform Act of 1986, which turned most investing rules on their heads, had something important to say about lump sum distributions. Before that time, taxpayers were allowed to pay tax on a lump sum distribution as if it were the only income received over a ten-year period. For example, under this formula, the tax on a $50,000 lump sum would be only $550.

But tax reform wiped out ten-year averaging except for people who turned 50 before January 1, 1986. That left Al with a couple of choices. He could pay taxes on the entire amount as if it were regular income. He could use the much less favorable five-year averaging. Or he could roll over the money into an Individual Retirement Account within 60 days and pay no taxes on it until he starts withdrawing it. Lou, the financial planner, suggests that Al take the lump sum. Then he gets control. No matter what happens to his company, the money belongs to him. Al wants to protect his retirement money from taxes now and put it to work so that it will be available when he needs it. So he needs to learn the rollover rules. But since he's never invested before, he doesn't know where to start. Naturally he doesn't have much tolerance for risk; he knows nothing about investing. Furthermore, this is his retirement income. He has to make some of the most important decisions in his life very quickly.

Perhaps you see something of your own situation in Al's dilemma. Do you:

- Have a sizable amount of money to invest?
- Feel torn between the need for current income from your investment and the desire to let your money grow?
- Think you need a quick primer on the tax implications of lump sum settlements?
- Feel intimidated by the enormity of managing more money than you've ever had before?
- Wish you had listened the last time you overheard a conversation on investments?

You, too, may have a fistful of dollars and no time to lose if you recently received an inheritance or a divorce or damage settlement, if you're the beneficiary of a life insurance policy, if you got an unexpected windfall in the buyout of your business, or even if you have a big lump of money sitting in some passive investment and you'd like to add a little pizzazz to your portfolio. If you suddenly have more money than you've ever had before, you're probably nervous about making a bad investment decision. Or perhaps you're feeling pressure from friends and relatives to make a particular investment (or to share your wealth). Maybe *you* feel that you'd like to enjoy the money a bit. If you've never had much extra to spend before, you probably feel a temptation to buy some of the things you've always wanted.

That's probably not a good idea, particularly if you're emotionally upset. If you've just lost your job or if a close relative died or if you got the money as part of a divorce settlement, blowing it on something frivolous is not your best move. Nor is locking it up in something illiquid like real estate or any other long-term or volatile investment. Your first step should be to get advice on the tax consequences of different investment choices. And your second should probably be to put the money somewhere where it's safe but where you can pull it out quickly as soon as you've had time to work through your situation and make some investment decisions.

If you are to receive the proceeds from a life insurance policy, many life insurance companies have a relatively new option that you should consider. They will put the life insurance settlement in a money market account and send you a checkbook. Whenever you're ready to make an investment decision—or you need the money for any reason—you simply write a check. You can write checks on it right away, or you can leave the money for as long as you like. Meanwhile, you're earning money market interest. This is an extremely attractive option because it allows you to deal with your immediate financial and emotional needs rather than attempting to make a long-term investment decision at a difficult time in your life.

Lump sum distribution
Single payment in lieu of a series of payments. This often refers to the payment of pension benefits in a single check rather than in regular monthly installments.

If, like Al Nikaloski, you've received your money as part of a severance settlement from your employer, chances are part of it is a **lump sum distribution** from your corporate pension plan. There are special rules that pertain to this money and, if you want to avoid tax problems, you must follow them. If you receive money that was contributed by your employer to your company pension plan on your behalf, you must either roll it over into an IRA within 60 days or pay tax on it. You do not, however, need to make a permanent investment decision about the money.

Say you receive $50,000 that is designated as a lump sum distribution. You must fill out the proper forms to roll that over into an Individual Retirement Account within 60 days. But you may simply roll it over into a money market account and leave it there for as long as you like. Once you've had time to investigate the other investment options, you can move as much as you like from the money market fund into other mutual funds in the same family. After you've designated the account as an IRA, the Internal Revenue Service doesn't care how you move it within that mutual fund family. You can also transfer it or roll it over to another investment at a different company provided that you do this only once a year.

If you've just been forced into early retirement from your job, you're probably emotionally upset and your confidence is bruised. You may be afraid to roll your money into an IRA because you don't know whether you'll be able to earn enough to support yourself and your family between now and the time you plan to retire. What if you need the money before then? How can you possibly make a decision in 60 days? Maybe this will help. You have not yet paid tax on the money that your employer contributed to the pension plan for you. You *will* have to pay tax on it at some point—either now or in the future. If you

"ROLL IT OVER" BY THE RULES

If you receive money that represents your employer's contribution to a company pension plan on your behalf, you have two choices. You can take possession of it and pay tax on it, or you can roll it over into an Individual Retirement Account. To roll over this money, you must follow these rules:

• You must receive the entire balance in one tax year.

• You must complete the rollover within 60 days of the time you receive the money.

• The money must represent either funds contributed to the plan by your employer or money that you contributed before paying taxes on it.

• You must be careful not to include any after-tax money that you contributed to the plan. Some plans allow employees to contribute both pretax and post-tax dollars. Only pretax dollars can be rolled over.

• If you withdraw money from this account before you reach age 59½, you must pay taxes plus a 10 percent penalty to the IRS.

• After you reach age 59½, you can take out as much money as you like without paying a penalty. But you must pay taxes at the current rate on whatever you withdraw.

• At age 70½, you *must* start withdrawing the money. And you must withdraw it according to a life expectancy formula. The money is intended to pay for your retirement, not to be left for your heirs. You are permitted, however, to use a joint withdrawal formula for you and your beneficiary.

put it in an IRA, you will postpone the time that you have to pay taxes on it. In the meantime, the earnings will also be building up, tax deferred, on your original principal.

For example, say you receive a pension distribution of $50,000. You're 50 years old. You plan to look for another job, but you don't know if you'll be successful. If you decide not to roll over the $50,000 and you pay tax on the $50,000 at 28 percent, you will have only $36,000 left. If you put the $50,000 into an IRA instead and you are able to earn 10 percent a year, your IRA balance in five years will be $80,525. If you need some of the money at that time, you can simply withdraw it. You will have to pay tax. And you must pay a 10 percent penalty on anything you withdraw before age 59½. But in the meantime, you have put your money to work—you've used it to make more money. Even if you withdraw all of it, you will still have $49,926 left after taxes, assuming the tax rates don't change. If you are successful in finding another job and you don't need to touch the money until age 65, by then it will have grown to $208,862.

ANNUITIES

Annuity Investment offered by life insurance companies that pays income for a specified period, for example, 10 to 15 years or longer. Annuities are usually used for retirement and often pay income for life. When you begin receiving payments, you must pay tax on the portion that represents earnings.

Underwriting Method of examining risks that are to be insured, classifying them, and setting the proper premium. Insurers use formulas and tables to determine how much premium each person should pay based on how substantial the risk of loss is.

As for Al and his $150,000, he's asked Lou, the financial planner, about an annuity. An **annuity**, which is sold by a life insurance company, is like a life insurance policy turned inside out. Whereas your life insurance policy pays a benefit to someone else when you die, an annuity pays income to you while you live. Annuities are used either to accumulate money for retirement or to provide income throughout retirement. For example, if you purchase a life annuity when you retire at age 65, the insurance company that sells it promises that you will never outlive your income. You will be guaranteed a specified amount of income each month or each year for the rest of your life.

Although life insurance companies do pretty thorough **underwriting** when you buy a life policy to make certain that you are in normal health, they generally don't underwrite an annuity. They're really not concerned whether the buyer is healthy or not. In fact, the worse your health, the better for them. They base your annuity income on the average life expectancy for people your age. If yours happens to be shorter, they save money. If you live beyond the average, they lose money on you. Insurance companies generally won't sell an annuity to someone over 85 years old, though. Although lifetime income is usually the purpose of an annuity, it could also be used to provide income for a specified period. For example, if you have a lump sum that you would like to have paid to you over a ten-year period, that can be arranged. And annuities can be purchased for a single life or they can be purchased for one person and a survivor, such as your spouse. The monthly benefit is higher if you buy an annuity that covers only your own life.

There are two ways you can use a lump sum to buy an annuity. If you are ready to retire, you can purchase an **immediate annuity.** You would start receiving monthly payments within the next month. Part of the monthly benefit is a return of your principal. The rest is taxable earnings. The insurer will inform you at the end of the year what your taxable earnings are.

If, instead of receiving immediate income, you would like to put money aside in an annuity for your retirement at some later date, you would choose a **deferred annuity.** The major attraction of a deferred annuity is that earnings on the money are not taxed until you begin to withdraw them, just like an IRA account. The tax savings can make a substantial difference in your earnings growth. For example, an investor in the 30 percent marginal tax bracket who invested $20,000 in a taxable mutual fund would have $77,394 after 20 years if he were able to get a 10 percent return. If he put the same money into a tax-deferred annuity, it would grow to $134,550 during the same period.

Further, annuities provide a means of sheltering capital gains. Until 1986, capital gains were taxed at a favorable 20 percent rate, compared with a top rate of 50 percent for earned income. Starting in 1988, though, capital gains were taxed at the same rate as regular income. If you lost the right to take a deduction for an annual contribution to an IRA, annuities are an attractive alternative to the nondeductible IRA, because there's no annual limit on the money you can invest in an annuity and it doesn't require the onerous record keeping necessary for an IRA account. Annuities can be purchased for a single lump sum, in a series of payments, or for variable premiums paid at irregular intervals.

The idea of an annuity appeals to Al. If he chooses one, he figures he will only need to make one investment decision. But Lou throws some cold water on this idea. Because Al's lump sum is from his company's pension plan, which is referred to as a ''qualified plan,'' it is pretax money. He will already have the tax advantages of a deferred annuity if he simply rolls the money into an Individual Retirement Account. Buying a deferred annuity, Lou explains, would be like a tax shelter within a tax shelter. Most investors who buy deferred annuities use after-tax dollars and take advantage of the tax-deferred earnings accumulation.

Insurance companies generally consider annuities to be an investment for people who are over 50. Younger people have different investment goals. They are not yet considering how to turn their retirement savings into retirement income. A typical annuity purchaser might be a 55-year-old man who buys a deferred annuity for $50,000.

Immediate annuity Annuity that begins paying income immediately. For example, you are 65 years old and plan to retire. You buy an immediate annuity for $250,000 on January 1. On February 1, you would start receiving monthly income of $2,283 if you are a man; $2,073 if you are a woman. The income is based on your life expectancy. Women receive less because they are expected to live longer.

Deferred annuity Annuity that is used to accumulate tax-deferred earnings for payout at some future date.

Let's say he is able to earn 12 percent on his annuity investment. In ten years, he would have $155,292. At that time, he's ready to retire. He could take the $155,292 in cash, but he would have to pay taxes on it. Instead, he might decide to buy an immediate annuity, which would begin paying him monthly income. For that sum, he would receive $1,417 each month for life. Each annuity payment is broken into two: one portion is taxable earnings; the other is return of principal. At the end of the year, he would receive a Form 1099 to tell him how much of his annuity income is taxable earnings. He would pay taxes only on the earnings, not on his original investment.

Even if you have not used an annuity to accumulate your retirement savings, you can still use it for retirement income. For example, say you have saved $250,000 for your retirement in a combination of accounts such as an Individual Retirement Account and a 401 (k) plan. You turn 65, retire, and need to start using your savings to live on. If you put the $250,000 into an immediate annuity, you could start receiving income of $2,283 a month if you are a man or $2,073 a month if you are a woman. You would receive that income for the rest of your life. (Women get less because they are expected to live longer.) Because annuities are considered a retirement vehicle, generally there is a 10 percent penalty on the taxable portion of the distribution if you take money out of the account before you reach age 59½.

Fixed annuity Annuity that earns interest at a fixed rate, set by the insurance company.

You might wonder what insurance is doing in a book on mutual funds. At one time, all annuities were called **fixed annuities** because they paid a fixed annual return. The money was invested in the insurance company's general account and managed by the company's investment managers. The company would announce the current rate for annuities and guarantee that rate for the first year after you purchased it. After the first year, you would be guaranteed an interest floor, or minimum—maybe 3 percent or 4 percent—for the life of the annuity. But the actual interest rate was determined at the sole discretion of the company.

Variable annuity Annuity that offers the investor an option of different mutual fund investments. In contrast to a fixed annuity, which pays a set interest rate, a variable annuity allows the investor to select his own investments and shoulder the investment risk and reward.

Over the last several years, though, investors have resisted the idea of having someone else control their investment returns. And companies have responded by passing on the investment reward, as well as the investment risk, to the investor. One product that does this is the **variable annuity.** These annuities, which have been around for years, became increasingly popular in the 1980s. They pay a return that is determined by the mutual fund selections made by the purchaser of the annuity.

When they were first introduced, variable annuities offered a small sampling of funds—sometimes just a stock fund and a bond fund. Today, though, you can find variable annuities with the full range of options, including aggressive growth funds, blue-chip funds, money market funds, junk bond funds, real estate funds, and government securities funds. You can switch mutual fund investments within your annuity, usually without a fee. Once you reach retirement and you want to start using your annuity for income, you can take the accumulated amount in your variable annuity in a lump sum, you can buy an immediate annuity and have the income paid to you over your lifetime, or you can choose to have the money paid over a specific number of years.

Annuities are an increasingly popular investment. This market has doubled every year from 1984 to 1988. But there is a downside. There are additional charges and fees connected to an annuity that you don't

BEFORE YOU BUY AN ANNUITY

Before you buy an annuity:

• Look for one with a top rating. Annuities are offered by insurance companies, which are rated by A. M. Best & Company, Standard & Poor's Corp., and Moody's Investors Service. The rating is supposed to reflect management expertise. It's also supposed to be a good indication of whether the company will be around to pay your benefit.

• Look at the money manager just as you would any other mutual fund manager. Although they're sold by an insurance company, annuities are managed by professional money managers. How long has he been in business? What's his track record? What investment options are offered?

• Check the fees. Annuities are sold by insurance agents and stockbrokers. That means they carry some type of sales fee. How much is it? How does it compare to other variable annuities? How is it structured? Some carry no front-end charge, but may have other types of fees instead. What are the annual fees charged to your accounts?

• What is the surrender charge if you change your mind and decide to liquidate your account in a year? In five years?

pay for a regular mutual fund investment. Some annuities also carry a front-end sales fee. And most have a surrender charge that starts at 7 percent of the premium payments if you decide to liquidate your investment early. (This fee typically decreases to zero over a five-year period.) For these reasons, annuities are not a liquid investment. Don't invest in a variable annuity unless you've decided that you will leave your money there for several years. Check the reputation and rating of the insurance company that issues the product. And check the performance of the mutual funds that are offered with it. The mutual funds offered in variable annuities are ranked by the major mutual fund ranking services, like Lipper Analytical Services, and listed in the tables in newspapers and magazines. (For more details on where to find information on mutual funds performance, see Chapter 13.)

CORPORATE BOND FUNDS

Lou has talked Al out of an annuity for now. Maybe when he retires. So, what else is available? Lou points out that if he wants a steady current income, Al should consider a corporate bond fund. If he buys a bond fund for his IRA account, the interest will be reinvested in his mutual fund. But, once he retires, he may choose to receive the dividends from a corporate bond fund as income. Many investors move from more aggressive growth investments to income investments when they retire. And they choose to receive their income in monthly checks because they need the money to live on. Lou gives this example: If Al has a retirement account of $200,000 when he's ready to retire, and he puts it in a bond fund that pays 8 percent coupon interest, he would receive $16,000 a year in income.

Unlike bonds issued by the government and municipalities, corporate bonds have no tax advantage. Both coupon interest and capital gains are taxable. For that reason, they are suitable for an investor who is not in a high tax bracket or for someone using a tax-deferred account such as an IRA. The range in quality of the investments made in corporate bonds is probably greater than the range of any other mutual fund category. They go from the debt issued by a corporation like IBM to the debt of small companies that have not yet established a credit rating to the debt of companies that are operating under protection of the bankruptcy laws.

Corporate debt is rated by two major agencies, Standard & Poor's Corporation and Moody's Investors Service. S&P gives four ratings for corporate stocks and bonds that it considers to be investment grade. Starting at the top they are AAA, AA, A, and BBB. Securities issued by corporations that are rated BB and lower are considered speculative. The lowest rating, for companies in default on their obligations, is D. You can find a corporate bond fund that invests only in bonds that are rated A or better. Or you could invest in a fund that selects bonds rated BBB. Bonds in this fund pay higher income because the risk is considered greater than that of bonds with a top rating. But they are still considered investment-grade bonds. You can also find a fund that invests in "high-yield" or "junk" bonds. These might include companies that are reorganizing, those that are in bankruptcy proceedings, or those that are carrying a heavy debt load due to a recent merger or acquisition. Naturally, junk bonds pay a higher interest rate because the risk to the bondholder is greater. (For more information on junk bonds, see Chapter 10.)

Top-rated corporate bonds are a relatively safe place to invest your money. But a bond mutual fund spreads your risk further—among many different top-rated corporations—offering you a portfolio of the debt of America's soundest corporations. They are a good way for you to diversify your portfolio.

When you invest in a bond, you must consider interest rate risk, which is discussed in Chapter 5. Most corporate and municipal bonds also have a **call provision.** This means that the securities can be redeemed, or called back, by the issuer within a certain period, usually ten years, at a specific price. If interest rates fall and a company wants to refinance its debt at the new, lower rate, it might take advantage of this provision to call in its outstanding bonds and issue new ones. U.S. government bonds are rarely callable. But **call risk** is another factor to consider in the corporate bond market. If interest rates fall and many of the bonds in your mutual fund portfolio are called, the fund manager will be forced to invest the money at new, lower rates, which will affect your return.

As with any mutual fund, you have to do some homework to pick a corporate bond fund. Decide how much volatility you can tolerate and

Call provision Part of agreement between bond issuer and bond buyer that spells out the terms under which the issuer may take the bonds back.
Call risk Risk that bonds you hold may be called back by the issuer. If interest rates drop, the investor will have to reinvest his money in a less favorable economic environment.

what you want the fund to do. Do you want to go for the biggest return even if it means you might sometimes have losses? Or do you want a lower but more consistent return? Remember that the yield is only one factor. It's not enough to simply compare yields and pick the highest one. For example, if you pick a fund that pays a 10 percent current yield over another that is paying 8 percent, that doesn't mean your total return will be higher. The fund offering the higher yield might have longer-term bonds. Or they might be lower-quality bonds. Even though the yield is higher, the bonds themselves might lose value. Total return includes both the coupon interest and the gain or loss in your principal. A bond fund with an 8 percent yield could have a 15 percent total return if the value of the bonds in the fund goes up. Or it could have a total return of 2 percent if the value of the bonds goes down.

The longer the average maturity of the fund, the higher the yield should be. But your exposure to interest rate risk is greater as well. Once you decide what you want—consistent yield or the best total return—check the historical records of different bond fund managers. See how they performed in bull markets as well as bear markets. (For more information on how to check fund performance, see Chapter 13.)

CONVERTIBLE SECURITIES FUNDS

Warming to his task, Lou explains to Al that there is another type of fund that is sort of "one step up" from a corporate bond fund. It's a bond fund with a stock kicker; a fund that blends the strengths of stocks and bonds into one conservative investment that offers both downside protection and upside potential. Well, Al understands what a bond is. And he understands what a stock is. So he's ready to listen to an explanation of this hybrid—a convertible securities fund.

Convertibles, Lou explains, are a type of bond or preferred stock that can be converted into shares of common stock at a set price. Here's how that works: Because they are bonds, convertibles offer a fixed return, which is likely to be higher than the dividend yield on a comparable investment in common stock. But, because they offer the option of conversion into common stock, the investor enjoys the possibility of more capital appreciation—or growth—than is available with regular bonds.

PRINCIPAL MATTERS: PILGRIM GROUP AND PRIME RATE TRUST

When interest rates moved up in 1987, the longest and strongest bond rally in history ran into trouble. Bond fund investors were alarmed as they watched the net asset value of their bond funds begin to sink.

In this the Pilgrim Group, Inc., spotted an opportunity. If it could come up with a fund that would protect invested capital from interest rate risk, yet pay a high current yield, it would have a winner. Before it came up with a solution, the stock market crashed in October 1987 and the ranks of disenchanted investors grew even larger. In May 1988, Pilgrim brought out its Prime Rate Trust. The attraction was that the fund offered a stable NAV, like a money market fund, but a higher rate of interest.

The way it did this was to invest in bank loans. The interest paid on bank loans floats up and down with the prime rate. That means, when interest rates go up, the rate on bank loans goes up along with it. So the bank—and other lenders—earn more income as interest rates rise. The Prime Rate Trust offered a way for individual investors to get in on this market.

When banks make loans to businesses, they turn around and sell off pieces of the loan to other investors, for a fee. This gives the bank fresh capital to make more loans. This bank collaterized loan participation market has been around for a long time. But the smallest chunk a single investor could buy was $5 million, which made it a market for big institutions.

Because the Pilgrim Prime Rate Trust is an institutional investor, it can buy the loans and open this market to individual investors with as little as $5,000 to invest. The portfolio manager is not a stock picker. He's a banker. But like other mutual fund managers, he offers professional management and diversification. He chooses what he considers to be the best quality bank loans. For example, he doesn't buy loans in the energy or agricultural industries and he avoids foreign loans, high-tech companies, and boom-or-bust industries such as children's toys.

Because of legal restrictions, the fund was structured as a closed-end fund with a unique twist. The shares are offered every day through brokers. But, because Pilgrim was determined to maintain the net asset value at ten dollars a share, it decided to control trading itself. Pilgrim offers to buy back shares from investors quarterly at ten dollars a share.

The result is that the net asset value remained stable at ten dollars a share throughout the first year. And, during that year, the prime rate—and therefore the yield paid by the fund—went up six times.

By late 1989, four additional mutual fund companies had these types of funds in the works.

Lou gives this example: Say a $1,000 bond pays a coupon or interest rate of 8 percent. The bond is convertible, at the discretion of the investor, into the company's common stock at a price of $20 a share. At the time the bond is issued, the company's stock is trading at $18 a share. There's certainly no incentive to convert then because it would cost an extra $2 per share over the listed price of the stock. But after one year, the stock takes off, moving up to $25 a share. The bond could be converted at the price of $20 a share, so one $1,000 bond would be converted to 50 shares of stock. But that amount of stock is currently worth $1,250. Meanwhile, you would have earned $80 in interest on your bond during the first year. So your $1,000 investment would appreciate by $330, or 33 percent, in one year.

This is what would happen in the best of all worlds. Although convertible bond funds are a conservative investment with upside potential, it can be tricky to determine whether they are selling for a good price. For example, convertibles performed poorly during the troubled market in 1987, underperforming both stocks and bonds. The stock market, as measured by the S&P 500, gained 5.23 percent for the year despite the devastating crash. After a roller-coaster year, with big nosedives in April and September, the bond market still turned in a total return of 2.29 percent for 1987, as measured by the Shearson Lehman Government/Corporate Index. But the average convertible securities fund, as measured by Lipper Analytical Services, lost 5.93 percent. It did survive the crash better than stocks. While stocks were down 20.21 percent in the fourth quarter of 1987, convertibles dropped 16.04 percent.

Convertible prices are determined by a mix of the coupon yield of the bonds and the conversion price for exchanging them for stock. They cost more than an equivalent amount of common stock because they offer a higher yield. Convertibles are attractive when they trade at a conversion value that is 5 percent to 25 percent over the current price of the common stock. Because of the premium and the yield, convertibles are generally limited a bit on each side in their performance. That is, when the stock market rallies, they might only gain 75 percent as much as the common shares into which they are convertible; when it falls, they typically lose only 50 percent as much. But in 1987, as stock prices soared, investors bid up the prices until the convertibles were overpriced, trading more as if they were equity funds rather than bond funds. When the stock market ran into trouble, the fact that they were bonds didn't provide a cushion. The convertibles didn't rally with the higher-grade bond funds. Instead, they sank like stocks. So, rather than giving investors the best of both worlds, they seemed to offer the worst of both. In a rapidly rising stock market, this could again be a problem. But in 1988 they did very well.

If you like the idea of a bond fund with a stock kicker, look at them when you are uncertain about the future of the stock market. If you're bullish on the stock market, choose a stock fund. If you're a bear, buy bonds. But if you're neutral, a convertible fund can provide steady income plus the opportunity to participate in a rising stock market. As always, look for a fund with a good track record. The fund manager must be able to pick issues that have a good yield without paying too much for the conversion premium. As an individual investor, you can't really analyze the issues in the fund. But you can tell if the manager has proven successful in picking winners.

FLEXIBLE PORTFOLIO FUNDS

Is there an investment, Al wants to know, where he can put his money and just forget about it? Not really. But Lou knows about some high-flying funds in which the portfolio manager does most of the work for you once you pick him. If, like Al, you've just received a big hunk of money and you know nothing about investing, maybe you, too, feel that the number and complexity of choices is formidable. As it happens, many mutual fund companies anticipated you. When the number of available mutual funds stretched well beyond 2,000, some mutual fund companies decided that investors were becoming confused by too many options. A number of companies responded by offering funds that gave the portfolio manager total flexibility in setting up and trading the portfolio of securities. Some of these funds resemble the asset allocation funds described in Chapter 4. But whereas asset allocation funds attempt to diversify your investment into different types of assets—gold, bonds, stocks, foreign securities—flexible portfolio funds just give the portfolio manager a blank check.

One flexible portfolio fund may invest only in bonds. Another may always be fully invested in the stock market, while still another allows the portfolio manager to time the market by moving out of stocks and into cash. These limitations on the portfolio manager allow an investor to make his own investment decisions. He can pick a fund that invests only in stocks if that's his desire. Flexible portfolio funds take the opposite approach: They assume some investors would rather let the portfolio manager, a seasoned professional, make all the decisions. So they put few restrictions on the manager.

Although the fund manager makes the decisions for you, these funds are certainly not low risk—quite the opposite. There are many ways to measure risk. One of them is volatility. And these funds are highly volatile. A common way to measure volatility is to compare a specific stock or a specific mutual fund to a broader measure of the market. In other words, how much does the net asset value of the fund change relative to the overall market? Highly volatile funds rise and fall more quickly than the market as a whole. They can be expected to outperform the overall market during a bull market and to do worse than the market average in a bear market.

MEASURING VOLATILITY

Beta *Measure of the relative volatility of a stock or a stock mutual fund. The market as a whole, as measured by the Standard & Poor's 500 stock index, is assigned a beta of 1. A mutual fund with a beta of 2 is considered twice as volatile as the market. One with a beta of .5 is considered half as volatile.*

One measure of market volatility is called a **beta** coefficient. Beta ratings, which are provided in many mutual fund rating books, help you to see how volatile a particular mutual fund is compared to the market as a whole. The stock market as whole, measured by the Standard & Poor's 500 stock index, has a beta of 1. If the market goes up 10 percent and a mutual fund gains the same 10 percent, it, too, would have a beta of 1. But if the market goes up 10 percent and the fund goes up 20 percent, it would be twice as volatile as the overall market and would have a beta of 2.

One particularly volatile fund, the 44 Wall Street Equity, an aggressive stock fund, has a beta of 1.9, which means it is nearly twice as volatile as the market as a whole. That's good news in a bull market, but bad news in a bear market. A mutual fund with a beta of less than 1 is less volatile than the market as a whole. If a fund rose only 5 percent over a period when the market rose 10 percent, it would have a beta of .5. Remember, that means that it should also fall only 5 percent when the market falls 10 percent. What betas are designed to do is to tell you which funds perform like a roller coaster and which are more like a carousel. It's one more way of helping you match your appetite for risk to specific investments. High betas are high risk.

Betas should not be computed over a short period. In fact, a period of less than three years is not considered long enough to get a good beta rating. There are other cautions about these measures as well. In order to give a good measure of volatility, the fund's investments must be spread across the broad market. Checking the beta of a fund that has no relationship to the S&P 500 will not tell you anything. For example, the Korea Fund or a gold and precious metals fund do not have a high correlation to the U.S. stock market, so the betas for these funds are meaningless. Other funds, like the 44 Wall Street Fund, may have high betas yet still not outperform the rest of the market in a bull market. That's because the fund is not broadly diversified across the market, but instead concentrates in only a few issues.

Most of the flexible portfolio funds are too new to have three-year performance figures or meaningful betas. We do know, though, that they are very volatile, and they will no doubt have high beta scores when they've been around for a while. They were designed for investors, like Al, who feel befuddled by the choice of funds available. But if you can't stomach any volatility—if you see yourself as a low beta investor—stay away.

EQUITY INCOME FUNDS

Al opts to stay away. The idea of not having to monitor investments closely appeals to him. The volatility doesn't. Still, he's learning. He likes the idea of corporate bonds—and corporate bonds with a kick, or convertibles. Anything else like that, Lou? Yes, as a matter of fact. Equity income funds are another conservative investment that combines growth and income. (See Chapter 4 for a discussion of growth and income.)

Equities, of course, are stocks. And by now you've probably come to associate the term ''income'' with bond or money market funds. For the most part, that's true. But stocks pay income, too, in the form of dividends. The portfolio managers of equity income funds seek stocks that pay higher-than-average dividends or income. How do you know that a dividend is ''higher than average''? Consider the average to be the dividend yield of the stocks that make up the Standard & Poor's 500 stock index, or ''the market.'' For example, at the end of 1988, the yield of the S&P 500 was 3.7 percent.

In times of high interest rate volatility, a stock income fund might provide more stability than a bond fund. Companies that pay a high dividend generally offer lower potential growth for your principal. But, as with most mutual fund categories, the men and women who manage these funds have many different approaches to stock picking.

Real estate investment trust (REIT) Company that manages a package of real estate investments. The portfolio is publicly traded. A REIT is similar to the investment companies that sell shares in mutual funds. But the REIT shares are traded on the stock exchange rather than bought and sold through the management company.

A typical equity-income portfolio might be heavy in utility stocks, which offer high dividends. They also might invest in **real estate investment trusts (REIT)**. Financial services stocks are another favorite. But after that, holdings in these funds vary greatly. Some buy bonds; some use many international securities; some buy convertibles; some use extremely conservative investments like bank certificates of deposit and money market instruments. Consider two top-performing equity income funds. The first, Fidelity Equity-Income, had a ten-year average total return of 20.4 percent for the period ending December 31, 1988, beating the S&P 500 by 4.05 percent. Three quarters of the fund's portfolio was in high-yield stocks of General Motors, Ford, big banks, insurers, and utilities. About 15 percent was invested in convertible securities and a small amount in bonds. Another consistent high performer is Lindner Dividend. In fact, 1987 was the first year that this fund did not post a double-digit return. Lindner's portfolio is split pretty evenly between common stocks, high-yield bonds, and preferred stocks. Nearly all the stocks are utilities.

Equity income funds generally are far less volatile than the market as a whole, as measured by the S&P 500. Because you've just learned that a beta measure is one indication of a fund's volatility, you may be interested to know that these funds sport low betas. For example, the Fidelity Equity-Income fund has a beta of .73. Lindner Dividend has a beta of .31.

FUND OF FUNDS

OK. Al is close to a decision. He'd also like to head out for a round of golf. Only one more shot, Lou. Give it your best. Lou offers one more way to get instant diversification: Invest in a mutual fund that invests in other mutual funds. These funds, which are sometimes called a "fund of funds," have been around for a long time. Like most investments, they've had their ups and downs. They've sometimes been used by scoundrels. For example, during the 1920s, they were used to create confusing layers of management so the owners could skim money off the top. In the 1960s, Bernard Cornfield set up the Fund of Funds, an investment that made millionaires of the managers at the expense of the investors.

Because this type of multifund investing has had such a troubled past, the Securities and Exchange Commission looks very carefully at proposals to set up new ones. Yet there are a few funds that do offer multifund investing today. Perhaps the best known is the Vanguard STAR fund, which was established in 1985. STAR invests in six Vanguard stock, bond, and money market funds, giving the investor the opportunity to diversify among them by buying just one fund. Roughly 60 to 70 percent of the money goes into stock funds and 30 to 40 percent into bond funds.

Similarly, the Republic National Bank of New York set up a series of funds called FundTrust in 1984. And Lincoln Investment Planning, Inc., set up the Rightime fund in 1985. This fund invests in funds of other managers such as Twentieth Century Growth and Vanguard Index Trust as well as options and futures. Rightime also relies heavily on market timing. In 1987, manager David Rights called the market right, moving into cash before it crashed and racking up a gain of nearly 19 percent for the year. Other companies are moving to get similar funds through registration.

On the plus side is the instant diversification. If your money is spread over several types of funds, it should weather market declines better than a fund that is invested only in stocks, for example. On the minus side is the fact that there are still only a handful of multifund products to choose from and some of them charge higher fees than an ordinary mutual fund. For example, the Rightime fund carries two sets of management fees, one for the fund itself and one for each fund it invests in. This is not true for the STAR fund, however. Because it is a Vanguard fund that invests in other Vanguard funds, STAR does not have separate expenses.

AL NIKALOSKI'S CHOICES

Based on Lou's advice, Al has reached some decisions.
• He's optimistic that he can find enough consulting work to keep him busy and comfortable until retirement. So he decides to roll over his $150,000 into an IRA. If things don't go as well as he hopes, he

Al Nikaloski's Portfolio

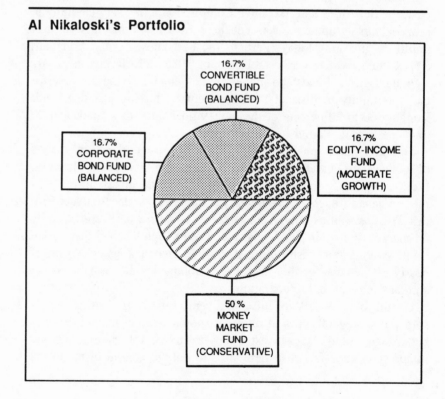

can start withdrawing it at age 59½ without paying a penalty. If he encounters disaster, he can take it out sooner, providing he pays taxes and a 10 percent penalty.

• No annuities yet. He's not ready for a semipermanent investment.

• Al wants conservative, somewhat liquid investments. Yet he knows he must diversify.

• The bulk of the money—$75,000—goes into a money market fund until he feels he's ready to make an informed investment decision with it.

• The rest is split into three pieces: $25,000 goes into a corporate bond fund.

• The second $25,000 goes into an equity-income fund. It's a conservative income investment, but it diversifies his investment into the stock market.

• The final $25,000 goes into a convertible bond fund—an income investment with the potential for growth.

POINTS TO REMEMBER

Maybe you like Al's choices. Maybe you found something else that appeals to you in this chapter, or in another chapter. But here are some principles to remember:

• If you receive a lump sum of money from a pension plan distribution, a divorce, or some other source, first check on the tax consequences.

• If the money is from a retirement account, consider rolling it into an Individual Retirement Account to avoid immediate taxes.

• Annuities are an investment option that will take your lump sum of money and pay you income for a specified period, usually for your lifetime. You can use an annuity to accumulate savings in a tax-deferred account. When you retire, you can use it to start paying you income for life.

• You could also get a steady income from a lump sum of money by investing it in a high-grade corporate bond fund or an equity income fund and requesting that the interest or dividends be paid to you in monthly checks.

• If you have some appetite for risk, but little investment knowledge, look at funds in which the portfolio manager makes all the investment decisions, like flexible portfolio funds. Or consider a ''fund of funds'' that diversifies your assets among several different mutual funds.

Chapter 9

Seeking Shelter—Tax-Advantaged Investment Strategies That Make a Difference

J anice Strickler makes a bundle as a top investment banker. She and her husband, Greg, the top financial executive of a small manufacturer, have an income that's well into six figures. Because both work in finance, the Stricklers spend a lot of time poring over magazines like *The Economist* and even the more arcane publications in their field, such as *Investment Dealer's Digest* and *Pension & Investment Age*. A great vacation for the Stricklers might mean lying on the beach at Bermuda's Coral Beach and Tennis Club and catching up on back issues of *Institutional Investor* magazine.

Although the Stricklers both depend for their living on digesting the latest financial and economic information, they haven't done a great job of investing for themselves. Like many of the professional couples who have been dubbed yuppies, the Stricklers spend pretty nearly everything they make. They have a condo in Manhattan, a weekend place in the country, expensive wardrobes, and expensive tastes.

They also pay a whopping tax bill each year. With federal, state, and New York City income tax, it seems that only a fraction of their substantial salaries ends up in their pockets. When April 15 rolls around, the Stricklers tell themselves they have to do something about their taxes. They certainly have enough information at their fingertips, but once the Form 1040 has been signed and filed, they find themselves back into the same old pattern of spending and watching the tax dollars go out the door.

Then the Stricklers had a baby. The first thing they thought about was how they would incorporate the added expenses into their bloated budget. The next was how to pay for Jennifer's college education at a good school. Greg has read about how the costs of college are outpacing the inflation rate. Still, he reasons, they make a lot of money now and, in another 18 years, they'll probably make a lot more. Why not wait?

Why indeed? The Stricklers are not neophytes in the world of finance. They don't need to be reminded about the importance of the compounding of interest. The earlier you put the money away, the earlier it starts working for you. But they are procrastinators. To bring the point home, Greg sets himself the task of performing a little exercise to see how much difference an early start can make. Let's say the parents of one girl put aside $200 a month for her from her birth until she reaches age 18. Her friend's parents start later, but they make up for it. They sock away $450 a month from her tenth birthday until she is 18. Both couples earn 8 percent on their investments. Who has more money for college? The first child has a college nest egg of $96,017 when she turns 18, while the second child, whose parents saved exactly the same amount of money—$43,200—has only $60,240.

The Stricklers can see that they have to get their spending under control if they're going to set up a college plan soon. And since investing means a whole new set of tax problems, Greg decides it's time to tackle their tax situation head on. They have many pluses: Although they don't have much savings, they make a good deal of money and can afford to cut back and put some aside. They have nearly 18 years to get the money together. They both know a great deal about finance and already spend a lot of time digesting financial and economic news. And the Stricklers are nothing if not risk takers. But they've wisely decided that their daughter's future is not something they want to put at risk.

Most of us see something of ourselves in the Stricklers. No matter how disciplined you are, chances are you sometimes feel that you spend more than you should; that you're not doing as much to meet financial goals as you'd like; and that taxes are eating away at your spendable income. You may have something in common with Janice and Greg. Do you:

- Have a high risk tolerance?
- Make a lot of money but spend even more?
- Pay a lot in taxes?
- Have a goal that is at least 10 or 15 years away?
- Know a Dow Jones from a General Electric?
- Need to save for college?

You, too, may be seeking shelter if you make a good deal of money and pay a lot in taxes. If you are comfortable with risk, spend a lot of time keeping up with financial news but feel that it's not doing you much good, this could be you. Even if college saving is of no interest to you, perhaps you want to get your spending and your taxes under control. Maybe you've decided it's time to start a retirement plan. Or maybe you know it's time to concentrate on building your wealth. In any event, you know it's time to address the tax issue as you move from consumer to saver to investor. It's time to take a careful look at the bill from Uncle Sam.

There are no secrets to getting your spending and taxes under control, and the purpose of this book is not to help you do a financial makeover. But perhaps you need to start at the beginning. Sit down and draw up a simple balance sheet. Do you have a large credit card debt? Owe a lot on your bank overdraft line? Are you paying a lot in short-term interest? Only 10 percent of that is tax deductible in 1990. By 1991, none of it will be. You need to get control of your finances. One basic rule of personal finance is that your net worth should grow each year. That's really not too tough. Even if all you do is pay down your mortgage a bit, you should see some progress, unless you're running up big credit card debts.

If, like the Stricklers, you're making plenty of money but you're heavily in debt, you probably need a basic overhaul. First off, you need to pay your bills. If you're carrying credit card debt at 18 or 19 percent, paying it off is your best first investment, because there's no other way you're going to get a guaranteed 18 or 19 percent return on your money. Next, think through your goals. You should be planning for retirement in a tax-efficient way. Do you have a 401 (k) plan at work? Are eligible for a Keogh plan for the self-employed? You should also be covering your insurance needs and building investing into your budget.

If you have a child, you should be planning for college. If you don't have the energy to tackle everything at once, pick one goal and start small. Set goals, one at a time. Work your investment goals into your budget and always consider the tax angle of your investment choices. Research and select an investment and then arrange to have the money regularly deducted from your bank account or your paycheck. If you need life insurance, consider variable life, a policy that allows you to combine tax-deferred investing in mutual funds with insurance coverage. Once you've found room in your budget for investing and you've learned to consider your investments from a tax point of view, you can build.

TAX-EXEMPT MONEY MARKET FUNDS

Even though the Stricklers aren't savers, they do have enough financial savvy to keep their money in a money market fund where it earns a market rate of interest, rather than marking time in a bank checking account. But, because they also pay a lot of taxes, they should consider a tax-exempt money market fund.

Municipals Bonds, notes, or other short-term loans issued by state, city, or other local governments to pay for projects. All are exempt from federal taxes; many are also exempt from state and local taxes. Sometimes called "munis" or "tax-frees."

These money market funds invest in short-term municipal bonds or municipal notes and other municipal paper or short-term loans. **Municipals** are simply securities issued by state and local governments and their agencies. These securities are exempt from federal tax. If you buy bonds or notes issued by the state in which you live, they'll also be free of state taxes. A few states—like Maryland and New York— offer triple tax-free funds that let you off the hook on local taxes as well.

If you live in a state with high state and local taxes, check into these funds. Consider this: In 1989, the top marginal federal tax rate was 33 percent. If you fell into that tax bracket and earned $1 in taxable

STATES WHERE YOU CAN BUY STATE TAX-FREE BOND FUNDS

Earnings on municipal bonds are almost always free of federal tax. If you buy the municipal bonds issued in your own state, you avoid state and local taxes as well. If you live in one of these states, you can also buy a mutual fund that invests only in the bonds of your state. Some of them, such as Texas, do not have state taxes. But many Texans still want to buy bond funds that finance projects within their own state, even though there is no tax advantage.

Alabama
Arizona
California
Colorado
Connecticut
Florida
Georgia
Hawaii
Idaho
Indiana
Kentucky
Louisiana
Maryland
Massachusetts
Michigan
Minnesota
Missouri
New Jersey
New York
North Carolina
North Dakota
Ohio
Oregon
Pennsylvania
Rhode Island
South Carolina
Tennessee
Texas
Virginia
West Virginia

interest, you kept 67 cents. If you earned $1 in interest that was free from federal taxes, you kept $1. In high-tax states like New York, tax-free funds are even more compelling. In New York City, where the Stricklers live, the combined state and city rate is 11.8 percent. Because state and local taxes are deductible from federal taxes, the effective state and local rate, net of federal tax, is 7.91 percent. But that brings your $1 in taxable interest on your investments down to 59 cents after taxes.

So what's the catch? Why doesn't every smart investor jump into muni funds whatever his tax rate? It didn't escape the notice of the issuers of muni bonds and municipal paper that they have an advantage in the marketplace. Because a tax-free investment is more at-

If you are in the 28% or 33% tax bracket, then tax-exempt funds may pay you considerably more than taxable funds, after adjusting for taxes. The table below compares the yields of tax-exempt funds with the yields of taxable funds.

Comparison of Tax-Exempt and Taxable Yields		
Tax-Exempt Yield	Taxable Equivalent Yield If Your Federal Income Tax Bracket is:	
	28%	33%
4.0%	5.56%	5.97%
4.5	6.25	6.72
5.0	6.94	7.46
5.5	7.64	8.21
6.0	8.33	8.96
6.5	9.03	9.70
7.0	9.72	10.45
7.5	10.42	11.19
8.0	11.11	11.94
8.5	11.81	12.69
9.0	12.50	13.43
9.5	13.19	14.18
10.0	13.89	14.93

The **taxable equivalent yields** in the above table are calculated using this formula:

$$\text{Taxable Equivalent Yield} = \frac{\text{Tax-Exempt Yield}}{1 - \text{Tax Bracket}}$$

For example, at the maximum 33% tax rate, you would have to earn 10.45% on a taxable investment to match the net income of a tax-free investment yielding 7%.

tractive, yields on tax-free funds are lower than those on taxable funds. All this means is that you need to spend a little more time determining if you still make out better in a tax-free account. For New Yorkers, for example, that means that if you can get a tax-

If you are considering an investment in a state tax-free fund, you must consider the effect of both federal and state taxes.

First, find the Effective Combined Federal/State Tax bracket for your individual state, in the table below:

Effective Combined Federal and State Tax Brackets				
State Tax Rates		Federal Rates:		
		28%	33%	28%
CA	9.3%	34.70%	39.20%	34.70%
CT	0.0–12.0	31.60	41.04	36.64
MA	10.0	35.20	39.70	35.20
MICH	4.6	31.31	36.80	31.30
DETROIT	7.6	33.47	38.09	33.47
MINN	8.0	33.76	38.30	33.80
NJ	2.5, 3.5	29.80	35.34	30.52
NY STATE	7.9	33.67	38.28	33.67
NY CITY	11.1, 11.3	36.08	40.55	36.12
OHIO	5.2, 6.9	31.74	37.62	32.97
PENN	2.1	29.51	34.41	29.51
PHILA.	7.1	33.08	37.73	33.08

For states with a range of tax rates, the highest tax rate that corresponds to the applicable Federal rate has been used to calculate combined rates.

Then, calculate the **taxable equivalent yield** for a state tax-free fund using the effective combined tax bracket found in the preceding table.

For example, if you are a resident of California and are in the 33% federal tax-bracket, your effective combined federal/state tax-bracket is 39.20% (from the table). Using the **taxable equivalent yield** formula, compare the yield of a hypothetical California state tax-free fund, yielding 7.14%, to a taxable fund; you would have to invest in a taxable fund yielding at least 11.74% to match the yield of this state tax-free fund:

$$\text{Taxable Equivalent Yield} = \frac{7.14\%}{1 - .3920} = 11.74\%$$

exempt yield that is greater than 59 percent of a taxable yield, it's attractive. In order to figure out how you'd fare depending on your tax status, see the charts above.

Like other money market funds, tax-free funds maintain a share value of one dollar. Only the interest rate on these short-term securities varies. There is one small note of caution. Tax reform has muddled the muni market. For one thing, it added an alternative minimum tax, which can make muni bond funds subject to taxation for the very wealthy in some cases. For another, some municipalities have begun to issue taxable bonds because they can't get the federal government to approve the purpose for which they are borrowing money. This means that, although they're *called* muni bonds, these bonds are not tax-exempt. But these are exceptions to the rule. For most purposes, you should consider that municipal bonds are tax-exempt. The advantage to investing in a tax-exempt money market fund has also narrowed since the tax reform act. And, in early 1989, some taxable funds were paying double the rate of tax-exempts. So your decision on whether to use a taxable or tax-exempt account requires careful consideration.

HIGH-YIELD TAX-EXEMPT FUNDS

Municipal bonds, including single-state funds, are also available in longer maturities, ranging up to 30 years. If you pay high federal, state, and local taxes, you might want to consider these funds for part of your portfolio. Remember, though, that a money market fund always pays a market rate of interest. If you buy a longer maturity, you are exposed to interest rate risk as discussed in Chapter 5.

But if you have plenty of money, plenty of knowledge, and a healthy tolerance for risk, take a look at intermediate- or longer-term municipal bond funds, particularly the high-yield funds. Like corporate bonds, munis are rated by Moody's Investors Service and Standard & Poor's. The higher the rating, the lower the risk and the lower the return. (For a discussion of credit risk, see Chapter 10.) High-yield bonds or "junk bonds" either have low ratings (a rating lower than BBB by Standard & Poor's or Baa by Moody's Investors Service) or they are not rated at all. Obviously the risk is significant. But the return can be, too. If you believe you can handle the risk, consider junk munis, which pay a higher tax-free yield than a general muni bond.

Junk bonds are not for the squeamish, or for the novice. But the experienced bond picker can find some real values in the bond bargain

YIELDING DIRECTION: PAY ATTENTION TO THE SHAPE OF THE CURVE

There's a good example of the risk/reward relationship of investing to be found in the bond market. Bond maturities range from extremely short to 30 years. Normally, the shorter the maturity, the lower the return. That's because the investor has only tied up his money for a short period of time. As maturities increase, so does the return and so does the risk. That's because the investor is locking up his money for a longer term. If interest rates rise before the bond matures, he is locked into a lower rate. For example, an investor who buys a 30-year bond at 9 percent will lose the opportunity to take advantage of higher rates if they subsequently rise to 12 percent.

Professional investors illustrate this relationship by plotting the bond market's maturities on a chart. This is called a yield curve. The bond market normally has a positive yield curve. That means that interest rates gradually increase along the line as the maturities increase. But when short-term rates are higher than long-term rates, the curve is called a negative or inverted yield curve.

Here's what causes an inverted curve: When investors expect lower inflation and lower interest rates, they are eager to lock in the current high rates for as long as possible. So they buy long-term bonds. As demand for these bonds increases, prices rise and yields go down. When they sink below the level of short-term rates, the yield curve is inverted. Some investors see an inverted yield curve as a good opportunity to buy long-term bonds. They reason that the yield curve will normalize and, as it does, the value of long-term bonds will increase.

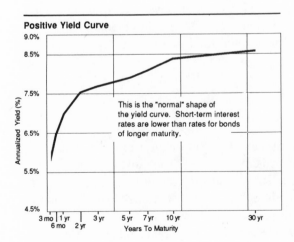

Positive Yield Curve

This is the "normal" shape of the yield curve. Short-term interest rates are lower than rates for bonds of longer maturity.

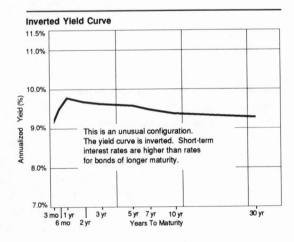

Inverted Yield Curve

This is an unusual configuration. The yield curve is inverted. Short-term interest rates are higher than rates for bonds of longer maturity.

basement. You might compare him to the aficionado of "junque," who spends free time scouring flea markets looking for collectibles. The knowledgeable shopper doesn't buy either a bond or a piece of art deco jewelry just because it's cheap. In both cases, they know what they're looking for—value at a deflated price.

However, it might be easier to recognize early Erté than to forecast the ability of a bankrupt company to repay its debt. Junk bond buyers are speculators in the bond market. Some take big risks. For example, the Washington Public Power Supply System, a utility that came to be known as Whoops, issued billions of dollars of tax-exempt bonds in the 1970s to pay for five nuclear reactors. In 1983, the utility defaulted on interest payments on the bonds issued to back two of the plants. Not surprisingly, two years later, prices of the bonds issued to back the other three plants were selling at a heavy discount. Although these bonds were not in default, their ratings had been suspended. So these junk bonds offered a tax-free yield of 16 percent compared to 10 percent on Triple-A–rated munis. But only a hard-core speculator would want to take a flyer on those bonds.

But junk bonds can be unrated for other, more benign reasons. If you found a Chippendale chair at a flea market priced at $50, you probably wouldn't walk away from it just because it was in dubious company. Similarly, many junk bond buyers look for value that has been disguised. Perhaps the reputation of a municipality or a corporation has been tarnished for no good reason. A talented junk bond buyer, just like an experienced junque shop buyer, can often find good buys in this market. Savvy investors, like the Stricklers, should consider seeking out a good junk muni fund as a tax shelter.

LIFE INSURANCE

The Stricklers do know that the Tax Reform Act of 1986 wiped out most tax-advantaged methods of investing. They lost their deductions for contributions to their IRAs. And they know that tax reform left affluent investors with only a few reliable tax shelters—their mortgages, 401 (k) retirement plans, and life insurance.

Life insurance? Can you be serious? Greg wants to know. That most boring of all investments? If you, like Greg, haven't looked at life insurance for the past several years, you might be surprised. One of the most popular investments in recent years is a tax-deferred mutual fund in a life insurance "wrapper." These policies, called variable life insurance, universal variable insurance, and variable annuities have been the fastest-growing investments of this decade. Here's how they work: Life companies have long offered **whole life insurance** (also called *cash value*) policies as an alternative to straight **term life insurance.** These cash value policies average out the cost of insurance over the policyholder's lifetime so the buyer pays a level premium for life even though it costs the insurance company less to provide the insurance coverage in the early years and more in later years. This premium is split between the death benefit and a separate savings or investment account. Unlike term insurance, which pays a pure death benefit, these policies offer a growing investment pot in the form of the cash value.

It is this cash value combined with the tax advantages that have become the focus of the new vogue in insurance. Until the mid-1970s, the cash value built up in a savings account with an annual rate of interest that might range between 3 percent and 5 percent. Most smart investors avoided cash value insurance. They figured they could do better with their money if they invested it themselves. "Buy term and invest the difference," was their motto. But in 1976, a new product, **variable life insurance**, which wraps an insurance policy around a tax-deferred investment in mutual funds, was introduced. While the policy offers a fixed, minimum death benefit, above that level both the death benefit and the cash value are determined by the performance of the investment portfolio.

There is no minimum cash value in the policy. The cash value depends on the performance of the investments. And there is nothing boring about the performance of some of the mutual funds that are available through these policies. Many of them are among the top performers. For example, The New England offers a capital growth fund in its Zenith Life policy that was the best-performing mutual fund of 1986, returning 95 percent! And in the roller-coaster year of 1987, the same fund returned 53 percent. Best of all, these earnings build up tax-deferred and you can tap them by taking out tax-free loans. Perhaps you, like Greg Strickler, are ready to learn more.

Whole life insurance
Policy that combines insurance coverage with a savings or investment account, sometimes referred to as "cash value" policies, because they build up a cash value over the years that the policyholder can borrow against.

Term life insurance *Policy that offers a death benefit for a specific period of time. The premium increases as the policyholder grows older. There is no investment or savings element in these policies.*

Variable life insurance
Policy that combines cash value life insurance with a tax-deferred investment, usually a stock or bond mutual fund. It is a type of whole life insurance. But instead of paying a fixed interest rate on the savings portion, this policy allows the policyholder to make his own investment choices and to take the additional risk as well as the additional potential reward.

A REVOLUTIONARY CONCEPT THAT MAKES SENSE: JEROME S. GOLDEN AND VARIABLE LIFE INSURANCE

The idea that a life insurance policyholder should get a guaranteed interest rate on the savings portion of his policy goes back to the Puritans. To many insurance companies, it is almost sacrosanct. In the late 1960s, when a couple of daring actuaries from the New York Life Insurance Company devised a way to offer an investment in common stock—which would provide a fluctuating rather than a guaranteed return—it was a shocking concept.

But some innovative insurers were ready to try something new. The idea behind the variable life policy was that "historically, common stocks have outperformed bonds and Treasury bills," says Jerome S. Golden, president of Golden Financial Services and one of the early developers of variable life. "If life insurance is the longest contract you'll ever enter into, it makes sense to offer common stocks."

In the early 1970s, it made sense to about 15 different life companies. But once they discovered that the new product would be regulated by both the Securities and Exchange Commission and the insurance commissioners of all 50 states, all but one company, the Equitable Life Assurance Company, backed out.

The Equitable introduced a policy in 1976 that offered an option of investing in a common stock fund managed by the company rather than in its general account. But the idea certainly did not take off. "It was a real struggle," Golden remembers. "You lived and died by what people heard about the market on the seven o'clock news." And what they were hearing about the market that year was not entirely good news. The new variable policy sold $400,000 in premium that first year, a pittance.

Then Golden got a brainstorm: "I saw that if you offered multiple options, you'd have something to sell in all markets." He took the idea to Wall Street to see if he could find a firm that would be interested in managing the assets and selling the policies. He ended up with an agreement between Monarch Life and Merrill Lynch. The product had five investment options: a money market fund; an intermediate government fund, a long-term, quality corporate fund; a blue-chip stock fund; and a growth fund. The policy was put on the market in 1981. That year it sold $4 million in premium.

After further fine-tuning, and the addition of more options—including zero-coupon bonds and a multiple strategy or asset allocation fund—the Monarch's premium jumped to $1.6 billion in 1987. But the company no longer had the industry to itself. By this time it was a $3 to $4 billion industry and variable life was the hottest insurance product around.

Life insurance has always had a special tax status. When federal income taxes were introduced in 1913, life insurance received special treatment. Legislators reasoned that taking care of dependents should be encouraged, so they provided various tax incentives to encourage people to buy insurance. Those who bought cash value life policies were given these benefits: tax-deferred accumulation of the investment portion of the policy; the ability to borrow the earnings tax-free; and tax-free distribution of the proceeds to the beneficiary if the policy is in force at the time of the policyholder's death. In addition, the proceeds do not have to go through probate.

This combination of tax advantages attracted millions of policyholders over the years. But the elimination of most other tax deductions in the Tax Reform Act of 1986 and the availability of a vast array of sophisticated mutual fund products with superior growth potential made these products among the most attractive investments around. Insurers also moved to sweeten the deal by making the policies more flexible.

Congress did add some restrictions in a 1988 tax law. You must buy a policy that requires at least seven substantially level premium payments in order to make tax-free loans on your policy. That doesn't mean you can't borrow money until you've made seven payments. Rather, the new law was intended to curb the use of policies that could be purchased for a single premium. Congress saw these single-premium policies as a tax-deferred investment account thinly disguised as a life insurance policy, because a policyholder could deposit a single premium of, say, $50,000, and then borrow the money from this tax-deferred account.

Here's how a variable life policy might work for 35-year-old Greg Strickler. Let's say he buys a policy with a face value of $125,000 by making premium payments of $5,000 a year for seven years, or a total of $35,000. Assuming he could earn a 12 percent annual return on the mutual funds he chose for the policy, the cash value after 20 years would be $152,170. During that same period, the death benefit would grow to $336,964. This assumes, of course, that Greg didn't borrow on the policy.

With these policies, the policyholder can dramatically alter the face value, cash value, and premium. He can skip premiums, add extra money to build up the cash value, and switch between various mutual fund investments whenever he likes. For example, if Greg needs the money for Jennifer's college education, he could borrow $20,000 a year for four years, tax-free. This would reduce the cash value of the policy to just over $40,000 and it would reduce the death benefit to just over $200,000. But he need never pay it back. If he doesn't need the money for Jennifer's education or any other purpose, he can simply let it grow until he retires at age 65. The policy would then have a cash surrender value of $359,784. If he no longer needs insurance at retirement, he could either cash it in or turn it into an annuity to pay him income for life.

Following tax reform, these policies were heavily promoted as the last remaining tax shelter. And they are, indeed, attractive for investors with a wide variety of needs. But there are three important things to consider before you buy a variable life insurance policy. First, it is not a pure investment. You pay for the cost of insurance as well as some hefty sales commissions. Commissions, administrative charges, and other fees can eat up 50 to 100 percent of the first year's premium. In the second year, that drops to around 25 percent. But one study found that over 20 years of the policy, fees still averaged 24 percent a year.

BEFORE YOU INVEST IN VARIABLE LIFE INSURANCE

Before you buy a variable life policy:

• Make sure that the insurance company has a top rating from the A. M. Best Company, Standard & Poor's Corporation, or Moody's Investors Service.

• Check the options offered for the investment portion of the policy. Does the policy offer a good range of funds?

• Determine how often you can move from one investment option to another. If it's three or four times a year, is that adequate for you?

• Find out what commissions and fees you will be paying.

• Find out what the surrender charge is if you decide you want to get out of the policy early.

• See if the company will waive the surrender charge if the tax law changes, making the policy less advantageous.

• Find out the minimum death benefit.

• Look for flexibility. Many policies allow you to skip premiums, to add to the amount of your investment portion, to change the amount that goes to insurance and the amount that goes to building the cash value. These are sometimes called universal variable policies.

This is not to say that you're being ripped off. But if you have no need for life insurance, you shouldn't buy one of these policies. Second, remember that insurance policies are illiquid. They are not short-term investments. There are surrender charges as well as tax consequences if you change your mind and decide to cash in your policy.

Third, check both the insurer that stands behind the policy and the performance of the investments that are offered. Standard & Poor's, Moody's Investors Service, and the A. M. Best Company rate insurers. Look for a top-rated policy from one or two of these services. Once you've isolated a couple of insurers, you need to make certain that they offer the range of mutual fund investments you want and that the funds have good performance records. Performance figures for the mutual funds that back variable life policies are published weekly in *Barron's*. These policies are available from most stockbrokers as well as from insurance agents who are registered representatives.

If your motivation in buying a policy is to put aside money for your child's college education, then you should know that borrowing on a variable life insurance policy is only one method of paying for college. There are others, particularly if you have some time before you need the money.

COLLEGE SAVINGS RULES

Janice Strickler has been studying the changes in the rules for saving for college. She learned that the 1986 tax act reduced the tax benefits of using **custodial accounts** under the **Uniform Gift to Minors Act** to give money to children. Before tax reform, the money deposited in custodial accounts under the child's name was taxed at the child's tax rate. Because a young child usually had no other income, this usually meant that no taxes would be due on the money earned in these accounts until it reached a significant amount. But tax reform changed the rules so that all the child's investment income over $1,000 a year is taxed at the parents' highest marginal rate until the child is 14 years old. Although this change makes custodial accounts less attractive, it doesn't make them worthless. It simply means the parents have to work harder to find the right investments.

Custodial account Account that is set up for a child by an adult, used for its tax advantages.

Uniform Gift to Minors Act Law that establishes rules for assets that are held in the name of a child. Since the Tax Reform Act of 1986 all earnings over $1,000 a year are taxed at the parents' highest marginal rate until the child reaches age 14, when they are taxed at his own lower rate.

Janice worked up this example. One couple saves $150 a month toward college, starting when their child is five. They keep it in a money market account, get 8 percent interest, and pay a 35 percent marginal tax rate, including state and local income taxes. Another couple with the same tax rate puts their college savings under the child's name in a custodial account. They start at the same time and get the same 8 percent money market deposit account interest. Although they also pay taxes at 35 percent marginal rate, they pay only on the earnings that exceed $1,000 a year until the child is 14. When he turns 14, he pays taxes at his own lower tax rate.

When the children are ready for college, the first couple's child has $33,339 in after-tax college savings. Because they have used a custodial account and saved money on taxes, the second couple's child has $38,425 for college. The advantages of this approach are even greater when the use of custodial accounts is combined with more sophisticated investment techniques. For example, when the child is around 10 years old, and the annual earnings on the account have begun to exceed $1,000, the money in the custodial account could be switched to a municipal bond mutual fund because earnings on municipal bonds are not taxed. Then, when the child reaches age 14 and is taxed at his own lower rate the money could be switched for a few years to a growth and income mutual fund that seeks high total return. As tuition time grows near, the money should be moved out of the markets and into the safety of a money market fund. Depending on market conditions, this approach could add several thousand dollars to the second couple's $38,425 college money and put them much further ahead. Even if the first couple also switched to different investments, they would have to pay taxes on their account at their own higher tax rate for the entire period.

What kind of mutual funds should go into a college account? If you're knowledgeable and comfortable with risk, you might want to consider aggressive growth funds that emphasize capital appreciation rather than income. These funds pay little if any dividends, which should reduce the income that would be taxable to the parents. Instead, the funds aim for capital gains. Even if the fund performs spectacularly, you don't realize your capital gains—and thus they're not taxable—until you sell the shares. (There may still be some capital gains realized by the fund manager from trading in the portfolio. These are distributed, and you will have to pay taxes on them, of course. But these funds can still be a good college investment.)

Consider how much time you have to sock money away until the college bills come due and how comfortable you are with a volatile investment. If you have a newborn like Jennifer Strickler, you're knowledgeable about the markets, and you can put money away regularly to take advantage of dollar-cost averaging, you can afford to be aggressive. But when you get close to college tuition time—perhaps within three years—start moving your child's college nest egg into a money market fund. Continue to monitor the investments. Don't move all the money at once, because your child's tax bill will be higher.

ZERO-COUPON BOND FUNDS

There is one type of bond that works very well for college accounts, as well as for tax-deferred retirement accounts: the zero-coupon bond. This bond functions quite differently from a regular bond, which pays interest, or a "coupon," every year (see Chapter 5). Zero-coupon bonds pay no coupon or interest. Instead, the bonds are sold at a deep discount to face value and then appreciate to face value or par over a period of 7 to 30 years. Interest rates at the time you purchase the bond determine the discount price. For example, in February 1989, you could have laid out $263.20 to buy a zero-coupon bond that would be worth $1,000 in the year 2004. The yield on that bond would have been 9.10 percent annually for 15 years until maturity. If you had a two-year-old child at the time, it might have been a good investment for his custodial account.

These investments have a couple of obvious advantages. First, you can target the exact year in which you want your bond to mature, which is handy if you have a specific goal, like college, in mind. Second, your initial outlay is small. Not surprisingly, these bonds were wildly popular when they first came out in 1981. Not only could they offer a specific return in any target year the investor chose, but they offered a form of tax-deferred earnings because the bondholder did not pay taxes until the bond matured and he got his money.

The IRS quickly closed this loophole, though, by declaring that the bondholder must pay tax on the interest each year, as if he were earning it, even though he did not actually receive it until the bond matured. This ruling on "phantom interest," as it was called, made zeros less attractive to most investors. But they still hold an appeal for tax-deferred accounts like IRAs and custodial accounts for children. As long as your child is not earning over $1,000 a year in "phantom interest," you don't have to pay any taxes.

There are a couple of other concerns about zeros, though. The prices of the bonds are extremely volatile and fluctuate wildly with movements in interest rates. This means that you could suffer a serious loss of capital should you need to get out in a hurry. The market for many of these issues is also thinly traded, making them difficult and expensive to sell. If you purchase the bond for your child's college account, that should not be a problem, since your intention will be to hold it to maturity and collect the face value.

Like regular bonds, zeros are available in bond funds. Instead of buying a bond, you simply buy shares in the fund. These funds have the same pluses and minuses as the bonds themselves. If you hold your investment until the "target date," you will receive the return that was promised to you. For example, if you put $10,000 into the Benham Target 2000 fund in January 1989, your $10,000 will be worth $26,428 in the year 2000.

Although the bond funds are more liquid, the net asset value is still very volatile. Prices may fluctuate wildly between the time you buy the shares and maturity, because you're making a long-term interest rate bet. In the above example, you would lock in 9.24 percent for 11 years. If interest rates move higher, the price of your bond fund shares will head lower. If interest rates drop, your shares will appreciate. For example, during the second quarter of 1989, as interest rates fell, five zero bond funds were among the top twenty-five performers of mutual funds in all categories. But that matters to you only if you want to sell before the year 2000. If you close your eyes and hang on, you get the $26,428, whatever happens to interest rates in the meantime.

SMALL-COMPANY FUNDS

The Stricklers are comfortable with risk and they have a long time horizon before they need the money for Jennifer's tuition. They know they shouldn't put all their eggs in one basket. To balance their income

SMALL STOCK BAROMETER: T. ROWE PRICE NEW HORIZONS FUND

How can you tell when it's a good time to buy a mutual fund that invests in the stocks of small companies? There's no guarantee, of course, but there is a barometer that's widely followed by investors.

Because small companies have more growth potential than large, established companies, their stock normally trades at a premium to the market as a whole. John H. Laporte, manager of the New Horizons fund, a small-company stock fund started in 1961 by T. Rowe Price, says small companies should trade at a premium of 30 to 50 percent over the large, established companies.

Because New Horizons contains stocks of 200 companies, it is considered representative of small-company stocks. And it provides a way to measure the relative value of small- and big-company stocks. Look at the price/earnings (p/e) ratio of New Horizons relative to the price/earnings ratio of the Standard & Poor's 500 stock index, which represents the larger companies.

When the relative p/e ratio of New Horizons is 1, that means small stocks are trading at the same level as the market. You don't have to pay a premium to buy them and they are considered a good buy. If the relative p/e is in the range of 1.3 to 1.5, they are trading at 30 to 50 percent over the market. Small stocks are then considered fairly valued. When the relative p/e is 2, it means they are trading at twice the price of the market as a whole and they are overvalued.

In the nearly 30 years since the fund was set up, the relative p/e ratio has moved between 1 and 2. Only twice has it fallen below 1. And only three times has it risen above 2. Laporte considers it very significant when it is at either end of the range.

Small stocks are very volatile. And they have long cycles during which they underperform and overperform the market as a whole, Laporte says. For example, from October 1976 to June 1983, they outperformed the market. By June 1983, the relative p/e was 2.2, indicating that the stocks were overvalued.

From June 1983 to October 1987, while the rest of the stock market was enjoying one of its longest bull runs in history, small stocks languished. But then on November 30, 1987, the New Horizons relative p/e hit a historic low of .9 and small stocks began to rally. From that date until the end of June 1988, New Horizons gained 34.6 percent compared to a 21.3 percent gain for the S&P 500.

investments, they need a portion of their portfolio in stock-oriented funds. A mutual fund that invests in the stocks of small, emerging growth companies appeals to them. Over time, the stocks of small companies have outperformed the larger, more stable blue-chip issues because the smaller companies are growing more rapidly from a smaller base. But, for the same reason, they are far more volatile. A strong stomach for risk and time to let your money grow—five years is a bare minimum, ten is better—are the keys here.

There is some support for the theory that small stocks outperform those of more established companies. Stock researchers Rex A. Sinquefeld and Roger G. Ibbotson at the University of Chicago divided Big Board stocks into five groups according to size. Stocks in the fifth group—representing companies that are under $100 million in market value—outperformed the stocks of larger companies over time. Ibbotson speculated that this was because these stocks are harder to buy, more difficult to analyze, less liquid, and characterized by more **insider ownership.**

Insider ownership
Securities ownership by officers or owners of a company.

But ''over time'' is the important qualification here. During the roaring bull market from 1982 to 1987, small stocks underperformed the market. One reason was that there was a lot of foreign money coming into the U.S. stock market and that money went into the big, well-known companies. The Japanese, for example, were pouring money into U.S. equities. And they didn't want to buy unknown and untested companies. They wanted blue chips. At the same time, big companies were profiting from massive cost cutting and restructuring. The declining dollar, which boosted earnings of big companies that do significant business overseas, did nothing to help small companies, which do most of their business here in the United States. The takeover boom and stock buyback activity further boosted big-company stocks without helping small companies at all. During that period, the small stocks lagged behind the overall market.

And some investors believed that small stocks would never again be in the limelight. They argued that the rules had changed, that the idea that small stocks should trade at a premium to the rest of the market was old hat. In fact, in nearly 1987, one fund manager, John Westergaard, closed his Westergaard Fund, which specialized in small stocks, for that reason.

Then, following the October 1987 stock market crash, the small companies began to outperform the larger blue-chip issues. From November 30, 1987, the low point for small-company stocks, until the end of June 1988, the best-known small-company fund, New Horizons, managed by T. Rowe Price, was up 34.6 percent, compared to

Small Stocks and Large Stocks Move in Different Cycles

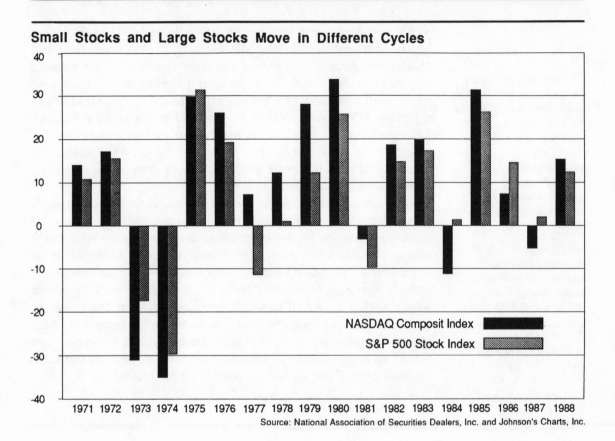

Source: National Association of Securities Dealers, Inc. and Johnson's Charts, Inc.

21.3 percent for the market as measured by the S&P 500. This performance left investors divided, though. Some, like Westergaard, still believed it was a false start. Others believed it was the first leg of a new up cycle. Small-stock cycles tend to be long—four or five years. The last up cycle was even longer, lasting from October 1976 to June 1983. That was followed by the four and a half years of underperformance, which temporarily ended in November 1987.

But because the stocks are volatile and the cycles are long, an investor who doesn't stick for the long haul can get walloped. Consider this: If an investor had put $10,000 into New Horizons in 1969, it

Over-the-counter market
Decentralized market for stocks that do not trade on the New York Stock Exchange or the American Stock Exchange. OTC stocks are traded through a regional telephone and computer network by brokers and dealers throughout the country.

NASDAQ Index   Index of over-the-counter stocks prepared by the National Association of Securities Dealers. NASDAQ stands for National Association of Securities Dealers Automatic Quotations Systems.

would have been worth less than $5,500 at the end of 1974. But if the investor had put in the same $10,000 in 1975, he would have had $61,060 by the end of 1983. If you have the stomach for a roller-coaster ride, consider these funds. And do remember to move your money well in advance of when you expect to use it. That shouldn't be a problem. Once your child is 14 years old and is taxed at his own lower rate, you should sell some, if not all, of the shares of this volatile fund, take the gains, and move into a more stable growth or growth and income fund for a few years until tuition time draws near, when you should move to a money market fund.

Most mutual fund companies offer funds that invest in small-company stocks. They may be called emerging growth funds, or OTC funds (a reference to the **over-the-counter market** where small-company stocks are traded). Other small-company funds might be pegged to the **NASDAQ Index,** which follows the over-the-counter market. There are many other types of aggressive growth funds that would work just as well in a college account. If you don't like the prospects for small-company stocks, look at the other options in Chapter 11. On the other hand, if volatile funds make you nervous, you should stick with a more conservative fund that makes you feel comfortable, even if you do have to pay tax on the income.

THE STRICKLERS' CHOICES

First the Stricklers will pay off their debts. Next they will set up Jennifer's college fund.

• They plan to open a custodial account for Jennifer and put $1,000 into a mutual fund composed of stocks of small, emerging growth companies. Greg will have $100 a month deducted from his paycheck to add to the fund. They realize that they'll probably never be able to cover all of Jennifer's education from this fund, but it's a start. And they'll try to increase the monthly amount as time goes on.

• They put another $500 in a zero-coupon bond fund and promise to add to that regularly, too.

• Greg and Janice each buy variable life insurance policies. For the investment portion, they pick balanced portfolios with 50 percent in an

Jennifer's College Portfolio

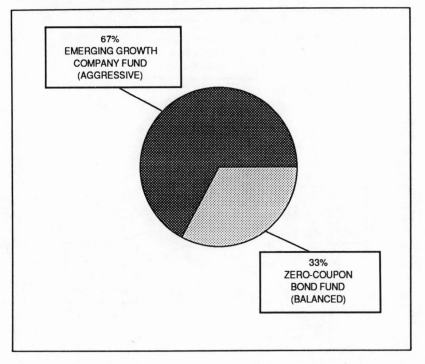

67%
EMERGING GROWTH
COMPANY FUND
(AGGRESSIVE)

33%
ZERO-COUPON
BOND FUND
(BALANCED)

aggressive growth fund, 30 percent in a balanced fund, and 20 percent in a bond fund.

• They promise to start an investment portfolio for themselves when Janice gets her bonus this year. Half of her bonus will go into mutual funds, with a hefty portion in aggressive stock funds.

POINTS TO REMEMBER

The Stricklers have made plans to set up a simple but aggressive portfolio. Jennifer's college fund is the first prong of a larger financial plan. They're aiming for 50 percent of their overall portfolio in ag-

The Stricklers' Portfolio

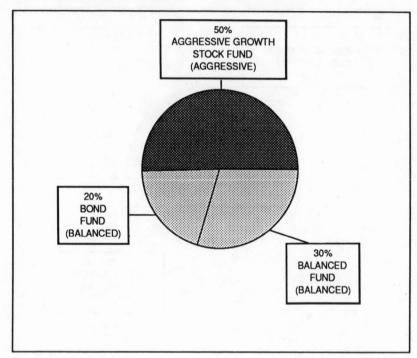

50%
AGGRESSIVE GROWTH
STOCK FUND
(AGGRESSIVE)

20%
BOND
FUND
(BALANCED)

30%
BALANCED
FUND
(BALANCED)

gressive growth stock funds. The other half will be split between balanced funds and bond funds. You might not make the same choices. But you should remember:

• If you're spending more than you earn, stop. Discipline yourself. First pay off your debts. Then pick one investment goal and start working toward it.

• If you're in a high tax bracket, consider tax-free municipal money market funds as well as longer-term municipal bond funds.

• Some life insurance policies allow you to set up a tax-deferred mutual fund account for the investment portion of your policy. They also permit you to make tax-free loans if you need to borrow the money.

• Custodial accounts for children lost some of their advantages with recent tax reform. But they still make sense for college saving.

• If you have considerable time to let college savings grow and healthy risk tolerance, try aggressive growth stock funds balanced with a bond fund.

Chapter 10

Aiming High—Aggressive Strategies for the Active Investor

Michael Grover was on the fast track at a big Chicago bank. He was moving up like gangbusters in the marketing department, leap-frogging lots of older men. He loved his job and knew he was good at it. And he spent much of his free time reading business and professional journals, as well as the mainstream business press—*Business Week, Fortune, Forbes, The Wall Street Journal, Investor's Daily*. He considered himself both well positioned and well informed, although he didn't have any investments. Instead of investing, Michael bought a small condo on Chicago's North Side. All in all, he thought he was doing pretty well. He expected to be made marketing director of his company before he turned 40.

One of the things he kept coming across in his business reading was how many people were becoming entrepreneurs—and how well they were doing. Although it was intriguing, he preferred the challenge of running a department at a major corporation. Then, shortly after he turned 30, Michael was passed over for a job. A promotion that he thought he had in his pocket went to a rival. What to do? No Casper Milquetoast, he went to see his supervisor. Well, there were company politics to consider, he was told. The next time it would probably be his turn.

But there wasn't going to be a next time for Michael. Although he'd never really considered himself a risk taker, he decided now that he was taking a big risk by sticking with his employer. He was putting his future position and salary in the company's hands. And he didn't like the way his boss was shouldering the responsibility. He wasn't going to bet his money on a company that wasn't willing to bet on him. Although he knew that many small businesses failed, he had more confidence in himself than he had in his employer. He quit and set up shop as a marketing consultant. It was a move that paid off handsomely. Now, three years later, his business is growing and he is making considerably more money than he had at his old job.

But he needs to do some personal financial planning. He's been so busy planning for his business that he hasn't done anything yet about his own financial future. It's true that he doesn't have much money to invest yet. On the other hand, his income is growing rapidly and he needs some tax breaks. Perhaps down the road, he might want to buy a house with a separate suite of rooms for his business or rent an office in the Loop.

A session with a financial planner convinces Michael that mutual funds offer many advantages for the small investor. Since he likes the idea of making his own investment choices, he doesn't simply want to pick a portfolio manager to do the work for him. He wants to select, monitor, cull, and trade his own investments. Although he has very little money to start, he has enough financial savvy to know that he needs some diversification. He's looking for mutual funds that put him in the driver's seat, that let him get started without a lot of cash, but still give him plenty of latitude.

After consulting his accountant, Michael learns about the unique investment opportunities that are available to him as the owner of his own business. When he points out that his tax bill is soaring as his earnings have grown, his accountant tells him that there is a way to address the situation. He advises Michael to consider opening a Keogh plan or an Individual Retirement Account Simplified Employee Pension (IRA SEP)—both retirement plans for the self-employed. Michael can deduct his annual contributions for tax purposes and use his account to launch his mutual fund investment plan.

Because these retirement accounts have special tax advantages, the investor enjoys a broad latitude for his investment choices. For example, Michael doesn't need to consider the tax consequences of heavy trading, because he won't pay any taxes on the money in his account until he begins to withdraw it when he retires. This means that he can be more aggressive in choosing mutual funds. He can try to actively time the market, moving in and out to catch the upswings and avoid the downdrafts. Or he can trade different industry sectors, moving from one to another when he feels the time is right. Or he can make use of gold and precious metals funds, which are highly volatile, because he has the chance to capture his gains without paying taxes on them.

You might have something in common with Michael. Do you:

- Know a lot about the financial markets and feel prepared to learn more?
- Feel comfortable with making your own trading decisions?
- Have some time to let your investments grow?
- Feel prepared to accept some setbacks, if necessary, for the chance to get bigger returns?
- Need a way to ease your tax burden?

You, too, may be aiming high if you have a high risk tolerance but not a large cash balance. If you plan to pay close attention to your own investments and have some time before you need to collect your returns and if you are self-employed, this may be you. Perhaps you don't have any special investment problems. You've just been too busy with the other business of your life to get started. But now that you're ready, you don't want ho-hum investments. You're an aggressive investor and you want to be in charge of your own portfolio. There are plenty of aggressive strategies that you can employ with mutual funds.

MARKET TIMING

Trying to time the market—or get into the right sector of the market at the right time—is considered to be one of the most aggressive investment strategies. It's also difficult to do. It's like trying to plan your vacation at the beach. You can gather all the past statistics on rainfall, sunshine, and average temperature. But you still may not be able to predict whether July 10, 1990, will be a good beach day. Timing the market is harder than predicting the weather, but the concept is deceivingly simple: When the stock market is surging, you keep your money in stock mutual funds. When it peaks, you switch to cash. Or, to take it one step further, you might switch to bond mutual funds to capture some gains there. Or you can track the movements of a specific fund or sector, and time your moves in and out. The problem is that no foolproof method exists for making these decisions. Market timing is an attempt to use backward-looking data to make forward-looking predictions. In other words, you're trying to use what's already happened to make a judgment about what will happen.

Market timing is hardly new. But it really wasn't practical to use mutual funds for market timing until the development of money market funds and telephone switching. Before that time, a market timer would have had to write to the mutual fund company with instructions to sell his stock mutual fund shares and send him a check or switch into another fund. Money market funds gave the mutual fund investor a cash equivalent so that he could move in and out of the markets and into a cash position to preserve gains. Telephone switching gave investors a quick way to execute the transaction from fund to fund.

Fundamental analysis The study of a company's assets, earnings, sales, products, management, and markets—the "fundamentals" of the company—for the purpose of predicting whether its stock price will rise or fall in the future.

Market timing is a controversial investment strategy. Its detractors claim that no one can accurately predict swings in the market. They argue that performance is determined by the underlying "fundamentals" of a security, the amount of debt a company has or its growth in earnings. Mutual fund managers who adhere to this philosophy use **fundamental analysis** to select companies with favorable fundamentals for their portfolios. And then they stay put until the fundamentals change. Some go so far as to say that they ignore the market.

Technical analysis Study of patterns of trading activity of a particular security. Technical analysts chart price changes and trading volumes, for example, to develop trading patterns. They use this "technical information" to predict what the market in general or a particular security will do in the future.

Advocates of market timing claim you can maximize gains and minimize losses by deciding when to be in the market and when to be out. They use **technical analysis** to time their investment decisions, focusing on trends and patterns in the market. Unlike fundamental analysts, they aren't particularly interested in whether a company has a lot of debt or its earnings are up. They study charts and use computers to spot buy-sell signals.

Some mutual fund investors attempt to time the smallest swings in the market, moving several times a year or even several times a week from fund to fund. Others take a middle ground, arguing that trying to time little peaks and valleys is futile. But they say that if you lose big—as some investors did in the October 1987 market crash—you may not be able to make up your losses for years. These investors may try only to time the real collapses. Like individual investors, some portfolio managers keep their eyes on company fundamentals and always stay fully invested. While others move almost entirely into cash when the technical indicators they follow point to a major downturn.

Should you develop a market timing theory? If you did and were successful, you would do better than most professional money managers because picking the right market can be more significant to your performance than picking the right security. Consider this. Let's say that over the past ten years, you decided each year whether to invest in the stock or the bond market. Each year you made the correct choice and picked the market that performed best. But each time you also picked the worst-performing stocks or bonds available. By picking the right market but choosing the worst investments, how would you do? Your performance would put you in the top 1 percent of all bond fund managers and the top 3 percent of all stock fund managers. That means that if, like Michael, you are willing to spend some time studying and doing research, trying to time the market could improve your returns. Professionals who follow these systems don't believe you need to pick the absolute top and bottom in order to do better than staying fully invested. You need to capture at least 70 percent of the swings. But the real question is whether you can do it successfully.

Market timing requires discipline. If you want to employ this strategy, you must determine how you will decide when to buy and how you will decide when to sell. The key to a market timing theory is an **indicator** or group of indicators that signal to you when the market has peaked or when it is poised for a takeoff. No perfect indicator exists— if one did, word would have spread and there would be many more millionaires than there are. But there are many different types of indicators that market timers use to make their predictions.

One group of indicators is called *sentiment indicators* because they show how other investors—particularly small investors—feel about the market. Most market timers use the sentiment of small investors as a contrary indicator. In other words, they feel that small investors don't

Indicators *Signals used by investment analysts to forecast the direction of the financial markets. An indicator is based on a specific measure of information, such as interest rate trends, insider trading activity, or stock trading volume.*

really know much about what's happening. They're just following the pack. When small investors do one thing, this theory goes, it's time to do the opposite.

For example, if you see that small investors are rushing helter-skelter into the market as they were in the middle of 1987, you would consider selling stocks. If small investors are nervously sitting on the sidelines, as in 1988, you would consider buying stocks. (In both cases, you would have been correct.)

There are some specific guidelines to measure the sentiment of investors. They show market timers whether investors are bullish or bearish. And many market timers use them as contrary indicators. Here are a handful of them:

• If you use the put/call ratio as a contrary indicator, you would consider selling when the ratio is low, because a low ratio indicates that investor sentiment is bullish. When it's high, you would consider buying. Puts and calls are options that give the buyer the right to buy or sell a security or an index at a specific price for a defined period of time. Although there are several indices of put/call activity, market timers look most often at puts and calls on the S&P 100 Index. Investors who buy puts on the index think the market will go down. Those who buy calls expect it to go up. The put/call ratio, which shows the volume of puts divided by calls, is a barometer of confidence in the stock market. You can calculate the ratio on a daily, weekly, or monthly basis. Market timers differ on what constitutes a high or low ratio. For example, *Barron's,* which publishes the daily/weekly numbers, uses .7 and above as bearish and .4 and below as bullish. However, some look for a ratio above 1.0 for a bearish reading and below .6 as bullish. In addition to *Barron's,* some major metropolitan newspapers have also begun to publish put/call figures. If you decide to track these for yourself, you'll want to look at the data over time.

CBOE Put-Call Ratio

| | Last Week | | Last Week's | Previous Week's |
	Puts	Calls	Ratio	Ratio
S&P 100	339,683	300,538	113/100	118/100

Source: *Barron's*

Put-Call Ratio

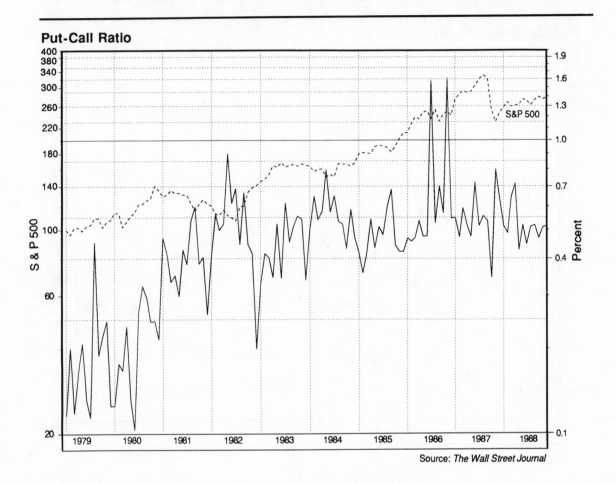

Source: *The Wall Street Journal*

Compiling the weekly data from *Barron's* would allow you to construct a chart, like the one shown above, that tracks the trend over time.

• If you use *odd-lot volume* as a contrary indicator, you would consider getting out of the stock market by selling stock mutual funds if odd-lot volume went up. If odd-lot volume went down, you would consider buying. Odd-lot volume also shows how many small investors are getting into the market, because odd lots of stock are usually purchased by small investors who may not be able to afford a round lot of 100 shares.

Odd-Lot Balance Index

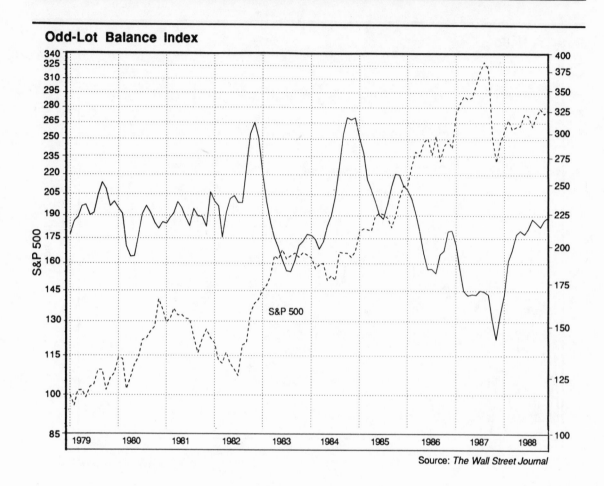

Source: *The Wall Street Journal*

• When *short interest* rises, a market timer would consider buying stock mutual funds. Short interest is the number of shares of stock that have been borrowed and sold short without a corresponding trade to close out the position. A large volume of short interest indicates that many investors have borrowed stock and sold it short because they expect the market to fall. They then plan to buy the stock back at a lower price, pay back the shares, and make a profit. What this indicates is that many investors expect the stock market to decline. But a market timer believes that the market will rise, partly because these investors

NYSE Short Interest

Source: New York Stock Exchange

must eventually buy the stock to cover their short positions and this pent-up demand will send the market up.

If you use the mutual fund cash position index as a contrary indicator, you would consider getting out of your stock mutual funds when cash positions trend substantially lower or drop precipitously. You would consider buying when cash positions trend substantially higher or rise precipitously.

Mutual fund managers report the percentage of assets in their portfolios that is held in "cash," virtually any safe, short-term security.

Mutual Fund Cash Position

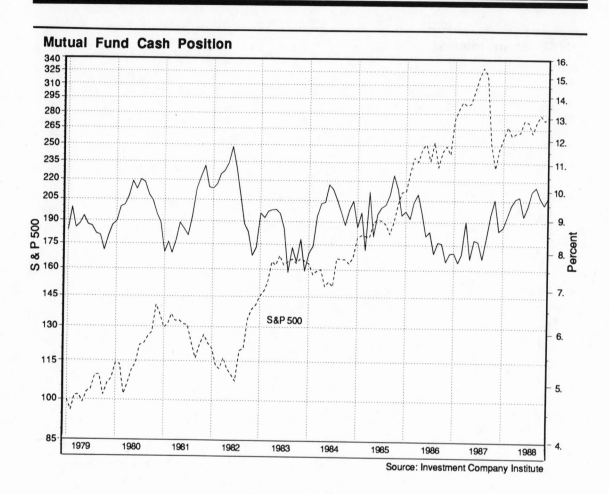

Source: Investment Company Institute

Some analysts use this information as a contrary indicator of the direction of the stock market. The theory is that when mutual fund cash positions are low or dropping, the stock market may be overvalued and due for a downturn. When managers increase their cash holdings, there is a lot of pent-up demand. As portfolio managers begin to see opportunity in the market, they will use their cash to purchase stock and thus push prices higher.

Other types of indicators require you to make some computations and develop some trends to determine when to buy and sell.

S&P 500 P/E Ratio

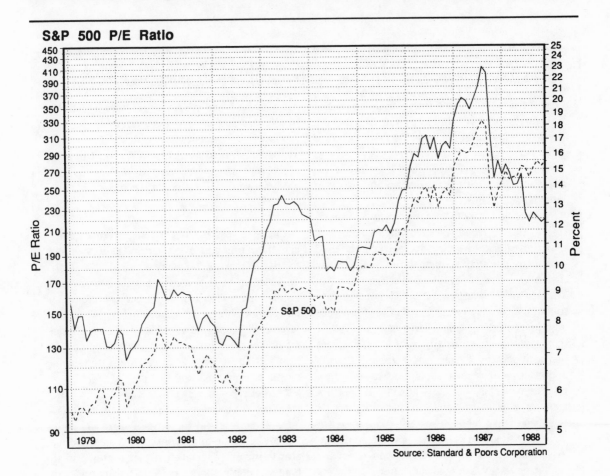

Source: Standard & Poors Corporation

• When the **price/earnings ratio** of the Standard & Poor's 500 stock index rises above 20, you would consider selling stock mutual funds. If it fell to 10 or below, you would consider buying. This ratio measures how expensive a stock is compared to the annual earnings it generates. The p/e ratio of the S&P 500 is published in *Barron's* and in *Investor's Daily*.

• When the price of your mutual fund fell substantially below its *moving average*, you would consider selling. If it moved above the moving average, you would buy. A moving average is the average

Price/earnings ratio or p/e ratio (also called the multiple) The price of a stock divided by its earnings per share. The p/e ratio gives investors an idea of how much they are paying for a company's earning power.

USING MOVING AVERAGES TO TIME YOUR MUTUAL FUND INVESTMENTS

One of the most common timing tools for mutual fund investing is charting the fund's "moving average"—a running tally of the fund's average price performance. Moving averages are useful for determining a mutual fund's overall price trend and, to some extent, determining when to buy and sell shares.

Market timing with moving averages is relatively simple, which is its strongest appeal to many investors. "Moving averages can be used with common stocks, mutual funds and broad market averages," says Royal LeMier, editor of *The Mutual Fund Specialist*. "They're an easy tool to use for the average investor, or for people who don't have the time or inclination to follow their investments on a daily basis." Market timing with moving averages is a *trend-following* approach. Rather than attempting to anticipate price movements, investors attempt to spot upward or downward trends in an equity fund's NAV and make their moves accordingly. When the equity fund's price moves upward, trend followers buy shares of the fund, and when the fund's price trends downward, trend followers sell shares and move into money funds.

According to LeMier, the basic rules for timing mutual funds with moving averages are:

1. When the fund's NAV rises above its moving average and the moving average is trending upward, buy shares of the fund.
2. When the fund's NAV falls below its moving average and the moving average is trending downward, sell shares of the fund.

The time span of your moving average is crucial: if your moving average is too *short*, you run the risk of making too many trades. That will not only run up your transaction costs if your fund family charges for switching, but also rack up a number of short-term capital gains, which are taxed at the same rate as ordinary income. If your moving average is too *long*, your switching signals will come too late to catch any significant movements up or down.

LeMier recommends either a 10-week or a 30-week moving average, depending on your investment objectives and the type of fund you own. "If you're a long-term, conservative investor in a growth-income, balanced or long-term growth fund and don't want to make too many trades in and out of the fund, then a 30-week moving average will probably be best for you," LeMier says. "If you're an active investor involved with

---

On August 24, 1987, the p/e ratio of the S&P 500 rose to 23, a strong signal to market timers.

price of a mutual fund calculated over a period of days or weeks. Market timers create these averages to smooth out the day-to-day zigs and zags of prices and make the longer-term trend clearer.

• When the *advance/decline ratio* moved down, you would consider selling stock mutual funds. When it moved up, you would consider getting into stock mutual funds. The advance/decline ratio is the ratio aggressive growth funds or sector funds, then a 10-week moving average will produce better results.''

Another method uses two sets of moving averages in addition to the fund's weekly price. According to Walter Rouleau, editor of *Growth Fund Guide,* the rules for this method are:

1. Plot the equity fund's 39-week moving average, its 13-week moving average and its weekly closing price.
2. When the 13-week moving average crosses below the 39-week moving average, sell your equity fund shares and park your money in a money fund.
3. When the equity fund's 13-week moving average crosses above the 39-week moving average, use your money fund investment to buy shares of the equity fund.

The advantage of this system, Rouleau says, is that the likelihood of getting ''whipsawed''— moving in and out of a fund when the overall trend is flat—is much smaller than if you use just one moving average. ''Generally, it takes some time for another signal to be generated after one has just occurred,'' Rouleau says.

Using moving averages to time your trades in and out of equity funds will not get you in exactly at the bottom or out exactly at the top. ''Because moving averages lag the price movements of the funds, you'll tend to get buy signals late and sell signals late, particularly if you use longer-term moving averages,'' Rouleau says. ''Still, you'll get 50 percent to 60 percent of the market move out of the middle.''

Moving averages work best with more volatile funds like growth and aggressive growth funds, says Rouleau.

While relying on moving averages alone for timing your trades has some drawbacks, plotting your funds' moving averages can be a useful aid in your investment decisions. ''Moving averages are helpful for investors, but only in conjunction with other information,'' says Lynn Elgert, editor of *The Lynn Elgert Report.* At the least, a change in your fund's price trend would signal you to evaluate your investment.

—*John Waggoner*

Reprinted with permission from *The Independent Investor.*

of stocks that move up in price to those that go down in price on a particular day. By plotting the advance/decline ratio, you can get a sense of the strength of the market. For example, even if the popular indexes are moving up, this indicator might show you that more individual stocks are declining in price than advancing, which indicates that the market is withering.

NYSE Advance/Decline (Cumulative)

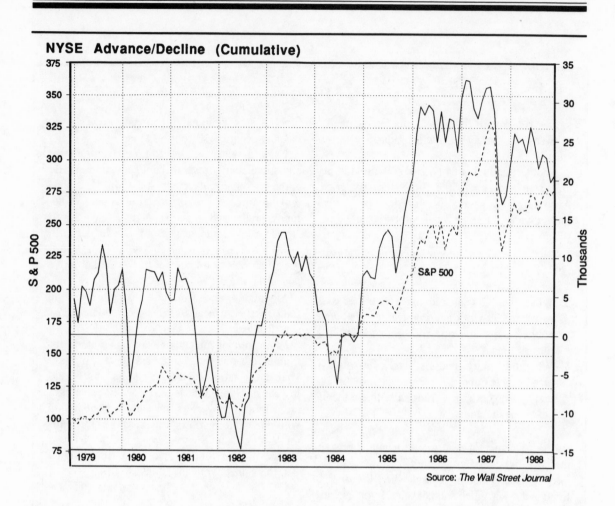

Source: *The Wall Street Journal*

• When the number of stocks making new highs outpaces the number of those making new lows, you would consider moving into stock mutual funds. When new lows outpaced new highs, you would consider moving out. *New highs and lows* is the difference between the number of stocks that are reaching all-time record high prices and the number reaching record low prices, averaged over a five-day period and charted on a cumulative basis so that you can see a trend, not just the short-term blips. Market timers who use this indicator believe that

NYSE New Highs/New Lows (Cumulative)

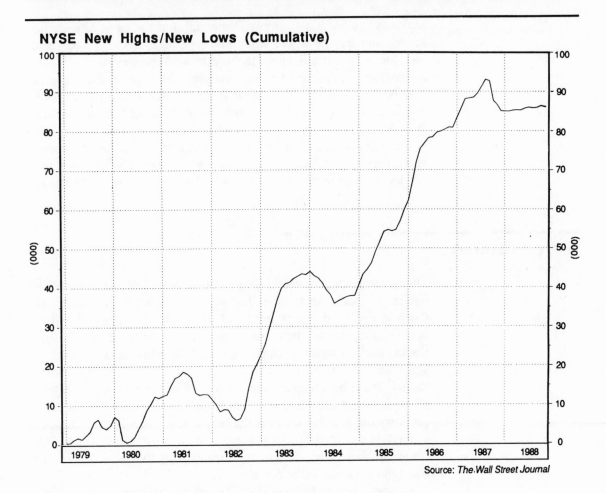

Source: *The Wall Street Journal*

in a rising market more stocks will hit new highs and fewer will fall to new lows. In a declining market, the opposite will be true.

• If you expected interest rates to fall, you would consider moving into the bond market. If you expected interest rates to rise, you would consider moving out of bonds and into short-term instruments like money market funds, because interest rates drive the bond market. When rates fall, the price of bonds goes up and vice versa.

Michael can see from his research that if he plans to time the market seriously, he needs a strategy. This handful of timing techniques persuades him that he would enjoy this type of analysis. If you decide you, too, want to try it, spend the time to work out a method. Get some information on different types of analysis. Do more reading. You can find books on timing in general or books that discuss timing with mutual funds, such as *Market Timing with No-Load Mutual Funds,* by Paul A. Merriman and Merle E. Dowd. You can also subscribe to one of the many mutual fund newsletters that give you advice on when to move your money (see Chapter 13). Or you can subscribe to a chart service or learn to maintain your own charts to stay up to the minute.

SECTOR TRADING

Michael learns that market timing involves more than just moving from one major market to another. Just as the stock market moves up and down in cycles, different sectors of the market move ahead and fall behind in cycles of their own. For example, interest-rate-sensitive stocks, such as those of banks and utilities, often show the first big gains when the market takes off. Next stocks of retailers, restaurant chains, and other companies in the leisure industry take over. Stocks of basic manufacturers that are expected to benefit from a healthier economy might move ahead in the rally's next stage. In later phases of a rally, stocks of drug companies or basic consumer products firms come into favor because investors reason that they will be hurt less when the economy turns down.

Michael's research shows that 70 percent to 80 percent of the movement of an individual stock is determined by the direction of the overall market and the direction of the industry group to which the stock belongs. That means that **sector trading**—determining which way the market will move and picking the sector that will outperform the rest of the market—can be a very rewarding investment strategy. Unfortunately, if you're trading in individual stocks, you can be right about the direction of the market, right again about the industry that is poised for a takeoff, but dead wrong about the individual company that you pick in that sector. Doing all that work and picking a lemon could be pretty discouraging. Sector mutual funds offer you a way out of this problem.

Sector trading Strategy of moving into and out of various industry and asset sectors to improve investment returns.

Industry sector funds invest in a single industry. They allow you to play your hunch that that sector will outperform the market as a whole without forcing you to do the research to select a single company within the industry. Although they do *not* offer a diversified investment portfolio, they do diversify your investment among companies within that sector, usually holding at least 30 stocks within that particular field. Another advantage over trading individual stocks is that transaction fees are usually lower for trading sector funds.

Sector funds have been criticized as a marketing gimmick. For one thing, critics contend, if a fund company fields funds in enough different market sectors, it is virtually assured that it will always have at least one fund that tops the performance list. And, they add, sectors are just another attempt to offer something trendy to bored investors. Furthermore, judging the portfolio manager's performance can be difficult because the performance of the fund depends so much on how well that particular sector performs.

But sector investing can be a way to earn terrific returns *if* you know what you are doing. You must do more homework and decide for yourself which industry will do well in an upcoming market environment. This is one case in which past performance can be a contrary indicator. If one sector has been outperforming the market, it may have run out of steam and a new industry will have its day in the sun.

Sector funds have been around for a long time. Some of the earliest invested in utilities, energy, or precious metals. Fidelity offered a new twist on sector investing in 1981 when it introduced sector portfolios that focused on four separate industries. Investors could switch among these industries when they believed the time was right, or even out of the market altogether and into cash when they didn't like their prospects. Today Fidelity offers 38 different industry sector portfolios. The sector funds have their own money market fund for traders who want to get out of the stock market altogether. Fidelity has also developed hourly pricing of the funds to make sector trading even more closely resemble trading individual stocks.

On the other hand, Fidelity and other companies that offer sector funds have tried to discourage investors from frequent trading by slapping stiff fees on switching. Many investors use these funds to time the market as well as individual sectors. Although that's possible, it can be expensive. You can also use a longer-term strategy for sector investing by choosing broader sectors that you expect to perform well over a long term. Some of the sectors offered by Fidelity are very narrow, such as the brokerage sector or computer software. Others are much broader, such as energy and health care.

The broader sectors—which are offered by other mutual fund companies as well—allow you to make a longer-term bet on a market segment. For example, if you believe that the United States will continue to move from a manufacturing to a service-based economy, you might choose Vanguard's Service Economy portfolio. If you think that over time the scarcity of oil will put that industry back in the pink, the energy sector might appeal to you. Or, maybe you see the aging of the U.S. population as a sign that the health care industry will boom over the next several years. In each case, you must remember that you are making a bet that the overall stock market will do well in addition to the particular sector you choose. If the entire market performs badly, an individual sector is unlikely to buck the trend.

JUNK CORPORATE BONDS

Junk corporate bonds
Bonds issued by corporations that have a low credit rating or no rating at all.

Michael likes the idea of sector investing. And he likes the prospects for the stock market. Still, he knows he must diversify. And he'd like to find something with the potential for big rewards in the portion of his portfolio that he plans to diversify into bonds. He knows where to look: at the highest-risk bonds—**junk corporate bonds**, or "high-yield bonds," as those who sell them prefer to call them.

Time was when interest rates governed bond prices. The investment choice was between government bonds and corporate bonds and there wasn't much variation between the quality of the credits. Although interest rates are still a factor, today credit risk may be the most important key to the bond market. The changes in bond prices can be very subtle. And many of them have to do with the changed perception of the marketplace to the bond issuer's credit.

The bonds issued by corporations and municipalities carry the ratings of their issuers, which range from AAA to C (to D if the company is in default). Ratings of BBB and above are considered investment grade bonds. A rating of BB and below is speculative. These ratings are bestowed by the Standard & Poor's Corporation and Moody's Investors Service as well as some other services. The higher the rating, the lower the interest rate or coupon on the bond. If you look at it from the issuer's point of view, this will explain why it is big financial news when a corporation's credit rating is lowered by one of these rating agencies. If, for example, Moody's lowers the rating of a corporation from Triple-A to Double-A, that company will have to pay investors a higher interest rate to persuade them to buy its bonds, which makes raising money more expensive.

But you're looking at it from the other side—as an investor. For you, the higher the rating, the lower the risk and the lower the reward. You can stick with corporate bond funds that are rated A or better if you want a relatively low-risk investment. Or you can move down in the ratings and take on more risk and potentially higher yield. Going into the junk market yourself to buy a single issue would be very risky indeed. Even junk corporate bond funds are not low-risk investments. But many portfolio managers of junk funds have done a good job of diversifying them to minimize credit risk.

Michael is on sound footing here. He happens to know that one of the reasons an experienced bond fund manager can venture into the junk market is that many companies with healthy balance sheets are forced to offer bonds that carry low ratings or that are not rated at all. For example, some small, emerging growth companies may not have enough credit experience to get an investment grade rating. But they still need to raise money in order to grow. Portfolio managers and their research staffs are in touch with these companies, constantly evaluating credit information to pick the best of these issues, something that an individual investor would have a hard time doing. Buying bonds—or stock—issued by a company like this can be a savvy move.

Other companies may have a low credit rating because they are struggling to reorganize. Consider this example: A few years ago, the management of the well-respected R. H. Macy & Company decided to take over the company in a **leveraged buyout.** Management planned to buy ownership of the company from shareholders. The company would go from a publicly held company to a privately held firm owned by private investors. In order to raise the necessary money, Macy's management had to issue junk bonds, because its credit rating was below investment grade.

Leveraged buyout (LBO)
Takeover of a company or a division of a company using a heavy amount of borrowed money. For example, management of a company may buy out a company division from the parent company. Or they may buy out the entire company from its shareholders, which means the company would go from publicly owned to privately owned. Typically, the assets of the company or the division are the collateral for the loan. The investors or managers who execute the buyout can go to a bank for the money. But they sometimes issue bonds to raise the money.

Bond fund managers and other institutional investors watch deals like this carefully. In this case, the word spread in the investor marketplace that Macy's management paid too much for the deal, so there was little demand for the bonds. Macy's management regrouped and came out with a second offering that gave the bondholders much better security. But the cloud from the unsuccessful attempt hung over the company and its second bond offering. There were few eager buyers. This is the kind of opportunity that experienced bond buyers look for. Some savvy mutual fund managers grabbed those bonds the second time around and they turned out to be a very good buy. But unrated bonds are volatile. A short time later, Macy's attempted to take over another company—Federated Department Stores. This frightened the bond market and the Macy's bonds dropped seven points. When Macy's got the part of Federated that it wanted, but didn't buy the whole company, the bond market interpreted this as positive and the bonds bounced back in two days. The bond managers who believed the bonds were a good buy in the first place were able to hold on to their investment with confidence. But this is clearly a market for sophisticated players.

Other good buys in the junk bond market might be companies with clean balance sheets that are in an industry plagued by problems. Such a company might be a good credit risk and the bond might also pay a high interest rate. But it takes an experienced bond buyer to pick the cherries and avoid the lemons. In the hands of such a manager, junk bonds can provide an opportunity to capture a higher return without taking on more risk than you can handle. The difference in yield may be 3 to 5 percentage points above U.S. Treasury bonds.

There is something else to consider here, though. Even if the fund manager has done a great job in assembling high-yielding bonds of companies with promise, the market may wreak havoc on the share price of your bond fund. Junk funds do not perform well in a troubled business environment. When bond prices start falling, investors bail out of the lowest-quality bonds first and their prices can plunge.

For example, although bonds in general rallied during the October 1987 stock market crash, junk bonds—which don't necessarily follow the rest of the bond market—did very poorly. In the fourth quarter of 1987, stocks, as measured by the S&P 500, dropped 22.5 percent while bonds gained 5.8 percent as measured by the two most common indexes—Shearson Lehman Hutton and Salomon Brothers. But junk bonds fell by 1.54 percent. Investors worried that if the economy really fell apart, the issuers of this unrated debt could **default.**

One way to measure market sentiment on junk bonds is to check the differential on the yield between the 30-year U.S. Treasury bond, which is considered the bellwether for the bond market, and junk bonds. It is usually 3 or 4 percentage points—or 300 or 400 basis points. But it widened to record levels following the stock market crash, when junk bonds yielded more than 5 percentage points or 500 basis points more than treasuries. Junk bond funds are for those investors who want high returns—and can also handle the accompanying risk.

Default   Failure of a bond issuer to make timely payments of interest and principal as they come due or to meet some other provision of the bond.

RETIREMENT ACCOUNTS FOR THE SELF-EMPLOYED

Michael's goal is to invest and cut his taxes at the same time. If you too are eligible to put pretax money in a **Keogh account** or Individual Retirement Account, do it. This is one of the best tax shelters left after the Tax Reform Act of 1986 and one of the best ways to accumulate a healthy retirement nest egg that you control. It's much more advantageous for you to have your own retirement account than a pension plan controlled by the company where you work, which is continued at your employer's discretion. One of your goals should be to put away some money every year in a retirement account that you control. There are several ways to do it.

Keogh account   Retirement account for the self-employed and small businesses. These accounts, which were established by Congress in 1962, allow people to put away a portion of their self-employment earnings in a tax-deferred retirement account and deduct the amount from their earnings for tax purposes.

• If you work at a company that does not have an employee retirement plan, you can contribute $2,000 each year to an IRA and deduct the money from your taxable income, provided that you earn at least that much.

• If you earn less than $25,000 as a single taxpayer or if you and your spouse earn less than $40,000, you can also put $2,000 a year into a tax-deductible IRA, even if your employer has a pension plan. If both you and your spouse work and you each earn more than $2,000, you can each sock away $2,000. If only one of you works, you may split up a limit of $2,250 in any way you choose.

• If you earn between $25,000 and $35,000 as a single taxpayer or between $40,000 and $50,000 as a married couple and you participate in a company retirement plan, the deductible contribution is phased out for you. But you are still entitled to a partial contribution. For married taxpayers, you subtract your adjusted gross income from the $50,000 ceiling and divide the result by $10,000 to determine how much you can contribute. For example, let's say you and your spouse earn $42,000. Subtract that from the $50,000 limit and you get $8,000. Divide the $8,000 by the $10,000 and you get 80 percent. This means each of you can contribute 80 percent of the $2,000 IRA, or $1,600.

• If you are self-employed, you can put away part of your pretax earnings in a Keogh plan or a Simplified Employee Pension, which is also called an **IRA SEP.** Don't overlook an opportunity to do this. Self-employment refers to the status of your earnings, not to whether you work for a company. For example, you may be employed full-time at a computer company. But perhaps you do some sideline software consulting. The money you make from that is self-employment income. Likewise, consider any lecturing, writing, carpentry, teaching, child care, handicrafts, or any other work that you do as a self-employed person. (Obviously, you must report this as taxable income in order to take a deduction for a retirement plan.)

Keoghs for the self-employed have been around for a long time— over 25 years. There are two different types of plans available. One type, called a money purchase plan, permits you to contribute from 3 percent to 25 percent of business income each year, or $30,000, whichever is less. (An accounting calculation reduces the real cap to 20 percent.) Although this plan allows you to put more money away, you must commit yourself to contributing the same percentage of your income every year.

The second type of plan, called a profit-sharing plan, lets you decide how much to put away, up to a maximum of 15 percent or $30,000 each year. (An accounting calculation reduces the real ceiling to 13.043 percent of income after business expenses.) With this type of plan, you can contribute the maximum one year and nothing the next if you like.

Obviously, the money purchase plan allows you a higher deduction up to the $30,000 limit. The problem, for some self-employed persons, is that you must put away the same percentage of your earnings every year. Of course, if your business has a bad year, the real dollar amount will be lower. But if you're worried that you might have some years when you can't contribute anything to the Keogh plan, the profit-

IRA SEP Retirement account for self-employed persons and employees of small companies. The employer can put in 15 percent of compensation or $30,000, whichever is smaller, for himself and for each employee. The account is in the employee's name and the employee has control over where to invest it. He is vested immediately. That means that if he leaves the company, the money in the account belongs to him. Employees also have the option of taking the contribution in cash, although they must pay taxes on it.

sharing plan will be more appealing to you. You can also use a combination of the two plans. For example, you could choose a fixed contribution of 10 percent for the money purchase plan and vary your contribution to the profit-sharing plan from nothing up to 15 percent. That means that in a good year, you could put away a total of 25 percent in the two plans. If you have employees in your business, you must include them in your plan, too. You can deduct the contributions you make for them as a business expense.

The IRA SEP allows the same 15 percent (or 13.043 percent) contribution as the profit-sharing plan. But it has some advantages over the Keogh. The IRS requires annual reports for the Keogh plans, while the SEP has no reporting requirements, like a regular IRA. This saves you either time or money, depending on whether you do your own tax work or use an accountant. It also costs less to maintain an IRA SEP than a Keogh account. That's because the companies that set up Keoghs for you—mutual funds, banks, or insurance companies—are also required to do more record keeping; and they charge you for it by slapping on a fee. It's possible to open a SEP with no fee at all. A final advantage is that a Keogh account must be opened before the end of the tax year, in other words December 31, in order to make contributions for that year. But you can open an IRA SEP any time before the April 15 filing deadline and make a contribution for the previous tax year. Again, you must make contributions for your employees if you have any.

Mutual fund companies typically have much lower minimums for both initial deposits and subsequent deposits for any of these retirement accounts than for a regular account. You must specify when you open the account that it is a retirement account, as well as what type it is.

TAX-DEFERRED ACCOUNTS: TWO POINTS OF VIEW

Michael decides to do some research before he goes any further in his investment planning. He learns that there are two theories on how to manage a tax-deferred account. The first makes this argument: Tax-deferred accounts are not the place for active securities trading because you can't take advantage of capital losses. In other words, if you lose money by trading mutual funds, you can't deduct it from your income for tax purposes because your transaction took place in a tax-free account. Devotees of this line of reasoning also usually argue that retirement money should be invested conservatively.

The second argument is just the opposite: A tax-deferred account is the perfect place for active trading because you don't have to pay taxes on gains. Michael likes the second argument better. Of course, his enthusiasm may be tempered if his trading is not successful. Still, the liberty of being able to make decisions without having to consider tax consequences is very appealing to him. And it fits very well with his plans to develop a market timing strategy and put his money in aggressive funds, which he expects to trade frequently. This is not the place for foolhardy trading, of course. But if, like Michael, you have 15, 20, 25 years, or more until retirement, you're very knowledgeable about investing, and you have the time and energy to monitor your investments, you should be able to ride out the market cycles.

MICHAEL GROVER'S CHOICES

Michael plans to open an IRA SEP.

• He plans to contribute to it regularly during the year, putting in as much as he can by April 15. His minimum goal is $5,000.

• Michael plans to trade actively. He chooses a large mutual fund company that offers industry sector funds as well as specialty funds in precious metals, real estate, international securities, and junk bonds. He is prepared to study the market to find out when to be in these funds and when to get out.

• He plans to set up his portfolio like this: 25 percent in high-yield bonds; 15 percent in international securities; 35 percent in industry sector funds; and 25 percent in specialty funds like gold or real estate, depending on the market environment.

POINTS TO REMEMBER

Michael's choices are aggressive. Not only is he making some high-risk investments, but he plans to study the market constantly and decide when it's time to get into and out of various industries as well

Michael Grover's Portfolio

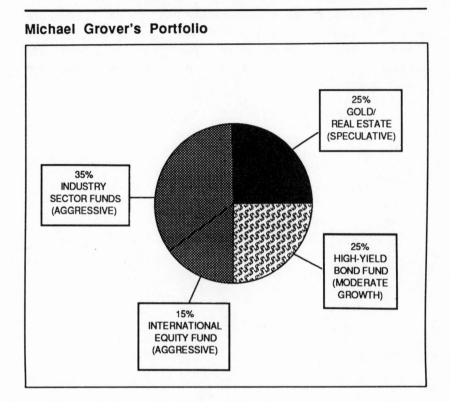

25%
GOLD/
REAL ESTATE
(SPECULATIVE)

35%
INDUSTRY
SECTOR FUNDS
(AGGRESSIVE)

25%
HIGH-YIELD
BOND FUND
(MODERATE
GROWTH)

15%
INTERNATIONAL
EQUITY FUND
(AGGRESSIVE)

as various asset classes such as gold and real estate. You, too, may want to invest for a retirement account. But you may choose to be more conservative. Still, you should remember these principles:

• Market timers use sophisticated techniques—or gut instinct—to decide when to move from one market to another to preserve gains and avoid crashes.

• When the market performs well, some sectors do even better. Being in the right industry sector or the right asset class can enhance your returns. Sector mutual funds provide a way to do this.

• When corporations that have low credit ratings or no credit ratings need to raise money, they are forced to issue bonds that pay higher yields. These "junk bonds" can yield 3 to 5 percent more than U.S. Treasury bonds. And sophisticated bond market players can often find good bargains here.

• Tax-deferred retirement accounts like IRAs and Keoghs offer one of the best tax breaks around. If you qualify, you should contribute.

• A tax-deferred account can be a good place for active trading because you don't have to worry about paying current taxes on your capital gains.

Chapter 11

Not Ready to Retire—Aggressive Strategies for the Portfolio in Transition

E llen and George Pope are nearing the conclusion of a long, happy, and successful work life. Ellen interrupted her career as a hospital nutritionist for five years while their two children were young, but she's been back on the job for nearly 30 years now. George has worked for longer than that as a chemical engineer. The Popes own a fine home in suburban Wilmington and a beach house at Rehoboth Beach in Delaware. They sent their son to the University of Pennsylvania and their daughter to Harvard. And they still have plenty of money for their retirement, which is about five years away.

They both make good salaries. But their affluence is largely due to their investing savvy. They started saving money as soon as they married in 1948. When they had a small nest egg, they bought a home. And then they began buying stock. The Popes quickly became knowledgeable and then aggressive investors. George, in particular, enjoys studying the financial pages, picking stocks, and tracking his investments. He checks with his stockbroker almost daily. And after 35 years as a stock picker, he figures he has an edge on many of the inexperienced players in today's market. Maybe he wasn't exactly *investing* during the Great Depression, but he was *alive,* for goodness sakes.

And he's weathered plenty of ups and downs since then. When the market crashed in 1987, he didn't give it a second thought. He knows that, over time, stocks outperform all other investments. He wants to be on the winning team. And he's picked plenty of winners. He spotted Subaru at $3 in 1981 and rode it to $39. And he bought Ford when it was trading at $7 and watched it move up to $60 before taking his gains. Because he's been in the market for so long, he's found favorite stocks that he's watched over the years and moved into and out of when the price was right. For example, he's done well by trading into and out of Exxon. And he's done pretty well with Wendy's. In fact, George enjoys stock picking as much as he enjoys the challenges of the engineering profession.

The Popes' accountant suggested that Ellen and George throttle back a bit and change their investment strategy as they get closer to retirement. Specifically, she says they should put their money into more conservative, income-oriented investments that will guarantee their lifestyle rather than high-flying stocks that could crash just when they need the money. She also suggests that they move their nest egg into mutual funds to get both diversification and professional management. To George, that sounds boring. It would mean that he would have to give up two of his favorite things—his job and his avocation—at the same time.

Besides, he is skeptical of mutual funds. It seems to George that each portfolio manager has something of a performance "window," a period when his investment philosophy meshes with what's happening in the world and he's on a roll. But none of them seem to last. He doesn't believe they're necessarily any smarter than he is. Instead, he believes that today's hot portfolio manager is probably the one with the best gimmick. It might be buying the "Nifty Fifty." Or seeking the stocks of unknown companies trading on the over-the-counter market. Or buying stock in companies that are in bankruptcy but have good prospects. The way he sees it, each manager has his day in the sun. And his day in the shadows. He would rather trust himself.

In fact, his goal is to increase their retirement nest egg substantially by trading actively over the next five years. Although they have plenty of money to live comfortably, he'd like to do something spectacular when he retires. If he could find a few sleepers, he figures he could bring in the money to finance an around-the-world cruise. Maybe then he'd be willing to lower his sights a bit and settle down to some safer investments.

But his accountant insists that he can be aggressive with mutual funds, too, by choosing aggressive growth stock funds. Futhermore, she says, the Popes' large portfolio is not truly diversified because all their investments are dollar-based. Mutual funds would allow them to diversify their investments internationally; to put some of their money in currencies other than the dollar.

Perhaps you have something in common with George and Ellen Pope. Do you:

- Have a chunk of money invested in the stock market?
- Have a healthy tolerance for risk, seasoned by some good investment picks over the years?
- Feel that you'd rather trust yourself with your money?
- Need to diversify into nondollar investments?

You, too, might feel that you're not ready to retire your assets to safe investments, even though you know you'll need a big chunk of them in a few years for a special project like starting a new business or making a major purchase. Perhaps you'd like to have money to buy a second home, yet you can't live with the idea of liquidating your investments a moment too soon. And you really don't trust your money to anyone but yourself. If you've made wise investment choices over the years, you may feel that there's no sense in paying someone else a fee to do what you can do very well yourself.

There are a couple of things you need to consider, though. First, investing savvy in the U.S. stock market is no longer enough. Some of the most spectacular gains in recent years have come from mutual funds that invest outside the United States. Although you may feel quite sure of yourself when it comes to analyzing a Big Board stock, do you feel the same confidence when it comes to trading on the Tokyo Stock Exchange? Regulations and accounting rules are different in every country, as are tax codes. And the way you've learned to judge a low p/e stock is meaningless if you're buying something in Hong Kong.

You also need to consider how aggressive you can afford to be when you need your money in a short period. What if the market dropped 25 percent—and your entire portfolio of stocks along with it—just when you needed to liquidate your investments? Another thing you need to think about is how individual stocks perform compared with mutual funds in up and down markets. It's true that many stock funds underperform the market averages during bull markets. Picking the right stocks can be dicey—for portfolio managers as well as for you. But when the market crashes, the professionals often have an edge on you.

Consider what happened in 1987. For the year, including the October market crash, the average stock fund gained a paltry 0.5 percent while the market, as measured by the Standard & Poor's 500 index, increased 5.23 percent. But during the last quarter of 1987 and the first quarter of 1988, a time when most individual investors were quaking in their boots and sitting on the sidelines, professional managers acquitted themselves nicely. In fact, the average stock fund gained 7.43 percent during the first three months of 1988 while the S&P index was up 5.69 percent. Furthermore, nine out of ten mutual funds followed by Lipper Analytical Services beat the market during the quarter, a pretty impressive performance. At the same time, many of the **large-capitalization stocks** that had fueled the five-year bull market performed very poorly during these two quarters. In fact, one of the more interesting things that happened after the market crash is that small-company stocks finally broke loose. For the first quarter of 1988, mutual funds that invest in small growth companies rose 12.98 percent.

What does this mean for you as an individual investor in the market? If you were smart enough to dump the big-name stocks in September, right before the market crashed, and to carefully select and buy the stocks of small companies immediately after the crash, you might have done quite well. But these trends are very difficult to spot. Even if you consider yourself a consummate stock picker, the experience of 1987 should have convinced you that you don't want to have all your money in individual stocks if your investment goals are short term; for example, if you need your money to live on during an imminent retirement.

It's true that some portfolio managers have had a meteoric fame, only to burn out as quickly as they flashed into sight. And others have their up and down years. But there are many consistent managers who

Large capitalization stocks
Stocks of major corporations. Market capitalization refers to the total value the stock market places on a company. It is calculated by taking the value of one share and multiplying the number of shares outstanding. Stocks with a market capitalization of $1 billion are considered large "cap" stocks. These stocks are also more liquid, widely held, frequently traded, and closely followed by investment analysts.

MUTUAL FUND MANAGERS: SOME STAND THE TEST OF TIME

Some investment experts maintain that money managers have a short investment life span, that they're one-gimmick people who burn out once their trick doesn't work anymore or that they are quickly overshadowed by others who adopt the same techniques and do it better. For some investors, this is an argument for managing your own money.

It's not necessarily a valid one, though. Not all money managers use gimmicks. Many go after value in the market. They've been around for years, they use time-tested formulas to decide what to buy at what price and when to sell it. And they are not swayed by the latest vogue in investing.

Consider John Neff, manager of the Windsor Fund for over 25 years. He's beaten the Standard & Poor's 500 index in 17 out of the last 23 years. In the five-year period ended December 31, 1988, Windsor was up 139.7 percent compared to 104.5 percent for the S&P. In the ten-year period, Windsor gained 565.8 percent compared with 353.7 percent for the S&P. Neff didn't turn in a single down year from 1974 to 1987.

Or how about John Templeton, manager of the Templeton Funds? Templeton's Growth Fund and World Fund both beat the market in the past ten years. Templeton Growth was up 373 percent for the ten years ending in 1988; Templeton World Fund rose 426 percent during the same period.

Neff and Templeton don't use the same technique. What they have in common is that they adhere strictly to a value investment formula that works for them. They decide when to buy and when to sell. And they avoid falling in love with their stocks and riding them down.

What they show—and there are other managers like them—is that portfolio managers can turn in consistent returns year after year after year. And that, in most cases, they can turn in returns considerably better than an investor can achieve on his own. Managers like these should also remind you, though, just how important it is to know who is managing your fund and when that management changes.

perform year after year. You need only check the rankings in one of the business magazines to see the five- and ten-year performance records of some of these men and women and reassure yourself that many are solid investment pros. Further, some funds are managed by committee. If you think several heads are better than one, you might want to take a look at the performance of these funds. Another twist is the system used by Capital Research. This fund management company believes that no fund manager hits a home run every year. So it splits each portfolio among three or four different managers, giving each total control over his section of the portfolio. If you feel you have a management style that's served you well, you may want to spend some time finding a portfolio manager who you think has the same approach.

CURRENCY FUNDS

Currency Money issued by a particular sovereign government. The currency in the United States is the dollar. In Japan, it is the yen.

You should also consider going global. It's hardly a secret to experienced investors like the Popes—or to most other Americans—that the U.S. dollar steadily lost ground against foreign **currencies** from late 1984 to late 1988. Foreign goods cost more. It costs more to travel abroad. U.S. goods have become more competitive in the world marketplace. Imported raw materials increased in price. Many sophisticated investors looked for ways to protect their investments against the decline in the dollar by putting them into other currencies.

One relatively new option is international money market funds that allow you to invest in short-term paper in other currencies. Like U.S. money market funds, these international funds invest in short-term, high-grade government and corporate debt. But they invest in foreign debt, not necessarily because the yield is higher but to diversify assets out of the dollar. In fact, interest rates in Germany and Japan are typically lower than those in the United States. For example, in late 1987, the yield on a money market fund investing in yen or marks was about 3.5 percent compared to about 6 percent for a U.S. money market fund. But investors are not looking for yield. They're looking for appreciation in the foreign currency. When the dollar drops against the yen, for example, the dollars you invested in these funds will be worth more.

These funds preserve your purchasing power on a global basis. If all your investments are in U.S. dollars, as the dollar falls, your purchasing power declines, even if your investments do well. If you are accustomed to buying foreign-made goods—a Mercedes, French wine, Japanese electronics—you've probably watched their prices climb as the value of the dollar has declined. Since a weak dollar affects your standard of living, the dollar's purchasing power is important to you.

A truly diversified large portfolio must be spread across more than one currency. Part of the purpose of diversification is finding classes of assets that are not highly correlated. In other words, there's little point in diversifying into three kinds of investments if they all collapse at the same time. Instead, you want to find assets that move in different cycles. International money market instruments have proven to be an excellent investment for this purpose. On October 19, 1987, when stock markets crashed around the world, the currency funds did very well.

At this writing, several large mutual fund companies have currency funds in the works. The first ones available were eight currency portfolios offered by Huntington Advisers. Although they are essentially

BEYOND THE DOLLAR: DONALD GOULD AND CURRENCY MUTUAL FUNDS

It was the summer of 1986. For nearly two years, the dollar had been dropping like a stone against foreign currencies. Foreign goods were growing increasingly expensive in the United States. Donald Gould spotted an opportunity. Why not a money market fund that invested in short-term, high-quality securities in currencies other than the dollar?

Gould set up Huntington Advisers international cash portfolios with two funds. One, the Global Cash Portfolio, was an actively managed multi-currency money market fund. The portfolio manager could select from among 12 different currencies, including the U.S. dollar. The other, U.S. Cash, was the standard money market fund that maintains a one-dollar-per-share price. In September 1987, Gould added six more portfolios, each investing in short-term paper in a single currency. They are the yen cash portfolio, deutschemark (DM) cash portfolio, Swiss franc, British sterling, Canadian dollar, and Australian dollar.

All eight portfolios invest strictly in money market instruments, including government bills, certificates of deposit, commercial paper, and other short-term, high-quality debt instruments. The global fund offers investors professional management and the opportunity to maximize total return by a combination of the interest yield and the gain from currency fluctuation. The single-currency funds are not actively managed. Instead the investor can make his own currency bets or simply put together a passive mix of different currencies. For example, he might want to put 25 percent of his investment in sterling, 25 percent in yen, 25 percent in DM, and 25 percent in dollars.

Hedge *Transaction used to offset the risk of another transaction or position. An investor with a large bond portfolio might use interest rate futures contracts to reduce the risk of loss in the value of his bonds that would be caused by rising interest rates. A U.S. investor with a large domestic portfolio might hedge against a falling dollar by diversifying into Japanese yen or British pounds.*

money market funds, they carry a 1.25 percent sales charge. U.S. money market funds, in contrast, don't impose a sales fee. You cannot write checks on the international funds as you can on Huntington's U.S. cash fund. There is no limit on switching between the currencies, but switching is not the idea of these funds. Rather, the idea is to **hedge** a part of your investment against the dollar. If you have a large portfolio and you want to be truly diversified, you should always have some portion of it in currencies other than the dollar.

INTERNATIONAL AND GLOBAL EQUITY FUNDS

This argument makes sense to George Pope. And he reasons that if it's true for the cash portion of his portfolio, it must be true for stocks as well. There are more than 60,000 stocks that trade on exchanges outside the United States. That's roughly 12 times the number of stocks that are available in this country. Yet, until the 1980s, foreign stocks were pretty much ignored by U.S. investors. There were a few mutual funds that offered overseas investment. But as recently as 1979, Americans had a measly $1 billion invested overseas. There were some good reasons for this. For one thing, there wasn't much research available on foreign markets. For another, there were many restrictions on international capital flows. Many countries prohibited the flow of money outside their borders and restricted the ownership of their companies to their own nationals. In addition, many foreign markets were small, illiquid, and largely unregulated.

But in the 1980s, investing became a global business. The Japanese plowed into the U.S. stock and bond markets. And U.S. investors began looking at many other attractive markets around the world: Hong Kong, Singapore, Japan, Australia, Great Britain, Italy. Thanks to deregulation of foreign markets, Americans could do more than just look. They began to buy. By the end of 1987, Americans had an estimated $60 billion invested overseas.

You can profit in two ways by investing in foreign securities. If the market or markets you invest in perform well, your investment will obviously grow. But even if the foreign stock market does little or nothing, you can profit just from fluctuations between the currency you invested in and the dollar. Consider this. Let's say you invest $1,000 in the German stock market when a dollar is worth 3 West German marks. Although the market languishes, the value of the dollar drops against the mark. When you're ready to sell the stocks, the dollar is worth 2 marks. In other words, the mark has appreciated from 33 cents to 50 cents. When you convert the marks back to dollars, you have $1,500 simply because the mark increased in value. Of course, the opposite could happen as well. The important thing to remember is that, when you make an international investment, you are betting on two things: the performance of the foreign stock market or markets and the value of the currencies vis-à-vis the dollar.

If you want to invest in the international stock market, you have a couple of choices. You can, of course, pick your own stocks. For most U.S. investors, that's not practical because of a host of obstacles, ranging from logistical (e.g., time zone differences) to legal (e.g., each country has a different set of laws governing foreign investors). Your second choice is to pick one of the dozens of international funds that are offered by mutual fund companies. In the 1980s, many of these funds were offering the best returns available anywhere, partly because they were boosted by the declining dollar.

Some of them have been around for a long time. The Templeton Growth Fund, managed by legendary money manager John M. Templeton, has been available since 1954. And it's turned in some very nice returns over the years. If an investor had put $10,000 into the fund when it started in 1954, it would have grown to over $1 million by the end of 1988. Each dollar grew to over $100. Yet Templeton's fund didn't keep pace with many of the funds that concentrated on the Pacific Basin in the 1980s. Although the gains in the Japanese market have overshadowed those in the rest of the world over the past several years, Templeton adheres to a strict value approach to investing. According to his philosophy, the Japanese market was overvalued in the late 1980s and he refused to participate. So, whereas funds that

THE APPEAL OF BOND FUNDS

Some high-flying investors say: Never buy a bond fund. To them, bonds are boring. With stocks, they argue, you always have the chance to hit a home run, to double or triple your money. That doesn't happen in the bond market. So why buy a bond fund?

Barbara Kenworthy, who manages nine bond funds for the Dreyfus Corporation, offers a couple of reasons: Bonds provide regular interest income that you can spend without touching your principal. They're also less volatile.

"A lot of people need the income that a bond produces year in and year out in order to live," Kenworthy says. "Typically an equity fund doesn't provide that." To get money from your stock fund, you'd have to sell it. "I think human nature says: I don't want to sell," Kenworthy says. "I don't mind having an income throw off, but I don't want to sell."

Some people don't have the stomach for the stock market's volatility, she says. "Although performance can be volatile in bonds, generally you don't see a down 40 percent year and then an up 60 percent year in a bond fund like you might in a stock fund." Instead, a bond fund might be up 10 percent or it might be down 7 percent.

"I think there are a lot of investors whose threshold for pain is such that they can't tolerate a bigger down year than that," Kenworthy says. "They very smartly have said: With an aggressive equity fund, I can hit a home run, but I can also get hit in the head."

went heavy into this area had spectacular performances—the G. T. Pacific Fund gained over 70 percent in 1986 and Financial Strategic Pacific Basin was up over 71 percent the same year—Templeton Growth gained a healthy, but less spectacular, 21 percent. (In some years the situation was different. For example, Templeton's Growth Fund gained a solid 26.86 percent in 1979 while the G. T. Pacific Fund dropped 22 percent.)

What does this tell you about international investing? Picking funds in the global arena is trickier than picking a fund that invests only in U.S. stocks. In addition to the currency play, you're also betting—if you pick a particular area of the world—that that region will outperform other geographic regions. The Japanese market has continued to confound most experts, who have considered it overvalued for some time. In fact, by 1987, many investment managers were bailing out of

Japanese stocks. But, it continued to outperform most other markets of the world. The DFA Japan Small Company Growth Fund was up over 32 percent for the 12 months ending December 31, 1988, proving that Japan again was a good place to be.

If you're very knowledgeable about international markets and spend a lot of time reading and doing research on world economies, you may spot an opportunity when a fund opens in a new market and you can get in on the ground floor. Or maybe your job gives you special insights into which market is about to take off. Aggressive international investing requires substantial knowledge of foreign markets, but the results can be dazzling. Even if you don't feel you have the expertise to zero in on a particular region, you can still make international investing work for you.

Before you start looking for a fund that suits your needs, you should be familiar with this distinction: **International funds** must, according to their charters, put most of their money in foreign stocks. **Global funds** have more flexibility. They can move their assets into the securities of U.S. companies or foreign companies, as the fund manager sees fit.

The riskiest international bet is a **one-country fund.** By mid-1988, there were about 15 funds that offered securities in a single country. They included Brazil, Thailand, Australia, Italy, Canada, Korea, Japan, and Mexico. Because foreign investments in many of these countries are limited by the governments, investors have been very eager to get a toehold in them and have paid a lot for the opportunity. But you must remember if you choose one of these funds that you are investing in a very volatile instrument. The markets in many of these countries are small and are dominated by a few large companies. Trading volume is insignificant. If the country faces a serious problem and the stock prices fall at the same time that the currency is devalued, your investment could be decimated.

Most of the single-country funds are closed-end funds. The funds trade on the major exchanges and trade at a discount or a premium to the NAV depending on their attractiveness to investors. Because one-country funds have been considered highly desirable and their availability is limited, the shares have been trading at a steep premium.

For example, in mid-1988, the Korea Fund had a share price of

International funds
Mutual funds that invest in stocks or bonds of companies and governments outside the United States. To be classified as an international fund, a fund must invest most or its assets overseas. The percentage varies with different funds.

Global funds *Mutual funds that invest in stocks of companies or bonds of governments all over the world, in the United States as well as in most other countries.*

One-country funds *Funds that invest in a single country. Many one-country funds are closed-end funds.*

$79.875—105.8 percent higher than the value of its assets. Shares of the Taiwan Fund were trading at a price of 112.5 percent higher than the value of its assets. Investors have made a lot of money in these funds. For example, investors who put $10,000 into the Japan Fund when it was started in 1962 would have had $1.14 million at the end of 1987. But these are clearly investments for aggressive, knowledgeable investors with a stomach for risk.

INTERNATIONAL BOND FUNDS

Ellen and George are warming to the idea of investing in other currencies—and to the potential returns. If international investing makes sense for a portion of cash and equity investments, why not bonds? Like their equity counterparts, international bond funds and global bond funds invest in foreign countries. The bonds in their portfolios usually represent the debt of a foreign government. International bond fund managers rarely buy the debt of foreign corporations because it is difficult to analyze. As with the stock funds, you get both the return on the bonds and the currency play. The difference in total return between U.S bond funds and international bond funds can be significant. For example, during the three-year period from 1985 through 1987, the internationals gained about 30 percent compared with just under 10 percent for U.S. treasuries. The foreign bond funds benefited from the steadily declining value of the dollar against foreign currencies.

In 1987, the six top-ranking international and global funds gained between 34 and 87 percent. The worst-performing world income fund gained 8.4 percent for the year. There's no guarantee that they will continue to outperform U.S. funds. In fact, in the first half of 1989, international bond funds declined 1.6 percent. They are aggressive investments that came along at a time when their performance was helped immensely by the declining dollar. Still, if you have a portfolio of any size, you should consider putting a portion of it in international stocks and bonds to diversify. In the years from 1974 to 1988, the U.S. bond market was the world's best performer in only two years—1982 and 1984.

OUTWITTING INFLATION: MASSACHUSETTS FINANCIAL SERVICES AND INTERNATIONAL BOND FUNDS

If high inflation and high interest rates are the worst of times for bonds, 1981 was a nightmare. The United States was experiencing the worst inflation in modern times. Interest rates hit record highs.

Anyone who wanted to sell bonds in such an environment needed a good sales pitch. Because bonds offer a fixed stream of income, as inflation goes up, the real value of the income goes down. And when interest rates go up, bond prices go down, so the underlying asset is decreasing in value.

Massachusetts Financial Services came up with a new twist: a fund composed of fixed-income securities from countries where inflation was not a problem—in other words, an international bond fund. "The first idea was to provide a fixed-income investment in this inflationary environment," says Leslie Nanberg, president and portfolio manager of the Massachusetts Financial International Trust—Bond Portfolio.

The international fund would also add a new element to the equation. In addition to interest income and possible appreciation in the value of the bond, investment in bonds of foreign governments would give investors another opportunity for profit: a change in the relative value of the U.S. dollar and the other currencies.

As it turned out, though, the timing was off. Inflation had peaked at 13.5 percent in 1980. In-terest rates peaked in 1981. And the U.S. dollar was very strong and continued to strengthen until 1984. In 1982, U.S. bonds started on their longest and strongest rally in history. Because investors had a roaring bull market in bonds at home, they didn't need to look to an international bond fund.

Massachusetts Financial may not have introduced the international fund at the ideal moment, but the concept was sound. According to statistics collected by the company, the U.S. bond market has been the best-performing bond market in the world in only two years between 1974 and 1988. Those were 1982 and 1984.

The opportunity to invest in different countries that are in different stages of the business cycle has turned out to be an important one. And, once the dollar started plunging against world currencies in late 1984, international investments became real dazzlers.

Although the fund got off to a slow start with investors, its performance the first year was spectacular—up nearly 30 percent. Once the dollar started to drop in 1984, the fund again picked up steam, returning nearly 30 percent in 1985 and 1986 and 24 percent in 1987. By that time, other fund managers were bringing out their own global bond funds and even conservative investors were beginning to look beyond U.S. shores.

Of the international funds, global funds offer the greatest flexibility to the portfolio manager because he can put most of the assets in the U.S. market if he likes its prospects. The one-country funds offer almost no flexibility. The international funds fall in between. If you have considerable money invested in the United States already, picking a global fund could defeat the purpose of diversifying. You may be better off with a solid international fund with a good track record that allows the portfolio manager to move from one country to another as their prospects change.

AGGRESSIVE GROWTH FUNDS

Even if you, like the Popes, have plenty of money to invest and a healthy appetite for risk, you don't want to put all your money in foreign investments. Although the U.S. stock market has been eclipsed in recent years by some spectacular gains in smaller foreign markets, George has done all right in U.S. stocks. Over time, U.S. equities are one of the best investments available. Even though he realizes he must diversify, George will always keep some of his money in the U.S. market. And he'd like it to be in something with potential for growth.

If you feel comfortable putting part of your portfolio in investments with potential for high return, consider aggressive growth funds. These stock funds seek to achieve maximum capital gains or appreciation. Their managers are not interested in current income, or dividends. Rather, they attempt to pick stocks that will increase in value. Some funds have a specific target of perhaps 15 percent or 18 percent a year or more. Of course, setting a goal is easier than reaching it. And these funds provide both the greatest potential rewards and the highest risk. That generally also means that the funds are the most volatile. They're meant for investors who don't mind some ups and downs so long as they are moving in the right direction.

It's important to realize that the downs can be significant. Experts say that when the market dips, you can expect aggressive growth funds to lose two or even three times as much as the market as a whole. This tells you two things: that you must expect to sit on an aggressive growth investment for a while and that market timing can be critical. Market timing here doesn't mean you should jump into and out of the fund. Instead, it's important to be able to buy and sell funds at the best opportunity. Don't wait to sell until the week before you need your money to start a business.

Another caveat here is that although these funds have the highest risk/reward ratio, they don't always top the fund categories in performance. For example, during the early 1980s, when both the stock and bond markets had a long bull run, growth and income funds as a whole did better than aggressive growth funds while exacting less risk. Furthermore, the smaller stocks that aggressive growth managers often favor were outperformed by the blue chips during the 1980s bull market, so many growth funds did better than the riskier aggressive growth funds.

The aggressive growth category offers a great variety of funds, because there are many ways to invest for maximum capital appreciation. It's easy for a fund manager to say that he plans to pick stocks that will grow in value more quickly than the market as a whole. But it's your job to figure out if he has a sound method for doing it. How does the portfolio manager expect to get growth? Does he plan to hedge? Leverage the fund? Trade actively? Look for out-of-favor stocks? Unknown stocks? Bankruptcies? How can you assess his chances for success? Should you worry about his method or just go for a proven winner?

Obviously, the fund manager is key to the aggressive growth fund. Perhaps many investors aren't able to analyze whether it's better to invest in bankrupt companies and try to turn them around or to use sophisticated trading techniques such as short selling and margin buying to boost the return. But, if you have an appetite for risk, you should also have the knowledge to understand the manager's approach and the time to examine the prospectus. Certainly, you should be able to determine whether the fund manager has been able to achieve a respectable rate of return using whatever method he chooses.

One final word of caution on aggressive growth funds. Some fund managers do have an uneven performance. The performance of the 44 Wall Street Fund and its sister fund, 44 Wall Street Equity, is an often-mentioned case in point: 44 Wall Street was a stellar performer

Mutual Fund Manager All-Stars

Bob Chesek,
Phoenix Fund Series
since 1951

Ken Heebner,
Loomis-Sayles Capital Development Fund
and
New England Growth Fund since 1977

Harry Hutzler,
AIM Weingarten Equity Fund since 1969

Kurt Lindner,
Lindner Fund since 1977

Peter Lynch,
Fidelity Magellan Fund since 1977

John Neff,
Windsor Fund since 1964

Michael Price,
Mutual Shares Fund since 1975

John M. Templeton,
Templeton Funds since 1959

in the late 1970s, up 73.69 percent in 1979 alone. That year it turned in the highest return of any mutual fund over the preceding five years. And again in 1988, both funds outperformed the market. 44 Wall Street Equity had a particularly good year—up 32 percent.

But in the five-year bull market—from 1982 to 1987—the fund turned in the worst performance, plummeting by more than 81 percent. It also took the dubious honors in the ten-year period ending December 31, 1987, losing almost 50 percent. As for the newer fund, 44 Wall Street Equity, it finished dead last in 1987 with a loss of 41.9 percent. The fund manager, David Baker, didn't change. He oversaw both funds throughout the period.

RETIREMENT STRATEGIES THAT MATCH YOUR INVESTMENT PERSONALITY

Ellen and George Pope see the value of international investing to diversify their portfolio. But can aggressive international funds fit into the portfolio of a retired couple? Indeed, how should one make the transition from a working investor to a retired investor? Many experts recommend that you move your assets from stock funds into bond or income funds because the latter provide more certain, although usually lower, returns. In the last decade, though, bond funds have provided a roller-coaster ride for some investors. If you decide to move from stocks to bonds because you have less appetite for risk than you did when you were younger, you might choose some of the shorter-term bond funds. A long-term fund can be whipsawed by changes in interest rates.

Perhaps, like the Popes, you are nearing retirement age. But maybe that's absolutely the only thing you have in common with them. You may be a very conservative investor who has just received a lump sum distribution from your pension plan. Then you should look again at Chapter 8. Or you may be a retiree with a modest nest egg and little investing knowledge. In that case, you might look again at Chapter 4 or Chapter 6.

How aggressive should you be in retirement? It depends a great deal on how knowledgeable you are, how comfortable you are with risk, and, more important, how much money you have. If, like the Popes, you have a very large nest egg, and you're comfortable with risk, you'll probably want to keep some portion of your assets in aggressive instruments with the potential for higher gains. But your retirement strategy must match your investment personality.

Whenever you reach a transition phase in your life, whether you're getting married, having your first child, putting the last one through college, or moving into retirement, you must look again at your investment personality. Transitional phases in life almost always demand at least a slight shift in investment strategy. But you should never go against your own grain. As a general rule, you will want to move into more conservative, predictable investments when you retire. But, as with the other passages of life, you will have to do some homework.

If you're planning to retire:

• Plan your budget. Figure out where your monthly income will come from. How much will come from pension and Social Security benefits? How much do you need to earn as income from your investments? Put enough money into income-producing investments, such as bond funds, Treasury securities, or bank certificates of deposit, to bring in the amount you need each month.

• Don't put any of the money you need for living expenses into volatile investments, which include investments in the stock market and stock mutual funds. Stock investments are to provide the opportunity for growth of money you will need in the future, not for the money you need for next month's rent.

• There is no magic formula for investing. If you have very little money for retirement, there is no way to safely invest it to turn it into a pot of gold. Don't believe anyone who promises you that. If you have only a few thousand dollars, you cannot afford to risk anything. You *must* stick with conservative, guaranteed investments like bank certificates of deposit or U.S. Treasury bills and do the best you can.

• If you have a very large nest egg and you're comfortable with risk, there's no reason you can't keep a portion of it in aggressive investments with the potential to provide growth.

• Diversify. Even if you are very conservative, don't put all your money in the same investment. You should be diversified at every stage of your life.

PROVIDING INCOME FOR RETIREMENT WITH SYSTEMATIC WITHDRAWALS

Systematic withdrawal
Plan that allows you to withdraw a specified amount from your mutual fund account at regular intervals, usually each month. Systematic withdrawal plans, which are most often used for retirement, are a method of converting your investments into regular income.

However, switching your entire nest egg overnight from a stock fund you bought 30 years ago into a money market fund probably isn't a good idea. When you liquidate your investments, you must pay tax on all of the capital gains. Under the 1986 tax law, there is no favored tax status for capital gains—you pay tax at the same rate as on your regular earnings. One solution is to use a **systematic withdrawal** plan. These plans, which are offered by most mutual fund companies, allow you to specify a certain dollar amount that you want to receive every month or every quarter from your mutual fund account. You pay tax only on the amount you receive.

Furthermore, if you have a substantial amount of money in a fund, you can stretch your income over a considerable period. For example, let's say you have $200,000 in a mutual fund that is growing at a respectable 9 percent a year. If you withdraw $20,000 a year—or $1,666.66 per month—your money won't run out for 26 years. And you will be spreading your tax liability over a much longer time period.

THE POPES' CHOICES

The Popes decide to begin to liquidate their aggressive stock portfolio. In general, they plan to pare their aggressive growth investments and diversify into international investments.

- Fifteen percent goes into aggressive growth funds.
- Another 10 percent goes into international equity funds, for diversification and growth.
- Fifteen percent goes into international bond funds.
- Thirty-five percent goes into municipal bond funds.
- The final 25 percent goes into a money market fund. The Popes choose one that is part of a family of currency funds so they can diversify their cash investment as well.

The Popes' Portfolio

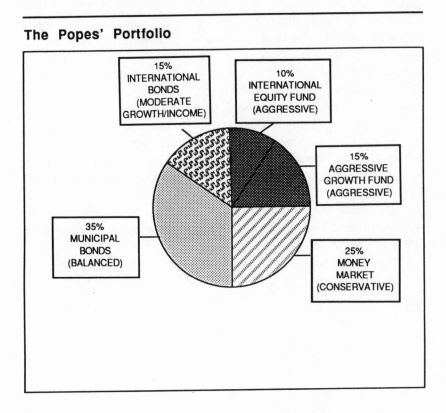

15%
INTERNATIONAL
BONDS
(MODERATE
GROWTH/INCOME)

10%
INTERNATIONAL
EQUITY FUND
(AGGRESSIVE)

15%
AGGRESSIVE
GROWTH FUND
(AGGRESSIVE)

35%
MUNICIPAL
BONDS
(BALANCED)

25%
MONEY
MARKET
(CONSERVATIVE)

POINTS TO REMEMBER

The Popes have taken one route to diversifying a large portfolio between income and growth investments. There are certainly other investments in other chapters that would work equally well for diversification. You should remember:

• If you're getting ready to retire, or facing a major transition in your life, you need to rethink your investment strategy.

• A diversified portfolio is a global affair. You need to think in terms of diversifying into different currencies as well as different types of securities.

• If you like hard-charging investments, but you need your money in a short period, you need to consider how aggressive you can be without leaving yourself stranded.

• Many mutual funds offer aggressive choices, but they still diversify your assets over a number of holdings, giving you a cushion against the volatility of individual stocks and bonds.

• The same investments that work in the U.S. market—stocks, bonds, and cash—are available in foreign currencies.

• Managers of aggressive growth funds use a variety of techniques in their attempt to achieve growth. If you have the appetite for them, these funds offer a smorgasbord of choices.

• Systematic withdrawal plans allow you to receive the money you've invested for your retirement as regular monthly income. You pay tax only on the amount you receive.

PART III:

Putting Your Knowledge to Work– The "How-To's" of Investing in Mutual Funds

Chapter 12

Ready, Set, Where Do I Go? A Shopper's Guide to Mutual Funds

I t seems that nearly everybody sells mutual funds today. You can buy them from stockbrokers. You can order them through the mail or by telephone. You can probably buy them at your bank. Many life insurance agents sell them. They're available from most financial planners. Or you can get them from a group like the American Association of Retired Persons.

This wasn't always the case. Twenty years ago, most mutual funds were available only from a salesperson, who was a broker or a **registered rep,** paid by the mutual fund company to bring in your business. You were charged a sales charge of perhaps 8.5 percent or 9 percent. In 1970, fewer than 10 percent of the mutual funds sold were offered directly to the investor without a sales charge.

The turning point came in the early 1970s. The stock and bond markets were in the doldrums and investors were deserting mutual funds in droves. Fund companies were looking for new products to woo them back. Money market funds, which were safe and convenient, seemed to provide an answer. But an 8.5 percent sales charge on a money market fund simply wouldn't work because it would take too much out of the investor's return. So money market funds were sold without a sales charge.

Registered rep
Securities salesperson who is licensed by the Securities and Exchange Commission and the New York Stock Exchange. Anyone who sells securities to the public must be a registered rep.

Understandably, brokers weren't enthusiastic about selling a product that didn't offer anything for them. When Fidelity began marketing money market funds in 1973, the company bypassed its broker sales network, which sold equity mutual funds. Fidelity placed an ad in the newspaper offering the fund directly to investors. Although Scudder, Stevens & Clark had always offered no-load funds—that is, funds without sales charges—and T. Rowe Price had offered them since 1950, Fidelity was the first of the large, established fund companies to switch from selling through a sales force to selling directly to investors. Other big companies, such as Dreyfus and Vanguard, followed. And new fund groups started that offered their products directly to investors.

Initially there was a stark difference between the two types of funds. Those sold through brokers, financial planners, or other salespeople generally carried an 8.5 percent sales charge and they were referred to as load funds. Those that were sold directly to the public through newspaper advertising, telephone sales, or the mail did not levy a sales fee and they were called no-load funds. During the mid to late 1970s, no-load funds started to gain market share. At one point, the market was divided about half and half between load and no-load funds.

Today the distinctions between load and no-load have been blurred because fund companies have added new kinds of charges, which will be discussed later in this chapter. But your first concern will be where to go to buy your mutual funds. As with most products, you can either do the comparison shopping yourself or hire someone to buy one fund or to put a package of funds together for you. You can even hire someone to manage your portfolio of funds so that you don't have to do anything but pay the fee. Which way do you fare best? It depends on many things. Certainly your knowledge of investing and how much time you're prepared to spend doing research are key factors. But before you decide to go shopping yourself or pay someone to provide the service, you should understand what you're getting into. You must consider the motivations of the people who are selling you the funds.

When you hire someone to pick a mutual fund for you, it's much like paying someone to perform any service that you don't feel you know much about—repairing your car or redecorating your home. If you know nothing about cars and don't care to learn, chances are you need a good mechanic. But you need to take the same care in selecting

FROM UP FRONT TO PAY-AS-YOU-GO: NEW TRENDS IN INVESTMENT FEES

Time was when you bought a load fund, you paid a sales charge. It went to the broker who sold you the fund. When you opted to go "no-load," you paid no sales charge because you bought directly from the company either by phone or through the mail.

Those distinctions began to lose their meaning when the no-load companies that sell funds directly started adding loads. Things were further complicated when the load funds began to get secretive about where the loads were. Rather than charging you 8.5 percent off the top, many companies found less apparent ways to pay the brokers they used to sell their funds.

For example, E. F. Hutton developed the first true back-end load fund in 1982. Hutton eliminated the front-end sales charge from its funds altogether. But it added what the company called a "disappearing back-end load." It disappeared if you left your money in the fund long enough, but if you took your money out within the first year, you paid a 6 percent exit fee. The exit fee was reduced by 1 percent each year until it disappeared after the seventh year. It's important to remember that these back-end fees are charged on the total assets you withdraw from the fund. If you've had your money in the fund for two years and it's performed very well, you will pay 4 percent of the total assets you take out, not just 4 percent of your original investment.

Fund companies argue that they use these disappearing back-end loads to discourage people from switching their money around too often and to provide stability of assets, for that is important to good portfolio management.

But it's clear that ingenious marketers, who have come up with permutations on the front-end and back-end load, have an opportunity to snag the unsuspecting investor, who may not understand the effect or even the existence of all these fees.

Fund companies are not necessarily doing something underhanded or disreputable because they have found new ways in which to charge fees or commissions. But information that spells out the effect of these fees has not always been clear to the investor. This problem has not gone unnoticed by government regulators, and in 1988, the SEC came to the rescue. New regulations forced fund companies to show in a chart how a $1,000 investment would be affected by fees the company charged over periods of one, three, five, and ten years.

the mechanic as you would if you were buying the parts yourself. Is he honest and reliable? Is he marking parts up excessively? Can you count on the quality of his work? Are his prices competitive?

When you're ready to remodel your home, if you don't feel confident of your own taste and ability, or if you don't have the time to plan, you may decide to go to a top-notch architect. But instead of choosing bathroom fixtures and deck planking, you're making a different choice. You have to choose the architect and builder. Does he have fresh ideas? Will he create a space with your needs in mind? Will he give you access to craftsmen that you couldn't get on your own? Will every subcontractor mark up his prices to give your builder a cut in addition to his fees? These are things you should know before you make your decision. You may decide you have strong feelings about the look you want and you'd rather spend the time yourself. Or you may decide you could never get the professional look and feel created by a top architect and it's money well spent. Deciding whether to invest on your own or go to an investment adviser requires the same sort of decisions. The first thing you need to know about people you hire to invest for you is how they get paid.

FINANCIAL PLANNERS

If you decide to get someone to help you to invest, chances are you'll go to someone called a financial planner. Before you do, you should know that anyone can call himself a financial planner. I could sell my services as "Mary Rowland, MA, Financial Planner." (The MA is in Russian history, but that doesn't matter.) Financial planning is an unregulated profession. Over the past decade, as Americans have focused more attention on their need for financial planning, the ranks of planners have been swollen by con men and hustlers looking for a quick buck.

This is not to say that there are not excellent professionals in this field. There are. And they are as eager as anyone to expose the charlatans who give their profession a bad reputation. But so far, there is no recognized way to separate the wheat from the chaff. Many financial planners carry a "CFP" designation from the College for Financial Planning in Denver. This means that they have completed a correspondence course from that school. There are both good and bad planners who have earned this designation, so in itself it is not a good way for you to pick a planner. The same is true for "ChFC," which is the Chartered Financial Consultant designation bestowed by the

American College in Bryn Mawr, Pennsylvania. Some planners carry both designations. That tells you that they've taken the time to complete some course work specific to financial planning. It still doesn't mean that they are *necessarily* good or bad.

Likewise, many financial planners may carry a ''JD'' after their name to signify that they are lawyers; an ''MBA,'' to indicate that they have completed a master's degree in business administration; a ''CPA'' to show that they are certified public accountants; or a ''CLU'' to indicate that they are a chartered life underwriter. These designations do show you that the person has certain kinds of education. Yet they do not show that he learned anything specific about financial planning. The International Association for Financial Planning, a trade group, is concerned about the problem of distinguishing between the ''good planners'' and the opportunists. The IAFP's effort to do something to help both consumers and planners is the annual *Registry of Financial Planning,* a directory that includes those planners who meet certain standards in their profession. This registry is available from the IAFP for $2.50. You can get it by sending a check to IAFP Customer Relations, Two Concourse Parkway, Suite 800, Atlanta, GA 30328.

The registry isn't foolproof either, of course. Your first question to anyone you propose to hire to give you investment advice should be: How will you be compensated? Some financial planners—only about 10 percent—work strictly on a ''fee basis.'' They charge a straight fee to set up a complete financial plan for you. After talking with you about your needs, they may prepare a list of options. For example, they may pick three or four mutual fund portfolios for you from three or four different mutual fund companies. You make the final choice and you can go wherever you like to actually buy the products. The idea is that these people offer unbiased advice based on your needs. They make the same amount of money whether you buy a fund from Scudder, Stevens & Clark or the Keystone group.

If you like this idea, you must make sure that the planner is, indeed, a ''fee-only'' planner, that he is not receiving any commission from the products you buy. If he makes recommendations and lets you choose the actual products, you can be quite certain that he doesn't receive a commission. If he sells you the products himself, ask him if he's getting a commission in addition to the fee. Fee-only planners are expensive. But if you are lost in the investment world and if you have enough money to invest to justify the planner's fee, they're worth checking into. Another twist on this is a fee planner who subtracts commissions from his fee. For example, the planner may tell you he will charge you $5,000 to set up a financial plan. Then, if he receives commissions on any of the products you buy, he will tell you what they are and subtract them from his fee.

Some planners receive a combination of fees and commissions. And other planners and salespeople make their money strictly from sales charges you pay for the products you buy. Even if the planner works only on commission, he might offer you a list of funds to choose from. And they might cut across the entire universe of available funds. But many planners who work on commission will select their recommendations only from a list of funds that carry a "load" or sales charge, because that's how they get paid.

BROKERS

Other "financial planners" are really stockbrokers. They might work for a national brokerage company like Shearson Lehman Hutton or Merrill Lynch or they might be with a regional firm like Piper Jaffrey in Minneapolis or Wheat First Securities in Richmond, Virginia. These people are financial planners in the sense that they help you define your investment goals and decide on a personal financial plan and a portfolio of investments. But they often have a vested interest in which products you buy. For example, major national brokerage firms sell a variety of mutual funds. Some of them are bought "wholesale" from investment underwriters or the people who actually manage the investments. They also sell funds that they manage themselves, so-called house funds, which are sort of their own private label. You should keep in mind that the brokers at these firms are paid more (and are heavily encouraged) to sell the house funds rather than the others, because the brokerage firm makes more money on its house products. This doesn't mean that the house products aren't good. Some of them are. But many are mediocre. And it doesn't mean that all brokers with national firms succumb to this pressure. Many sell very few house funds. They consider their clients' needs first and look for the best investment products for them. But it's something else you must consider when you are shopping for an objective financial adviser.

Smaller regional brokerage firms are less likely to manage their own mutual funds. And thousands of brokers and financial planners are not affiliated with any major brokerage firm. Instead, they work for themselves and use the trading service of an independent broker/dealer. Unfortunately, this doesn't mean that they'll necessarily do a better job of recommending funds for your portfolio. Mutual fund companies work hard to get these brokers to sell their funds. They sponsor contests and offer prizes, such as trips abroad, for the brokers who sell the most of their funds. Consider this, too, when you're looking for an objective adviser.

INSURANCE AGENTS

Insurance agents, too, got on the financial planning bandwagon. Because many new insurance products are combined with mutual fund investments, many insurance companies set up their own mutual funds. In order to sell them, agents, who are licensed by the states, needed to become registered reps as well. Thousands of them did. If you are comfortable with your insurance agent, and if he is a registered rep able to sell you mutual funds, you might be comfortable with the choices available. Remember, though, if the agent works for a large insurance company, his recommendations will be limited to those funds offered to you by his company. Some agents are "independent," which means they are not linked to one specific company. They might offer you mutual funds from a number of different companies. Some of them, who have really moved into financial planning, may offer you funds from a larger universe.

BUYING DIRECT

What if you decide that your taste in investments is better than anyone else's, that you want to make your own investment decisions? You have some choices here, too. Many fund companies sell direct to investors. You can buy funds from them over the telephone or by mail. They also have representatives who will answer your questions about their fund selections. But they will not give you any advice. For example, if the markets grow really turbulent and you need someone to hold your hand, these companies will not do it. If you want to sell, they'll take your order. If you want to know the latest price, they'll tell you. But they will not advise you to hang in there as a broker or financial planner might. They will not call you up and suggest that you move from one fund to another because your financial situation warrants it. They will take your order and answer your questions. Period. And some of the companies that sell funds directly to investors are no longer strictly no-load funds, either. Some—Fidelity is the most prominent example—now carry a sales charge.

DISCOUNT BROKERS

Some discount brokers offer funds from a variety of different mutual fund companies. This can be very convenient if you choose to keep all your investments in one account. For example, let's say you have a growing retirement account. You're a knowledgeable investor and you don't want to be limited to the funds of a single mutual fund company. You want to buy funds from several companies or maybe even actively trade into and out of different fund families. A discount broker will allow you to do this. Charles Schwab & Company, the country's largest discount broker, offers a variety of funds from a number of fund families.

Discount brokers are not permitted to give you any advice. They simply execute your orders. Unlike the individual fund companies, they do not even answer questions about specific funds. If you want to deal with a discount broker, you must be confident about what you want to do on your own. Another thing to consider is that you pay a fee for the convenience of doing all your investing through one outlet. Even if you buy funds that carry no sales charge, you must pay the discount broker a fee to buy and sell them.

BANKS

If you plan to buy mutual funds from your bank because you think they will be guaranteed by the Federal Deposit Insurance Corporation, you should reconsider. There is no greater level of security in buying mutual funds from a bank than in buying them from a stockbroker or a mutual fund company. The bank does not "back" the mutual funds it sells. Selling mutual funds is just one way that banks, like insurance companies, have moved to compete in the new financial services arena.

In fact, technically, banks don't actually sell mutual funds. In words carefully chosen by the legal minds, they "make them available." That means that they work as a conduit for other fund companies. They will provide the literature, take your orders, process them, and provide customer service. But they are just like a department store that puts the product on the shelf. They don't make the sneakers or the microwaves. They pick the brands they'll carry and let you put them in your shopping cart. Banks make the mutual funds available to their customers because they believe they have an edge in getting the business of customers who are already loyal to them. If you like your bank and have a good relationship with the bankers, you may feel that they will do a good job in picking their mutual fund partners. You should still check to see what variety of mutual funds they offer before you buy.

You can see that you have many choices and you need to do some work to sort them all out. Even if you choose to pay someone for advice, you cannot be a know-nothing investor. Many investors have complained of being taken to the cleaners by investment advisers. And many investors have claimed that the investments they made didn't keep the promise of the company that sold them. In both cases, the real problem was no doubt that the investor didn't do enough homework to figure out what was going on.

FEES

Before you can really make a final decision about what type of person or company you want to buy your mutual funds from, you need to consider fees. When you pick your own funds, you may or may not pay a sales charge. Some funds tout themselves as strictly no-load, and they are. Vanguard is one good example. But some former load companies simply reduced the front-end load—from the traditional 8.5 percent to 4 percent—and added an exit fee. Keystone and Kemper are examples of companies that offer what the industry calls "mid-load" funds because they charge a sales commission of about 4 percent. But these two companies usually make up for the lower front-end load with other charges. Other companies, like Franklin and G. T. Global funds, simply offer the mid-loads without the additional fees. And some of the direct marketers—most notably Fidelity—have added "low-loads" of 1 percent to 3 percent on some of their funds. These fees are not commissions, because they don't go to a salesperson. Instead they go directly to the fund company and are called "sales charges." The only real difference is in who pockets the 3 percent.

Another wrinkle that blurred the distinction between load and no-load funds was the creation of Rule 12 (b) 1 in October 1980 by the Securities and Exchange Commission. This new rule allowed funds to charge a fee for marketing and distribution costs—called a 12 (b) 1 fee. This is something of a "hidden fee" because it is simply subtracted from the assets of the fund year after year after year. These fees are used for a variety of purposes, including providing additional compensation to the people who sell the funds. But fund companies are required to disclose to shareholders in the prospectus how much they charge as a 12 (b) 1 fee.

Here are some questions you need to ask:

- Does this fund carry a 12 (b) 1 fee?
- How much is it?
- What is it used for?
- Does any of it go to compensate the broker for keeping his clients in the fund? (This type of compensation is referred to as a **trailing commission**.)

Trailing commissions
Commissions that are paid to the sales agent each year that his clients' money remains in the account. These commissions usually range from .25 percent to .75 percent of total assets, or 25 to 75 basis points.

Talk to your broker about trailing commissions. Remember that many brokers select those funds that offer these trailing commissions over those that don't pay them. And, although there's nothing unscrupulous about it, the big brokerage houses, like Merrill Lynch, Dean

"NO-LOAD" IS THEIR TRADEMARK: SCUDDER, STEVENS & CLARK

Back in 1919, two small rooms at 53 State Street in Boston were partitioned to form tiny private offices for the principals of Scudder, Stevens & Clark, a fledgling investment banking firm. The idea that set the firm in motion came to Ted Scudder one day when he was out trying to peddle some bonds to a Boston banker. The banker wasn't interested. He thought Scudder was simply trying to make a buck and that he didn't really have his client's best interest at heart. "I'd be willing to pay for unbiased advice if I could find it!" the banker told Scudder.

Voilà! Scudder and Haven Clark decided they would sell advice rather than investments. (Stevens didn't go for the idea and bailed out, but his name stuck.) The firm set up a research department and began signing up clients and looking for good investments. By 1924 it was charging a fixed fee of .5 percent of assets under management. And Scudder was coming up with investments that clients couldn't get anywhere else. For example, the firm found a contact in Hartford, the country's insurance capital, to buy insurance stock when estates in the area were settled.

In 1928, the firm took the idea a step further, offering a mutual fund for those who didn't have enough money for personal management. Scud-der stuck to the same principle, though—it didn't charge a sales commission. The Scudder, Stevens & Clark Balanced Fund was the first no-load fund. Of the handful of mutual funds on the market at the time, it was alone in not charging a front-end sales charge. Instead, a management fee was charged on assets in the fund.

Like other early financial services firms, SS&C had some tough sledding through the early 1930s when stock prices continued to slide. It was not until 1933 when President Franklin Roosevelt closed the banks, created the Federal Deposit Insurance Corporation, and took the United States off the gold standard that SS&C was able to report to clients: "Your account has shown an increase in value equivalent to 25 percent."

Not only was Scudder's the first no-load fund, but it didn't have much company for decades. Load funds dominated the mutual fund scene until the 1970s when a moribund stock market made mutual funds a tough sell. At that point, several fund companies took the loads off their funds or came out with new "no-load" funds. But by the late 1970s, Scudder, Stevens & Clark had been a "no-load" company for 50 years. "Scudder has never had a load fund," says Burke Walker, a company spokesman. "We have a trademark on 'Pure No-Load Fund.'"

Witter, and Shearson Lehman Hutton, pay brokers a higher trailing commission if they put clients' money in the company's house funds. This is merely something else you need to consider when you're deciding where to buy your fund and examining the fees. Even if you like your financial planner, don't be a gullible investor. Always consider how he is getting paid and how that might influence his decisions.

Fortunately, figuring out how much a mutual fund will cost you is a lot easier than it used to be. A recent SEC ruling requires mutual fund companies to identify all fees they charge and to show in a table how they might affect a hypothetical $1,000 investment. The ruling became effective in May 1988. Although fund companies were always required to disclose their fees, the information could be sprinkled throughout the prospectus so that even the most diligent reader couldn't uncover all of it. In addition to the sales charges and the 12 (b) 1 fees, all funds charge a management fee that ranges from .5 percent to 1 percent of assets under management, as well as administrative fees. And some funds charge the sales fee on all reinvested dividends, while others only charge it on your initial purchase.

The fee table in a prospectus, which is divided into three sections, shows all the fees you're required to pay. The first section includes maximum sales charges on purchases and reinvested dividends, deferred sales charges, redemption fees, and exchange fees, stated in percentage terms. Specific charges and flat fees must also be included. The second section shows the annual operating expenses, also expressed as a percentage. They include management fees, investment advisory fees, accounting costs, 12 (b) 1 fees, distribution costs, and other expenses.

The third section of the table will be most helpful to you. It shows how a $1,000 investment would be affected by these charges over a one-year, three-year, five-year, and ten-year investment period. The calculations assume that you earn a 5 percent rate of return. Naturally, you hope to do better than that. But the standardization helps you compare different funds. Sheldon Jacobs, editor and publisher of the *Handbook for No-Load Fund Investors,* collected 92 of the new prospectuses—26 for load funds and 66 for no-load funds, in mid-1988. This is what he found: The projected one-year costs ranged from $4 to $93. The ten-year projections ranged from $35 to $306.

When you compare the operating expenses of different funds you are considering, remember that the lowest expense ratio is not the only thing to consider. Larger funds typically have lower expense ratios because there are economies of scale. Some types of specialty funds that do business overseas or invest in the OTC market may incur larger expenses, because it costs more for them to trade. And if a fund provides you with spectacular performance, that may offset higher fees. But here are some guidelines on fees. Total operating expenses for stock funds average about 1.4 percent. For income funds, the average is about 1 percent for taxable bond funds and .8 percent for tax free bond funds. For specialty funds, the average is just over 2 percent. According to Morningstar, Inc., the organization that tracks these figures on a regular basis, an expense ratio over 2% in any category other than specialty funds should prompt some questions of the investment company.

The SEC also issued a ruling, effective July 1, 1988, on how funds may advertise yield and total return. In the past, fund companies had considerable liberty in deciding how to calculate yield on income funds. The result was that they picked whichever method made their fund look better. For example, if interest rates were rising, bond funds would quote a seven-day average yield. If rates were falling, they might quote a one-year yield. Shareholders were poorly served and had no decent basis for comparing one fund with another.

Income funds that advertise yield must now use a standardized 30-day yield figure. And any fund that advertises yield must include average annual compounded total return figures calculated in a method prescribed by the SEC for the past one-, five-, and ten-year periods. The same standards apply to **automated phone messages** that provide yields. The early effect of this ruling seemed to be that funds are advertising their yields less. But this information is available to you, and you should find it easier to compare mutual fund yields.

Automated phone messages   Service offered by some mutual fund companies that lets you use a Touch-tone telephone to get up-to-the-minute information about the funds you own—e.g., net asset value, your account balance—and switch money from fund to fund. Computer-generated instructions guide you through the process of using the service. Some automated phone services operate 24 hours a day.

READING A PROSPECTUS

Even before these recent rulings, you had rights to information from the mutual fund company before you made your investment and the right to receive regular reports on how your investment was faring. The prospectus provides information on the fund's objectives and policies as well as the restrictions on the portfolio manager. It describes how shares are bought and sold, what fees are involved, and what other charges you must pay.

HOW TO READ A MUTUAL FUND PROSPECTUS: THE FIVE FLAGS

Don't be put off by the small print of the prospectus. You can make this important exercise much simpler by looking first for the following five items. They appear in different places from one prospectus to another, but you should find them all listed in the table of contents.

1. Summary of Fund Expenses

Here's where you'll find a breakdown of all the sales loads, management and operating fees on a percentage basis, and a table that shows how those fees would affect the value of a $1,000 investment over time.

	1 Year	3 Years	5 Years	10 Years
You would pay the following expenses on a $1,000 investment, assuming (1) 5 percent annual return and (2) redemption at the end of each time period.	$16	$50	$87	$190

A. Shareholder Transaction Expenses

Sales Load Imposed on Purchases.None
Sales Load Imposed on Reinvested Dividends ....None
Deferred Sales Load Imposed on Redemptions ....None
Exchange Fees................................None

No sales fees here – this is a true "no-load".

B. Annual Portfolio Operating Expenses

(as a percentage of average net assets)
Management Fees..........................0.57%
12 (b) 1 Fees....................................None
Other Expenses 1.03%
Total Fund Operating Expenses....1.60%

Expenses are important. They show you what percentage of the assets of the fund go back to the fund's management to pay various fees. Sometimes they can be sizable. In the prospectus above, you can see that the total expenses are slightly higher than average (average, remember, was about 1.4 percent). You should find out why. There are some answers that you might find acceptable. For example, if the fund is fairly new, there may be substantial one-time start-up costs. If the fund is small, the expenses are spread over a smaller asset base. If securities in the fund are very actively traded, the expenses are probably due to high transaction costs. But even if these explanations are acceptable to you, they suggest that you should look at comparable funds before making an investment.

2. The Fund's Financial History

This is a table that shows up to ten years (depending on the date the fund began) of the fund's detailed financial history. It repeats some of the expense information from the expense table. The two most important things to look at here are the sources of investment gain (or loss) and the payout to investors. This exercise can be very revealing, as in the following example:

Per-Share Data and Ratios

				Years Ending January 31						
	1988	1987	1986	1985	1984	1983	1982	1981	1980	1979
1. Investment Income	$ 1.72*	$ 1.92	$ 2.09	$ 1.92	$ 2.02	$ 1.98	$ 1.90	$ 1.71	$ 1.47	$ 1.17
2. Expenses	.18*	.19	.18	.16	.21	.17	.17	.18	.19	.16
3. Investment income—net	1.54	1.73	1.91	1.76	1.81	1.81	1.73	1.53	1.28	1.01
4. Dividends from investment income—net	(1.51)	(1.70)	(1.70)	(1.63)	(1.70)	(1.68)	(1.57)	(1.42)	(1.19)	(1.00)
5. Realized and unrealized gain (loss) on investments—net	(2.73)	4.87	2.67	2.11	3.92	5.28	.14	2.97	3.65	2.30
6. Distributions from realized gain on investments —net	(3.92)	(3.08)	(.52)	(3.12)	(1.42)	(1.49)	(2.59)	(1.84)	—	—
7. Net increase (decrease) in net asset value	(6.62)	1.82	2.36	(.88)	2.61	3.92	(2.29)	1.24	3.74	2.31
Net asset value:										
8. Beginning of year	29.93	28.11	25.75	26.63	24.02	20.10	22.39	21.15	17.41	15.10
9. End of year	$23.31	$29.93	$28.11	$25.75	$26.63	$24.02	$20.10	$22.39	$21.15	$17.41
10. Ratio of expenses to average net assets	.66%	.65%	.66%	.72%	.80%	.82%	.83%	.90%	1.00%	1.00%
11. Ratio of investment income —net—to average net assets	5.5%	5.8%	7.1%	7.9%	7.0%	8.5%	8.3%	7.4%	6.8%	6.1%
12. Portfolio turnover rate	120%	110%	118%	123%	118%	138%	107%	149%	144%	135%
13. Share outstanding at end of year (000's omitted)	157,996	127,554	84,037	52,481	29,320	16,614	9,587	6,381	4,529	3,948

[handwritten note:] Fund has elected to pay out distributions and cut into the net asset value. You should ask why.

[handwritten note:] Expense ratio is declining over time. This looks good.

[handwritten note:] Fairly consistent turnovers. Another favorable sign.

Another important piece of information in this table is the *portfolio turnover rate*. You should be looking for two things (1) a rate that is consistent with the objective of the fund, and (2) a general consistency from year to year. There are legitimate explanations for certain deviations, but you should ask for them. In the example below, you should ask why the turnover nearly doubled from 1984 to 1985. If the fund was taken over by a new manager who restructured his holdings, you might be satisfied.

	1988	1987	1986	1985	1984	1983	1982	1981	1980	1979
12. Portfolio turnover rate	88%	63%	85%	133%	74%	90%	70%	66%	66%	49%

3. The Investment Objective

A brief statement of the fund's objective is usually given on the cover page of the prospectus. You should look further and read the full and more lengthy statement that appears inside. Here are some things to look for:

• The amount, in percentage, of assets the fund will normally invest in certain types of investments. For example:

> The fund's Manager, will normally invest at least 80% of the fund's assets in income-producing common or preferred stock. The remainder of the portfolio will tend to be invested in debt obligations, most of which are expected to be convertible into common stock.

• The options for investing the remaining percentage of assets. For example:

> Manager can also make temporary investments in securities such as investment-grade bonds, and short-term notes, for defensive purposes when it believes market conditions warrant.

• The flexibility the fund gives its manager in using derivative securities such as options. For example:

> The fund may write exchange-traded covered call options, which means that it sells to another party the right to purchase securities it owns at a fixed price. The fund may buy exchange-traded put options on stock indexes or on individual securities it owns to protect against a decline in market prices.

• If the fund invests in bonds, the quality criteria the manager will use in selecting bonds. For example, here, buried in about the fifth paragraph of a statement of the investment objective of a growth and income fund with a reputation for being conservative, is a statement that indicates the manager is free to invest in junk bonds:

> The fund may invest in lower-quality bonds which have moderate or poor protection of payment of principal and interest. These bonds involve greater risk of default or price changes due to changes in the issuer's creditworthiness.

4. Performance

You can read quickly through the explanation of how the fund calculates yield and total return. These calculations are governed by SEC regulation and the language has been largely standardized. However, you should spend some time with the table that will show the fund's total return performance over a period of time. Usually it will be compared to an index such as the S&P 500. This table should reveal how well the fund lives up to its investment objectives and how consistent its performance record has been.

Years Ended 7/31	Total Return	S&P Total Return
1979	8.90	8.63
1980	16.21	23.63
1981	14.45	12.90
1982	1.52	−13.12
1983	51.60	58.97
1984	2.89	−3.03
1985	37.95	32.21
1986	21.20	28.34
1987	24.05	39.21
1988	−2.03	−11.58

5. A Statement About the Fund Organization

Think of this as the fund's pedigree and examine it accordingly. Look for language that suggests stability and reputation ("is one of America's largest investment management organizations"), longevity ("founded in 1940"), and any special interests ("owns more than 50 percent of voting stock and is its 'controlling person' ").

You don't have to read every word of the prospectus. But you should definitely request one. There are five "red flags," things you should check in the prospectus before you invest. You want to know the objective of the fund, the strategy the manager will use to try to achieve that goal, and the type of securities the fund holds. For example, the objective of a stock fund might be to achieve growth and the strategy might be to invest in the stocks of established blue-chip companies that will grow as the economy expands. The prospectus outlines what the portfolio manager is permitted to do and what, if any, are his restrictions. It also tells you about the history or investment record of the portfolio manager. It does not tell you how he actually manages the portfolio.

But you can get a good idea about how the fund is managed from the statement of objectives and investment policy. You can also tell by noting which securities are in the portfolio and the **turnover rate.** The turnover rate may reveal whether the manager is following his investment objectives. For example, if the objective is to pick solid, undervalued stocks and hold on for the long haul and you see that the portfolio has a 100 percent turnover rate, you can see that something is amiss. In other words, he is turning over (or trading) the securities in his portfolio once a year, which is hardly the same as holding on for the long haul.

Investors have traditionally looked askance at a high turnover rate. For one thing, constant trading increases the fund's expenses, because the commission costs are heavy. For another, high turnover makes the portfolio manager appear indecisive. He couldn't pick the right securities the first time, so he had to keep trying over and over again. But recent innovations in the securities market, such as the introduction of different types of investments that allow the manager to hedge, have brought with them entirely new types of funds that are traded constantly to take advantage of the volatility in the market. Turnover, by itself, is no longer always a negative. It must be considered in conjunction with the fund's objectives and performance.

Part B of the prospectus is called the **statement of additional information**. Like Part A, it's free from the mutual fund company. But you have to request Part B specifically. It provides details on things not included in Part A, such as the name, occupation, and compensation of directors and officers. It also includes the name of any person who

Turnover rate
Frequency of trading of assets in a portfolio, expressed as a percentage. Although there are many other things to consider, a high turnover rate and heavy trading can result in high transaction costs. Every time securities are bought and sold, the fund must pay commissions.

Statement of additional information   Document provided by a mutual fund company that elaborates on the information found in the prospectus and provides additional information. The prospectus and the statement of additional information were once combined in the same document. Several years ago, in an effort to simplify the prospectus, fund companies put the additional information that they are required to provide to shareholders into Part B of the prospectus or the statement of additional information. Although the mutual fund company is required to send you a prospectus before you invest, it is not required to send you the statement of additional information. This information must be available to you, but it will be sent only if you request it.

THE MOST COMMON COMPLAINTS ABOUT MUTUAL FUNDS

Here are the things shareholders complain about most, according to an informal poll of mutual fund companies:

- Performance.
- Statement errors.
- Confusing or unclear statements.
- Errors in transactions.
- Unclear instructions for figuring taxes.
- Bounced checks.
- Errors in sales charges when money is transferred between funds.
- Statements and reports that arrive late.
- Mistakes that take too long to correct.
- Lost correspondence.
- Problems with signature cards.
- Checks that take too long to clear.
- IRA fees that are confusing, too high, or unfair.

The most common non–investment-related request is for a change of address, and shareholders complain a lot about the handling of this request. Many of them are irritated that the fund company requires the request in writing. Others complain that the company acts too slowly when it has the request or that it loses the request altogether.

One major fund company customer service executive, who has been tracking these complaints for the past ten years, says the list hasn't really changed much over that period. While service enhancements have given fund shareholders such things as automated quotations and statements that show all of their transactions and balances in all of their fund holdings on the same statement, the basic problems are still the same. In fact, the complexities introduced by automation, technology, and the vast array of products have added to problems. That said, it's worth noting that most fund companies take the problems very seriously and have committed increasing resources to solve them.

KNOW YOUR RIGHTS

As a mutual fund shareholder, you:
- Elect the fund's directors.
- Approve any proposed change in the fund's investment practices, policies, or objectives.
- Approve any change in the fund's investment adviser *but not* the portfolio manager.
- Approve any proposed changes in method of calculating the fund's price and the management (or other) fees.

owns 25 percent or more of the fund shares and the fund's complete financial statement.

You might also be interested in how a fund company operates and how it generates investment ideas. Some companies give their managers total autonomy. Others operate on a top-down approach, generating investment ideas in a policy committee and communicating them to individual managers. In some companies, top-performing managers are big stars. Others set up committees to manage funds specifically to avoid the star syndrome. Some funds use two or three independent managers on each fund, who don't work together. The idea is that they counterbalance one another. If you're interested in how fund companies operate, call the company's toll-free number and ask if the company has a corporate profile or a statement of its investment philosophy. Go to the library and look for articles in the *Business Periodicals* index. See if the company has been profiled in any of the business magazines so you can get a sense of its management style.

FUND REPORTS

Once you become an investor, the SEC requires that your fund send a shareholder report twice a year as well as a confirmation of every transaction. The annual report can be almost as important as the prospectus. All of the information about what is being done with your investment portfolio is in the annual and semiannual report. Read them. These statements are important for tax purposes as well as for figuring your returns and determining how well your investment is doing.

POINTS TO REMEMBER

• You can buy mutual funds from banks, brokers, insurers, financial planners, or the fund company itself.

• Before you decide where to buy your funds, think carefully about the vested interest of the seller.

• Many people call themselves financial planners. Picking a good one requires time and effort.

• Brokers and insurance agents sell you their investment advice as well as a mutual fund. When the chips are down, they'll hold your hand. But you must be sure they're not reaching into your pocket at the same time.

• Banks, discount brokers, and direct sellers of mutual funds offer no advice. They will answer your questions and execute your trades. But if you panic and don't know whether to sell or hold, don't expect them to help you out.

• Mutual fund fees come in the form of front-end loads, redemption fees, and annual charges such as the 12 (b) 1 fee and management and administrative fees.

• New SEC rules help you compare fees by forcing fund companies to show the effect their fees will have on a $1,000 investment in one, three, five, and ten years.

• Mutual fund prospectuses and annual reports unlock the mysteries of mutual funds. They'll tell you what's in the portfolio, how it's traded, who manages it, what the fees are, and what the performance has been.

Chapter 13

Staying on Top of Your Mutual Fund Investments: All You Ever Needed to Know, and Then Some

You've gotten a handle on your goals, a feel for your risk tolerance, and an idea of the different kinds of mutual funds that suit your needs. Maybe you've already picked the types of funds you want for your portfolio and you're ready to buy them. But you still need to learn where to go to get up-to-date information.

READING THE DAILY FINANCIAL PAGES

Most of the information you need as a mutual fund investor is available in the daily newspapers and the popular business and investment magazines. Let's start with the newspaper. When you pick it up in the morning, you'll probably want to find out whether the NAV of your fund changed. But you really need to do a little more work to be an informed investor. You should build to the level of knowledge you need for the amount of action you plan to take as an investor.

Each of the three major exchanges—the New York Stock Exchange, the American Stock Exchange, and the over-the-counter (OTC) market—has an overall index to show how that market performs. The *Wall Street Journal* and most other major newspapers print these indexes every day. Start by reading the newspaper's summary stock market and bond market stories, which give a synopsis of the previous day's activity. The stories will report on the performance of the indexes and, in the case of the bond market, will tell you how bond prices moved the previous day. In addition to finding out whether the market moved up or down, you'll also learn the trading volume, or how many shares changed hands, and what affected the markets.

As you watch the indexes over a period of time, you'll learn what constitutes a strong upward or downward movement and what represents heavy and light activity. Although these indexes are important measures of market activity, there are several other barometers that are more closely watched. Best known is the **Dow Jones Industrial Average,** composed of 30 blue-chip industrial stocks. This average, which was devised to give a quick fix on market movement, has fallen out of favor with some investors in the past several years as the U.S. economy has moved from industrial to service-based. Yet if you listen to radio or television news reports or look at the "snapshot" statistics provided by most newspapers, the Dow is inevitably the market measure you'll get. So whether it's as relevant as it was in the past or not, get accustomed to it and get a feel for how much of a movement is significant.

To give you some perspective, the Dow reached a high of 2,722 on August 25, 1987. It dropped nearly 500 points over the next several weeks, then, on October 19, it plummeted 508.32 points—losing 22.6 percent of its value—to 1,738.42. In percentage terms that one-day decline far exceeded the 12.82 percent drop of October 28, 1929, which ushered in the Great Depression. Movements of that magnitude are highly unusual. But changes of 50 points or more in one day are no longer particularly startling.

Although the Dow is the most quoted market index, the S&P 500 is a broader measure of market activity and the one that most individual investments are measured against. For example, when you check the performance of your mutual fund, chances are it will be measured against this market barometer rather than the Dow. The broadest measure of the market is the **Wilshire 5,000 Equity Index,** which includes

Dow Jones Industrial Average Average of 30 actively traded blue-chip stocks. At one time, the Dow 30 were all industrial stocks. As the United States has moved from an industrial to a service economy, stocks like American Express have been added to the average. The index, which is the most widely quoted indicator of the market, is prepared by Dow Jones & Company. It is quoted in points rather than dollars.

Wilshire 5,000 Equity Index Index of all stocks traded in the United States. Although the index, which is published by Wilshire Associates of Santa Monica, is called the 5,000, it actually contains 5,900 stocks.

all 5,900 stocks that are traded on all U.S. markets. While the S&P 500 measures the movement of the largest issues, the Wilshire index shows the movement of the entire market.

You'll quickly learn that nearly everything can affect your investments—politics, the trade deficit, the value of the dollar, a movement in interest rates, unemployment figures, inflation, reports on economic growth, and meetings of OPEC. The better handle you have on these economic indicators, the more confident you'll feel about making decisions on when to invest.

Most newspapers also carry regular reports—at least once a week—on short-term interest rates. For example, *The New York Times* lists money market fund rates on Thursday and Sunday. Accompanying the list is a story that summarizes the direction of short-term rates, the rates paid for bank certificates of deposit and Treasury bills, and the average yield on money market mutual funds and bank money market accounts. The report also indicates whether assets in these funds are growing or shrinking.

CHECKING UP ON YOUR INVESTMENTS

Now you've got a sense of what's happening in the markets as well as the rest of the financial world. Next you want to know how these events affected the value of your mutual fund investment. Did it move with or against the tide? It's easy to find out. Major metropolitan papers list mutual fund share prices daily. Look through the tables that list prices for individual stocks and bonds until you spot the section with the "Mutual Fund" heading.

The fund listings are alphabetized under the name of the mutual fund management company. That's where you start. For example, let's say you own the Affiliated Fund managed by Lord, Abbett & Company. You first find Lord, Abbett in the listings. Then look for Affiliated. You will probably see three columns of numbers. The first column tells you the closing NAV (net asset value) of the fund on the previous day. The second column, which might be called "Buy," indicates what you would have to pay for the fund. If the column says "NL," the fund is a no-load fund and there is no sales charge. But if the "buy" column is different from the "NAV" column, it means you must pay a sales charge. For example, one day in mid-1988, Lord, Abbett Affiliated had a NAV of $9.16. The "buy" column indicated that you would pay $9.88 per share if you wanted to purchase it. If you subtract 9.16 from 9.88 and divide the difference by 9.16, you will see that this fund carries an 8 percent load or sales charge.

In 1988, the National Association of Securities Dealers developed guidelines to further help you distinguish between funds that carry no sales charges and those that do when you check their performance in the mutual fund tables of the newspaper. Before that, those funds that imposed 12 (b) 1 fees and exit fees or redemption fees could use the "NL" designation, which was confusing to investors. Beginning in 1988, funds with a 12 (b) 1 fee were required to carry a footnote "p" to let you know that they levy this charge. Because of this rule, some fund companies dropped the 12 (b) 1 fees for new funds. Funds with redemption fees are marked with an "r." A footnote "t" means the fund carries both a 12(b)1 fee *and* a redemption fee.

Some people think that managing their mutual fund investments means checking to see if the price changed or if the market went up or down. But that's just one part of it. It's important, but not the most important part. Tracking prices is like following the weather reports. Six gloomy days in Miami may be miserable to endure, but it probably doesn't suggest that it's time to pack your bags and move if the fundamental reasons for picking the location are still sound. On the other hand, if you find yourself buffeted by hurricanes, discover there is a bug population vicious enough to consume your weekly groceries, and look out the window one morning to find a gas station going up next to your swimming pool, it may be time to rethink your position. Gathering information about mutual funds, and using it wisely, calls for the same common sense.

Even if you consider yourself a "buy and hold" investor, you need to monitor your investments in the newspaper periodically and read the information you receive from your mutual fund company. But if you want to become a more active investor, you'll want to know more. You'll want to see how your funds stack up against other funds, which fund categories are hot, and which are not. There's certainly no shortage of information about mutual funds today. Nearly every consumer magazine, whether it's a business publication or not, has some piece of advice. But there are a couple of sources that you'll want to be sure to get.

PERFORMANCE RANKINGS

There are several different tiers of information available to you, depending on how serious you are about investing. They range from shelling out a couple of bucks at the newsstand for a magazine to going to the library to do research to asking your financial planner for information or—if you're really insatiable—buying some source books yourself. Many companies monitor the mutual fund industry, collect statistics, and publish regular reports that give returns of individual funds and their rankings within categories. The reports might measure them for the most recent quarter, the past year, three years, five years, and ten years. The best-known ranking service is Lipper Analytical Services. Morningstar, Inc., CDA Investment Technologies, and Wiesenberger Investment Companies Service are also known for their performance rankings. Lipper publishes information for large institutions in the securities industry as well as a publication for individuals, the S&P/ Lipper Mutual Fund Profile. If you use a broker or financial planner, you may be able to get access to these publications from him. Morningstar and Wiesenberger publications are available in libraries. You can also purchase them, if you like.

But before you go that far, check what's available to you through business publications that you can buy on the newsstand or get through the mail. *Barron's,* a weekly business publication that comes out every Saturday, is an important source of information on mutual funds. At the end of each quarter, *Barron's* publishes a special section on mutual funds that includes the rankings by Lipper Analytical Services and an overview plus lots of stories about individual fund categories and how they performed. It also provides features on which funds may do well in the future, discusses which funds are having trouble and why, and profiles top fund managers. This issue generally comes out about six

PICKING A MUTUAL FUND: A SAMPLE EXERCISE

Once you've decided what type of fund you want to invest in, the next step is to pick one particular fund within that group. How do you do that? Although performance is most important, consider how much you're willing to pay in fees as well. When you're doing your research:

• Do consider performance first. You want a steady, long-term performer, not a flash in the pan.

• Don't be distracted by the hottest or trendiest fund. Today's winner might end up on the bottom of the heap in a couple of months.

• Don't make a decision based on quarterly statistics. One quarter is not long enough. Look at one-year, five-year, and, if possible, ten-year performance.

One good way to find a fund that meets your criteria is to look at a sourcebook like the loose-leaf *Mutual Fund Values*, published by Morningstar and available in many libraries.

Suppose you've decided that you want a growth fund. First, look at the section that lists growth funds that have earned the top 5-star rating for at least three years—five or ten would be even better—all the strongest performers. Select several names. Then, find the section with the latest growth fund reports. At the top, next to the name of the fund and the objective, "growth," you will be able to see if the fund carries a load, or sales commission, and how much it is. You will also see the yield, which is not of prime importance in a growth fund, the asset size, and the net asset value.

Next look at the chart that provides the total return of the fund for each of the last ten years. This is key and it's much better than a cumulative five- or ten-year return. Here you can see the best year and the worst year over the ten-year period. You'll also see how it compared to the Standard & Poor's 500 stock index and how it ranked with other funds. There's also a list of securities in the portfolio, an analysis of the fund, and a rating.

Once you've narrowed your choice to a couple of funds, call the fund companies and ask how long the current portfolio managers have been on the job.

Ask each fund to send you a prospectus. Browse through it and look for the five key things you learned about in Chapter 12. Then you should be ready to pick your fund.

weeks after the end of the quarter. For example, the year-end rankings might appear about February 15. Results from the third quarter, ended September 30, might be in an issue in early to mid-November.

Money magazine reports on mutual funds in nearly every issue. It also provides a regular mutual fund column. And, like *Business Week*

Ivy Growth

	Objective	Load%	Yield%	Assets $mil	N.A.V.
	Growth	None	2.7	172.9	13.97

Ivy Growth Fund seeks long-term growth of capital. Current income is a secondary consideration.

The fund invests primarily in common stocks and securities convertible into common stock. At times, however, it may invest all or part of its assets in debt securities, preferred stocks, or short-term notes. The fund invests primarily in securities traded in the United States, but may invest up to 25% of its assets in foreign securities.

Return	Risk
Above Avg	Low

Rating ★★★★
Above Avg

N.A.V.

	Mar31	Jun30	Sep30	Dec31	Yr. End
1986	15.63	16.05	16.18	13.44	13.44
1987	14.52	14.88	15.69	12.09	12.09
1988	12.73	13.23	13.29	13.21	13.21

INCOME

	Mar31	Jun30	Sep30	Dec31	Total
1987	0.59	0.00	0.00	0.321	0.911
1988	0.00	0.00	0.00	0.379	0.379
1989	0.00				

CAPITAL GAINS

	Mar31	Jun30	Sep30	Dec31	Total
1987	0.30	0.00	0.00	0.00	0.30
1988	0.00	0.00	0.00	0.00	0.00
1989	0.00				

PERFORMANCE/RISK

THRU 02/28/89	TOTAL RETURN%	+/- S&P500	PERCENT RANK ALL FDS	PERCENT RANK OBJ
3 MONTH	5.56	-0.93	43	77
6 MONTH	9.74	-2.73	35	59
1 YEAR	9.65	-2.17	41	54
3 YR AVG.	8.14	-3.94	43	54
5 YR AVG.	14.07	-3.18	35	44
10 YR AVG.	19.63	3.03	10	21

	MFV RISK PCT. RANK ALL OBJ	MFV RETURN RISK 1.00=Equity Funds Avg		MFV RISK-ADJ RATING
3 YR	45 9	1.08	0.72	★★★
5 YR	40 6	1.18	0.65	★★★★
10 YR	30 5	1.29	0.66	★★★★★
Weighted Avg. →		1.22	0.67	★★★★

ANALYSIS

03/24/89

Ivy Growth Fund is a 4-star fund with a caveat. The fund has rapidly gone from 5-stars for the 10-year period to 3-stars for the 3-year period--and for the worst of reasons: a management change.

It started when Ivy fired its sub-adviser in 1986. Though the fund's claim to stardom had largely rested in its ability to combine staid portfolio holdings (sector weightings generally mimic the S&P, and undervalued blue chips tend to be the picks of the day) with an eagerness to flee to bonds or cash, it found such timidity onerous in the late great bull market of the mid-1980's. Ivy didn't like the fact that its sub-adviser was holding low-upside T-notes when blue chips reigned; nor did it like the fact that the fund was lagging the rapidly rising 1986 bull market.

So, Ivy ousted its sub-adviser and got the fund more fully invested. Unfortunately, since that decision, the fund has posted its two worst years of relative performance in the past decade. Not only was a more aggressive position damaging during the crash, but holding 40% in cash in 1988 caused the fund to miss much of that year's rebound.

Recently, Ivy is back to being aggressive (it is now 95% invested), though so far to little avail. Also, management has made an unexpected 10-15% foray into foreign equities (it hopes to reap some of the rewards evident in Ivy International).

Ivy Fund has changed much in recent years, and it remains to be seen if Ivy is as good at picking stocks as it was at picking sub-advisers.

OPERATIONS

40 Industrial Park Road
Hingham   MA 02043
617-749-1416   800-235-3322

ADVISER	Ivy Management Inc.
DISTRIBUTOR	Ivy Financial Services Inc
PORTFOLIO MANAGER	Peers/Watson (1986)
MGMT FEE	1.10% flat fee
FEES	No-load
TICKER	IVYFX	MIN. INITIAL PURCHASE	1000
PHONE SWITCH	Yes	MIN. SUBSEQUENT PURCHASE	100
SHARE HOLDERS	44809	INCORPORATED	1961

	1979	1980	1981	1982	1983	1984	1985	1986	1987	1988	2/89
N.A.V.	7.86	10.16	10.38	12.99	15.49	13.88	15.90	14.10	12.10	13.21	13.74
TOTAL RETURN%	28.86	34.90	5.94	32.94	29.97	7.93	29.43	17.30	-1.87	12.40	4.01
+/-S&P500%	10.56	2.68	11.02	11.48	7.51	1.80	-2.21	-1.33	-7.09	-4.11	-0.62
TOTAL RETURN PERCENT RANK — ALL FDS	31	28	25	30	12	35	29	35	73	46	41
— OBJ	55	49	17	29	12	11	44	26	73	57	67
INCOME	0.13	0.34	0.36	0.59	0.74	0.78	0.96	0.46	0.91	0.38	0.00
CAPITAL GAIN	0.00	0.00	0.00	0.00	0.38	1.78	0.76	4.48	0.30	0.00	0.00
EXPENSE%	1.37	1.26	1.27	1.28	1.22	1.29	1.27	1.29	1.27	1.34	---
INCOME%	4.20	4.90	5.80	7.30	5.90	5.40	4.70	4.50	2.40	3.10	---
TURNOVER%	90	103	74	86	59	97	132	95	74	---	---
NET ASSETS $ MIL	32.6	54.2	54.3	76.7	114.4	63.5	136.7	158.1	173.7	172.9	

	ALPHA	BETA	R²	STD.DEV.
	-2.5	0.74	92	4.60
PCT. RANK — ALL FDS	55	68	22	56
— OBJ	44	90	26	92

PORTFOLIO

NO. OF STOCKS 191   TOP 30 EQUITY HOLDINGS AS OF 12/30/88

SHARE CHANGE	AMOUNT	STOCK	VALUE $000	% NET ASSETS
9500	46700	WARNER-LAMBERT	3660	2.12
5000	65600	TENNECO	3177	1.84
40000	60400	BF GOODRICH	3126	1.81
41200	96200	CHAMPION INTERNATIONAL	3090	1.79
	54000	REYNOLDS METALS	2903	1.68
9400	26900	QUANTUM CHEMICAL	2835	1.64
10000	55000	FNMA	2791	1.61
-7000	46700	HOUSEHOLD INTERNATIONAL	2656	1.54
12500	55000	MCA	2503	1.45
	30000	MONSANTO	2453	1.42
28000	28000	GENERAL MOTORS	2342	1.35
10000	85000	CITICORP	2199	1.27
2500	22500	DOW CHEMICAL	1974	1.14
17900	53700	UNIVERSAL FOODS	1866	1.08
15000	50000	WARNER COMMUNICATIONS	1831	1.06
	70000	TELE-COMMUNICATIONS CL A	1829	1.06
8000	15000	IBM	1826	1.06
20000	50000	MAY DEPARTMENT STORES	1813	1.05
15000	55000	SCHLUMBERGER	1794	1.04
	40000	HERCULES	1780	1.03
	50000	K MART	1744	1.01
22500	50000	CBS	1705	0.99
10000	10000	HEWLETT-PACKARD	1598	0.92
15000	30000	MOBIL	1593	0.92
10000	35000	GULF & WESTERN	1569	0.91
38500	38500	JP MORGAN	1564	0.90
8000	45000	ALBERTSONS	1502	0.87
	39645	UNION PACIFIC	1484	0.86
8000	23000	POLAROID	1475	0.85
	40000	EASTMAN KODAK	1467	0.85
	32500			

PORT. STATS.

02/28/89

	PORT. AVG.	% OF STKS. S&P500	REL S&P500
P/E	11.9	73%	0.94
PRICE/BOOK	2.6	74%	1.04
5YR. EARN. GROWTH	16.2	48%	1.36

COMPOSITION

12/31/88

CASH	14.2 %
COMMON STOCKS	85.8 %
BONDS	0.0 %
PREFERREDS	0.0 %
CONVERTIBLES	0.0 %
OTHER	0.0 %

B = 12b-1 plan in effect   I = Income Fee   R = Redemption Fee
D = Deferred Sales Charge   L = Max. Sales Charge   Percentile Ranks: 1=Highest 100= Lowest
G = Group Fee   P = Performance Fee   Except MFV RISK 1=Lowest 100=Highest

Page 234

and *Forbes, Money* provides rankings at least once—and usually twice—a year. Because these magazines use different ranking services, your fund may not be listed in the same category in each one. Or the performance return listed in one may not match the return in another because there are various methods to calculate performance. But it's not necessary to read all four publications to get the essential information.

In addition to looking for fund rankings, you should be using these publications to get acquainted with the investment philosophies of the stock and bond pickers who manage your mutual fund portfolios. Although the prospectus will give you the outside limits of what these traders can do with your money, many managers are far more conservative in their actual trading. Getting to know your portfolio manager and his strategy is important and reading these articles and interviews is a good start.

If these newspapers and magazines aren't enough for you, the next step is the library, where you can most likely find the outsized, 1,000-page Wiesenberger guide. This book provides a history of the industry as well as a history of each fund group. It details services and fees and offers statistical histories of the funds. Morningstar provides a couple of sources for consumers. The *Mutual Fund Sourcebook,* a large paperback survey of funds, is published quarterly. It's available for about $200 a year. This book lists funds by objective and provides information on performance, expenses, and outlook as well as the investment criteria used by the fund manager.

Another publication by Morningstar, *Mutual Fund Values,* is a loose-leaf portfolio that lists funds by category with ten-year performance figures, their objectives, their major holdings, and an analysis. It also ranks them and assigns them a risk rating and a volatility number. This service is the mutual fund equivalent of the Value Line Investment Survey for individual stocks. The short 200-word analyses are particularly helpful and perfectly accessible even to the beginner. Here you can learn that, although the fund might state income as its objective, in fact it has focused on growth. You can get a quick fix on the type of investments it makes, how volatile it is, and sometimes, how the fund manager has reacted to a recent crisis. If browsing through statistical books appeals to you, you might find some small but highly consistent performer in here that perfectly meets your needs.

MANAGING YOUR PORTFOLIO

Once you've found the information you need, there's just one more step for you to finish your primary education in mutual funds. You have to decide how you want to manage your portfolio. Whether it's large or small, whether you have 2 funds or 20, as poker players know, it's important to know when to fold. Managing your portfolio means staying on top of your funds, and an important part of that exercise is knowing when it's time to sell. The time to settle on your strategy is not when something happens in your life, your fund, the market, or the economy. Something unexpected always happens sooner or later. The time to develop your selling strategy is when you invest. Resolving your selling strategy is part of your investment decision.

You should be able to tell yourself, in a few sentences, why you've chosen a particular fund, what you expect from it, and what could make you change your mind. If you've invested in a fund because you like the services it offers, the way it responds to its customers, then a reduction in services could make you reconsider your investment. If you've invested in a fund company with an impeccable reputation, you'll want to reevaluate if the company's reputation is tarnished by scandal or even minor bungles in handling your account. But let's face it, these are not day-to-day issues that are likely to unsettle your confidence. Performance is what keeps most investors happy and poor performance is what drives most investors to sell.

In theory, that makes sense. Why bother with a mutual fund if it doesn't perform? But in practice, the art of selling is riddled with contradictions. Study after study reveals that most investors are inclined to get into a fund or bail out at precisely the wrong moment. By building your selling strategy into the investment decision up front, you can avoid this all too common fate. Here are some general do's and don'ts for selling your mutual funds:

Do Sell

1. *Do sell* or begin to sell when you're within one to three years of needing your money—for retirement or college expenses, for example.

If you've invested in a growth fund with an eye to letting it grow until you reach retirement, don't wait until the gold watch is in your hand before you decide what to do with your investment. Historically, the market moves in cycles, and allowing yourself adequate time to move your money slowly will help you achieve your investment goals more fully without the risk of getting caught in a bad market precisely when you need to liquidate your investments.

2. *Do sell* when your fund's performance slips below the averages for an extended period of time, two years, for example.

Mutual fund performance is best judged over the long term. When your fund doesn't make the list of top performers for a month, a quarter, or even a year it doesn't mean it's time to sell. Use a longer yardstick, but once you're convinced that mediocre performance has become the norm for your fund, it's probably time to sell.

A word of caution: Be sure that you are, indeed, measuring performance against some standard. Following several years of rates that rose as high as 17 percent, many investors were disappointed when money market yields plummeted in the mid-1980s. Investors who reassessed their money market investments in light of lower yields moved into something with higher potential. For them, it was a calculated move. But for the investor who was looking for another safe place for his assets plus performance that was reminiscent of those 17 percent days, the party was over. The defectors who jumped into Ginnie Mae funds, for example, were in for an unpleasant surprise when they learned their assets could erode despite high yields.

3. *Do sell* when your fund's performance is making you anxious.

If your fund's performance makes you anxious, you're in the wrong fund. The advice of points one and two notwithstanding, it's time to sell. But, before you make the same mistake again, try to determine why you felt the way you did. A friend of mine took his $10,000 family inheritance and put it into a top-performing growth fund just before the market took a tumble and his fund with it. He was furious: this fund was supposed to be a top performer! He sold out, pocketing $9,000 instead of his original $10,000, and invested in *another* top-performing growth fund. It's always risky to give advice to a friend, but I think his money belonged in a bank. It's clear that he didn't consider the selling part of the investment decision when he decided to buy. And he set himself up to incur further losses.

4. *Do sell* when the reasons you invested in the fund have changed.

This last point really summarizes all the earlier ones. If your goals have changed, if, for example, you invested for retirement and now you need the money to add on to your house, if your tax situation has changed, if the fund slaps on new fees or sales charges, if you invested because you liked the fund manager and he's gone on to a different company . . . it may be time to sell. Any change in your life or the fund calls for a reevaluation of your investment decision.

Don't Sell

1. *Don't sell* just because the market is declining.

The moment you decide to invest, accept the fact that the market *will* decline. It's bound to. That's what financial markets do from time to time. Unless you are following the discipline of a market timing strategy, it's usually not a good reason to sell. Peter Lynch, manager of the Fidelity Magellan Fund, claims his fund has declined at least eight times in the past ten years. Still, Fidelity Magellan holds the top spot for ten-year performance. The investor who sold on the basis of a declining market missed participating in those rewards.

But what if the market is in for a long-term correction? One popular investment book advises investors to "plan to miss" long-term corrections. A neat trick! Unfortunately, the book doesn't go on to tell the reader how to do it. Unless you think you've got a "system" that works, and are prepared to spend a lot of time employing it, you're probably better off riding out the declines.

2. *Don't sell* in a panic, when the market takes a big dive in a single day, as it did in October 1987.

Many investors who cashed out of their mutual funds in those final days of October 1987 were twice burned. They lost money selling shares into a declining market, and then they missed out on the fine performance of 1988, when the market climbed 16.5 percent, as measured by the S&P 500, and the first half of 1989, when it climbed another 16.5 percent.

3. *Don't sell* because you get a tip from a friend or adviser.

Consider the source. Then do your homework. Only *you* know what's best for your portfolio. One man's tip is all too often another man's trap.

4. *Don't sell* on the basis of artificial stop/loss limits that you've placed on your fund.

Can you imagine the basketball coach who would tell his team to quit when the opponents go up by ten points? That's a pretty good analogy to the stop/loss limit. Some financial advisers advise investors to set a percentage limit—say 10 to 20 percent—and if the NAV of your fund falls to that level, you would automatically sell. However, if you are so concerned about the volatility of your fund that you are uncomfortable at the thought of a 10 to 20 percent drop, you're probably in the wrong fund. Declines of these magnitudes are not uncommon in some types of mutual funds. You should consider this possibility when you make your investment decision and choose a fund that is not so volatile. If you're inclined to employ a stop/loss limit on a fund you own, sell it and reread ''Sell'' number 3.

That said, there is one situation in which it may make sense to use a stop/loss limit. If you've enjoyed substantial gains in a fund *and*—the important word here is *and*—you are near the time when you'll need to take your money out, it may make sense to set a limit that would preserve your gains. You can stay in and enjoy any future gains but limit your losses by setting that point at which you would sell. It's important to remember that this is not a foolproof method. On a day such as October 19, 1987, some prices fell so far so fast that only luck could have gotten an investor out at a precise stop point.

5. *Don't sell* because your fund has performed so well you can't imagine that it will continue.

This is the reverse of the stop/loss limit. And in some ways, even worse. If your fund is performing well *and* you're checking in now and then to make sure the reasons you invested have not changed, why do you want to limit your gains? If nothing has changed and you're still anxious, go ahead and sell. But reread ''Sell'' number 3 before you make a new investment.

MANAGING YOUR PORTFOLIO WITH MARKET TIMING

If you've adopted a market timing strategy, your buy/sell guidelines are already built into your system. You should be prepared to follow your indicators religiously and act on the signals for buying and selling. If, over time, you don't like the results, it's time to rethink your strategy for buying *and* selling. Remember, the two decisions always go hand in hand.

If you're going to do any market timing, mutual fund market timing newsletters are a good source of information. Their editors use popular market indicators to decide when the market is too high and when it should be ready to take off. These newsletters advise you on when to switch from one mutual fund to another or when to move out of the stock market and into cash or a money market fund. Some even tell you which industry sector looks like the best bet. Others will manage your mutual funds for you, calling your fund company and requesting a telephone transfer.

Some investors swear by newsletter advisers. Others find the offerings full of hype, hot air, and back patting. They certainly aren't an essential part of being an informed investor. But if you do feel that you'd like to try them, it's important to find a newsletter editor whose investment philosophy you're comfortable with. Some may be too fast-paced for you. You may not like the style of others. But you might find one that speaks right to you. If you're interested, the best way to get a feel for what's available is to get trial subscriptions to three or four. You can find ads that offer trial subscriptions in most business publications, like the *Wall Street Journal*.

You also need to consider the costs involved. Every time you sell shares at a profit, you must pay taxes on your gains unless you are trading in a tax-deferred account. You also need to consider the fees imposed by mutual fund companies. Some companies encourage market timers. Others find them a nuisance. That's because every time shareholders redeem their shares, or move their money out of a mutual fund, the portfolio manager must raise cash. He can do this by selling stock or by borrowing. Consider what happens if an investment guru who writes a newsletter advises his 150,000 subscribers to sell Zebra Fund. If they all sell, the fund manager must quickly come up with the money to redeem their shares. If he is forced to sell stock into a falling market, it will hurt the fund's performance.

For this reason, many fund companies have taken steps either to thwart market timers or to limit their activity. Some funds, for example, do not allow telephone transfers. Or they permit a maximum of anywhere from two to eight a year. Other companies charge a fee every

A BRIEF & SELECTED GUIDE TO MUTUAL FUND INVESTMENT NEWSLETTERS

The Graphic Fund Forecaster
(formerly *Time Your Switch*)
508-470-3511
Charts performance of selected mutual funds with heavy emphasis on sector funds. Recommends selected funds on basis of technical indicators. Began publication: 1984. Twenty-six issues per year.

Growth Fund Guide
800-621-8322
Publishes charts and detailed technical analysis of no-load and low-load funds and fund categories. Makes recommendations and forecasts. Began publication: 1968. Monthly.

Income & Safety
800-327-6720
Provides performance information and assigns "safety" ratings on money market and income-oriented mutual funds. Began publication: 1981. Monthly.

Insight
800-444-6342
Reviews Fidelity fund performance and makes recommendations on fund selection. Not associated with Fidelity Investments. Began publication: 1985. Monthly.

Jay Schabacker's Mutual Fund Investing
800-722-9000
Provides commentary and forecasts on the market and the economy. Recommends general strategies and positions as well as specific mutual fund selections. Began publication: 1984. Monthly.

Muni Bond Fund Report
714-897-9511
Provides commentary on the tax-free bond market and the bond market in general. Provides performance data and makes recommendations. Began publication: 1985. Monthly.

Mutual Fund Forecaster
800-327-6720
Reports performance, assigns risk ratings, and makes profit projections on more than 400 mutual funds. Makes specific recommendations. Began publication: 1985. Monthly.

The Mutual Fund Letter
312-649-6940
Provides performance information on top mutual fund performers. Offers strategic investment advice for building an investment portfolio using no-load and low-load mutual funds. Began publication: 1983. Monthly.

Mutual Fund Specialist
715-834-7425
Tracks moving average trends of selected mutual funds and makes specific buy/sell recommendations based on technical trend data. Special sections are devoted to sector and gold funds. Began publication: 1978. Monthly.

Mutual Fund Strategist
802-658-3513
Employs market timing and relative strength to select mutual fund positions in advancing and declining markets. Began publication: 1982. Monthly.

Mutual Fund Trends
800-621-8322
Provides performance data and detailed charts on selected mutual funds. Also publishes widely followed market index charts. Makes no recommendations or forecasts. Monthly.

No-Load Fund Investor
914-693-7420
Ranks and reports performance of no-load and low-load mutual funds from list of more than 800 funds. Makes specific recommendations and offers general outlook commentary. Began publication: 1979. Monthly.

***Noload Fund*X**
800-452-4445
Uses proprietary formula for scoring funds on basis of performance and recommends selected no-load and low-load funds. Began publication: 1976. Monthly.

Switch Fund Advisory
800-722-9000
Provides performance data on more than 500 no-load and low-load mutual funds. Publishes general stock and gold forecasts based on proprietary models. Regular section on sector funds. Began publication: 1977. Monthly.

Telephone Switch Newsletter
800-950-8765
Recommends selected mutual funds based on relative strength performance. Transmits switch sig-nals to subscribers via telephone hotline and express mail service. Began publication: 1976. Monthly.

Subscription prices range from around $50 to more than $150, with $100 as the median. Most of the newsletters will send you a sample copy.

In addition to requesting a sample issue, here are some questions worth asking the publisher or editor:

• Is he a registered investment adviser? There's no guarantee that a registered investment adviser gives better advice, but this is information worth knowing. It means the newsletter has to meet certain standards, and it also allows the adviser to offer money management services.

• Does the newsletter include "model portfolios"? Most do. Some monitor a variety of portfolios for different investment profiles or objectives. Ask about them.

• How have the model portfolios performed over the past few years? Were sales charges, transaction fees, and taxes figured into the performance results? (Since many of these model portfolios involve heavy trading, you could end up with a real tax and fee nightmare.)

• Does the newsletter have a telephone hotline or does it send switch signals by mail? By express mail? Many do; some include these services in the subscription fee, others charge extra for it.

time you switch from one fund to another. And some fund companies have asked certain active market timers to take their business elsewhere. If you're thinking of timing the market by trading actively, check the rules for the fund family you plan to use before you sign up. Find out how often you are allowed to make switches, whether you can do it by telephone, and what fees are involved. If the fund group carries a load, or sales charge, must you pay it again when you move to a new fund? If there is an exit fee, do you pay it each time you leave a single fund? Or do the funds operate as a group, giving you free exchanges between, say, a money market fund and a range of stock and bond funds? If you want more options than a single fund family can offer, consider an account with a discount broker that allows you to buy and sell funds from different families.

Nearly every investor should have his account set up so that he has the opportunity to switch if he wants. However, studies show that more switching does not equal better results. Although there are a few investors whose active trading of mutual funds has brought them spectacular gains, more common is the investor who ended up getting out of the market too early or getting back into the market too late. In order to make switching pay off, you must make two correct decisions each time you switch. You need to switch out of the market and into cash when the market tops and you need to get back into the market at the bottom. If you don't get in at the bottom, you're worse off than if you had simply held on to your fund all along.

TAXES

Mutual funds do not pay taxes on their earnings. Instead, they pass on the entire taxable gain or loss to the shareholders and these shareholders pay taxes as if they owned the securities outright. Investors receive two types of income from mutual fund investments: dividends and capital gains. Dividends and interest are the earnings on the securities held in the portfolio. Capital gains income comes from the profits the portfolio manager makes by trading securities throughout the year. You can, of course, choose to have dividends and capital gains reinvested rather than receiving them when they are paid. But whichever

HE FOLLOWS THE EXPERTS AND INVESTORS FOLLOW HIM: MARK HULBERT ON MUTUAL FUND NEWSLETTERS

Every investor wants to be in the stock market when prices are soaring and somewhere else when they collapse. But how to recognize a market that's ready to take off or one that's headed for a crash landing?

Like the fountain of youth and the origin of the universe, market timing is a subject of endless fascination, an industry unto itself. Many people have made lots of money selling market timing advice over the years. But does anyone do it very well?

Bailing out of the market before a serious crash like the one in October 1987 can do a lot to preserve both your capital and your peace of mind. On the other hand, most of the evidence suggests that investors who try to switch into and out of the stock market to catch the small ebbs and flows don't do so well.

There are a dozen or more mutual fund newsletters that will provide you with advice on how to time the market if you want to try it. But Mark Hulbert, editor of *The Hulbert Financial Digest*, who has been analyzing these investment advice letters since 1980, suggests it may not be worth your while.

"Most people tend to believe that more switching makes the odds go in your favor," Hulbert says, "and that's not the case. My data seem to suggest that switching quickly reaches the point of diminishing return. Switching holds value, but more switching does not add up to greater gains."

In fact, he says, if you compare performance to the number of switches, "you find that the portfolios with the most switches generally had the worst performance."

What switching should be measured against, according to Hulbert, is a "buy-and-hold" strategy. In other words, compare how your investment performed as a result of your switch with how it would have performed if you simply held on to the first fund you bought.

In order to beat buy and hold, you must make two good switch decisions, he says. You must switch out of the market and into cash when the market tops. And then you must move back into the market at the bottom. "If you don't get in at the bottom, you're worse off," he says.

Hulbert regularly studies switch advisory newsletters to see whether they timed the market right. In one recent study of 32 cases, only 3 newsletters timed the market right and got readers back in at a lower price than where they got out, he said. "In 29 cases they got in at higher prices than where they sold. When you take tax consequences into account, you're much worse off."

you decide, you still owe tax on the income. By early February of each year, your fund will send you a statement, IRS Form 1099-DIV, just like the one you receive from your employer or your bank, indicating what your income was for the year. If the amount conflicts with other information you receive, you should find out why. But when you report your income for tax purposes, stick with the 1099. This is the same information that the fund reports to the IRS.

The Tax Reform Act of 1986 made some significant changes in the way mutual fund shareholders are taxed. Most important, it eliminated the favorable tax status for capital gains, the profit you make when you sell or switch a mutual fund. They are now taxed at the same rate as earned income. The new law also decreed that any income declared by your fund by December 31 and distributed by February 1 of the next year will be taxable on the earlier year's return.

You will also have taxable income if you sell your shares at a profit and receive a *capital gain* during the year. If you sell your shares for less than you paid and have a *capital loss*, you can use it to offset capital gains. In other words, if you have a capital gain of $1,500 and a capital loss of $900, your capital gains income would be $600. If your losses exceed your gains, you can deduct the excess losses from your ordinary income up to $3,000 for single taxpayers or married taxpayers filing jointly. Married taxpayers filing separately are allowed $1,500 each. If your losses exceed the limit, you can take them forward to offset them against the next year's income.

Obviously, you need to keep good records of your investments for tax purposes. If you don't, you may end up paying taxes twice on the same money. You need records of when you made an investment, how much you invested, the price per share, and how many shares you bought. Whenever you have dividends reinvested, treat this as purchase of additional shares for record-keeping purposes. These records are used to determine the *cost basis* of your shares.

If you have good records and you decide to sell some shares, you can tell the mutual fund company which shares to sell, which can result in tax savings for you. For example, let's say you've been buying Capital Fund over the years at various share prices ranging from $10 a share to $20 a share. Capital is now selling at $16 a share. You need to sell 100 shares. You can instruct the fund to sell 100 shares that you bought at $20 a share. That means you will have a capital loss of $400. If you haven't kept records that allow you to use this method, the IRS assumes that you are selling the 100 shares that you purchased first. If that purchase was made years ago, you probably paid less for them. For example, if you bought them for $10 a share and you are now

with
it's
anize

u buy
mation
mpany
sends y... trades
you've made during that p...... number
of shares you bought and sold on each day and
the share price as well as records of reinvested
dividends, you can toss the individual confirmation statements once you get the quarterly reports.

• *Form 1099-B*. This form, which the company sends you in January, reports the money
you got from selling fund shares. Use the form to
determine your capital gain or loss.

• *Form 1099-DIV*. This form reports your
share of the fund's income from dividends or
capital gains.

• *Retirement account fees*. If you are self-
employed you can deduct maintenance fees for
an IRA or Keogh account from your taxable income *if* you pay them separately by check. If you
are an employee, these fees are miscellaneous
expenses and can only be deducted to the extent
that they exceed 2 percent of your income.

selling 100 shares at $16 a share, you have a capital gain of $600. This
example should make it clear why you need to keep good records.
(Keep a copy of your instruction letter.)

There are two additional methods of figuring cost basis, both of
which use an average cost per share. Both require that you have a
custodian for your account and that you specifically request from the
IRS that you be allowed to use one of these two systems. Further, you
cannot change from one of these two systems to another without written permission from the IRS. For these reasons, one of the two methods described above makes more sense.

One further point about your cost basis. If you pay a sales charge or
an exit fee, figure this into your cost basis. If the fund you buy has a
load, it is taken off your investment up front and that money is never
invested in shares. Your statement should indicate this. But you need
to check. For example, say you invest $2,000 in a fund that is selling
at $10 a share and carries a 4 percent load. The 4 percent, or $80, is
subtracted from the $2,000 before the shares are purchased. So you are
buying 192 shares rather than 200.

The *1990 Mutual Fund Tax Guide* (Fidelity Publishing, 1989) offers an example of how the two most common methods might work for one mutual fund shareholder. Below is a record of Molly's purchases of the no-load Great Fund:

Date	Amount of Purchase	Share Price	Shares
2/88	$2,500	$10	250
1/89	225 (reinvested dividend)	15	15
7/89	2,800	14	200
8/89	1,200	12	100
TOTAL	$6,725 invested		565

Let's say that it's October 1989, and Molly has decided to sell 200 shares of the Great Fund. The selling price is $11 per share. Molly wants to know whether she's selling at a gain or at a loss, and she wants to figure the tax consequences of her sale.

Here are the four ways she can treat the transaction.

Method One—Sell Specific Shares

Since Molly has kept good records, she knows how many shares she has purchased, at which prices, and on what days. So she can instruct Great Fund to sell specific shares. This method gives Molly choices about whether to realize a gain or a loss on the sale.

In this case, Molly asks that the fund sell the 200 shares she purchased in July 1988 at $14 per share. Because she specified which shares she was selling, figuring her basis in those shares is easy. For this case it's $14 per share—the price she paid for them.

So, if she sells the 200 shares for $11 per share, Molly will have a *short-term capital loss* of $3 per share—that is, her $11 selling price minus her $14 basis. Her total loss is $600 ($3 times 200 shares). It is a short-term loss, because she's owned the shares less than one year.

Molly may use this $600 loss to offset some of her capital gains income from other transactions. What if she has no capital gains? Uncle Sam allows her to subtract the $600 from her ordinary taxable income.

Method Two—First In, First Out ("FIFO")

If Molly hadn't kept good records, she couldn't have told Great Fund precisely which shares to sell. Or she may have had some other reason not to specify. Either way, the IRS would generally require that Molly sell the first 200 shares she had purchased.

The first 200 shares of Great Fund that Molly bought were part of her original purchase. She paid $10 per share, which, in this case, is also her basis. So the sale would result in a $200 *long-term capital gain* (the $11 selling price less the $10 basis, times 200 shares).

The tax consequences of these two methods are substantially different, of course. With Method One, Molly would have a $600 short-term loss, which would reduce her taxable income in 1988. But Method Two would add $200 to Molly's taxable capital-gains income.

SOME ADDITIONAL WRINKLES

If a fund earns capital gains on its investments and does not distribute them to you, this may also affect your basis in the fund. Also, calculating your basis becomes slightly more complicated if your mutual fund shares are inherited or are a gift. You should consult a tax professional or invest in a good book on tax calculation to understand fully how each of these special situations should be handled.

Keep in mind . . .

• You must keep very good records of your purchases, sales, and fund distributions for figuring cost basis.

• The IRS allows four different methods for calculating cost basis. Before you make a final selection, you might consider calculating your results using the two most common methods. Make sure your mutual fund company can accommodate your choice—call them and ask.

• Once you've made a choice, you cannot change methods without asking Uncle Sam. You can use different methods for different funds, but it's apt to be confusing. Don't try unless you have a very good reason.

And a final note about *when* to buy a fund. Naturally it would be great to buy just as the fund hits a new low and is poised for a takeoff. Needless to say, most of the time you won't be that precise. What you *can* do is avoid buying a fund just before it makes a big dividend

Ex-dividend *Effective date of a dividend distribution. When the dividend is paid, the NAV of the fund drops by the amount of the dividend. Since you receive the dividend, the total value of your investment is unchanged. However, you must pay tax on the dividend.*

distribution, or goes **ex-dividend.** These large distributions usually occur once a year. Here's how they work: The fund makes a dividend distribution that lowers the price of your shares and, at the same time, gives you a capital gain. So although your investment has not changed in value, you must pay taxes on something you didn't actually receive. Say you put $10,000 into a fund, buying 1,000 shares at $10 a share. The next day a $1 a share distribution goes ex-dividend. This means you get $1,000 to reinvest and your NAV drops to $9. Your investment is still worth $10,000, the same as the day before. But now you have a $1,000 taxable capital gain. You can call the fund group before you make your purchase and find out if a dividend distribution is planned.

POINTS TO REMEMBER

• Most of the information you need to track your investments is available in the daily newspapers and popular business magazines. The *Wall Street Journal* and the financial sections of most metropolitan dailies report on what happened in the stock and bond markets as well as reporting news on broader economic indicators. You can also learn how your particular mutual fund investment performed by checking the tables that list the price changes in the net asset value.

• Many companies rank the performance of mutual funds. You can find their reports in the library. Or you can ask your broker or financial planner for this information, if you use one. You can also buy many of these services yourself. Or you can find the performance rankings in many popular business and personal finance magazines, such as *Money, Business Week, Forbes,* and *Barron's.*

• An important ingredient of investment success is a regular checkup. Even if you consider yourself a buy-and-hold investor, take a look at your portfolio at least once a year, maybe when you're doing your tax planning.

• Stay in touch with the basic economic indicators. Keep tuned in to the direction of interest rates. Get a sense of the general health of the economy and your portfolio.

• Figuring out when the markets will move can be as frustrating as contemplating the Mona Lisa's smile. If you're determined to try to make money by timing the market, you need a strategy, an approach. To make timing pay off, you must make two correct decisions. You need to get out of the market at or near the top and back in at or near the bottom.

• Maybe you want more than just objective reporting on investments. If you're looking for advice, check the newsletters on the mutual fund industry.

• Frequent trading can give you an unpleasant surprise at tax time. Whenever you make a profit, you must pay tax. Whether or not you are a frequent trader, you must keep careful records of your mutual fund accounts for tax purposes.

Glossary

Accumulation plan   Method of buying mutual fund shares through small, regular, voluntary purchases.

Annuity   Investment offered by life insurance companies that pays income for a specified period, for example, 10 to 15 years or longer. Annuities are usually used for retirement and often pay income for life. When you begin receiving payments, you must pay tax on the portion that represents earnings.

Assets   Property with value. Your personal assets include your home, car, furnishings, jewelry, clothing, and investments. When money managers talk about assets, they mean the amount of money they're managing, which they refer to as "assets under management."

Automated phone messages   Service offered by some mutual fund companies that lets you use a Touch-tone telephone to get up-to-the-minute information about the funds you own—e.g., net asset value, your account balance—and switch money from fund to fund. Computer-generated instructions guide you through the process of using the service. Some automated phone services operate 24 hours a day.

Basis point   One one-hundredth of one percent. Basis points are used to express such things as expenses and yields that are less than 1 percent; 1 percent equals 100 basis points.

Beta   Measure of the relative volatility of a stock or a stock mutual fund. The market as a whole, as measured by the Standard & Poor's 500 stock index, is assigned a beta of 1. A mutual fund with a beta of 2 is considered twice as volatile as the market. One with a beta of .5 is considered half as volatile.

Call provision   Part of agreement between bond issuer and bond buyer that spells out the terms under which the issuer may take the bonds back.

Call risk   Risk that bonds you hold may be called back by the issuer. If interest rates drop, the investor will have to reinvest his money in a less favorable economic environment.

Cash management account   Brokerage account developed by Merrill Lynch in 1977. This type of account, which is now offered by many financial service companies, allows investors to buy and sell securities as well as to tap the account by writing checks or by using a credit card to make purchases. Idle cash is swept into a money market fund.

Certificate of deposit (CD)   Time deposit at a bank or savings and loan institution. When you buy a CD, you agree to leave your money in the bank for a specific period of time, which may range from 30 days to several years. In exchange, the bank guarantees you a specific interest rate, higher than that paid on a passbook account. If you take your money out early, you pay a penalty. Bank CDs are insured by the FDIC. You can also buy CDs from a stockbroker. The broker can canvass the country and get you the best rate. However you must pay a fee for the service.

Clone   A new mutual fund that takes its name from an established "parent" fund in the same fund family. A large, successful mutual fund is sometimes cloned when the fund company decides that the fund has grown too large to manage well. The large fund closes to new investors; the clone fund hopes to attract investors through name recognition, which may create a favorable association with the original fund.

Commission   Portion of the purchase price that is paid to a salesperson or middleman. You pay a commission to a real estate agent when you sell your house. You pay an insurance salesman a commission when you buy a policy. And you pay a commission to a stockbroker when you ask him to buy or sell securities for you.

Commodities   Bulk goods such as metals, oil, grain, and livestock traded on a commodities exchange. Funds that invest in commodities or commodities futures are highly volatile. But some of them have turned in spectacular returns.

Contractual plan   A mutual fund investment plan that requires an investor to sign a contract agreeing to invest a predetermined amount of money periodically over a certain number of years to reach a set investment goal. The plans have been criticized for their high up-front sales commissions and have fallen off in popularity. Nonetheless some investors still choose them because they offer the discipline that enables them to invest.

Coupon   Interest rate on a bond, based on the face value of the bond when it is issued and set until maturity. Coupon refers to the detachable coupons that were once part of the bond. Every six months the bondholder removed a coupon and presented it to the issuer to receive his interest. Although few bonds today have these coupons, the interest rate is still referred to as the coupon.

Covered call option   Option that is sold on a security held by the option seller. Differs from a naked option, which is a call option written by someone who does not own the stock.

Currency   Money issued by a particular sovereign government. The currency in the United States is the dollar. In Japan, it is the yen.

Custodial account   Account that is set up for a child by an adult, used for its tax advantages.

Default   Failure of a bond issuer to make timely payments of interest and principal as they come due or to meet some other provision of the bond.

Deferred annuity   Annuity that is used to accumulate tax-deferred earnings for payout at some future date.

Discount broker Brokerage house that executes orders to buy and sell securities at a price significantly lower than that charged by a full-service broker. To keep their costs down, discount brokers don't offer advice, recommendations, guidance, or other related services. Their employees are paid salaries rather than commissions, which also helps keep prices lower.

Dollar cost averaging Method of buying stock or mutual fund shares by investing the same amount of money on a regular schedule regardless of the market price. Dollar cost averaging allows investors to avoid guessing whether the market is going up or down. The advantage of this method is that your dollars buy more shares when the price is down, fewer when the price is up. Studies show that investors who use dollar cost averaging tend to pay less per share over time than those who purchase shares in a lump sum.

Dow Jones Industrial Average Average of 30 actively traded blue-chip stocks. At one time, the Dow 30 were all industrial stocks. As the United States has moved from an industrial to a service economy, stocks like American Express have been added to the average. The index, which is the most widely quoted indicator of the market, is prepared by Dow Jones & Company. It is quoted in points rather than dollars.

Equity Ownership interest in a corporation, which distinguishes stockholders from bondholders; a term often used interchangeably with stock, as in "He's invested in equities (stocks)," or "the equity (stock) market."

Ex-dividend Effective date of a dividend distribution. When the dividend is paid, the NAV (net asset value) of the fund drops by the amount of the dividend. Since you receive the dividend, the total value of your investment is unchanged. However, you must pay tax on the dividend.

Expense ratio Percentage of a fund's assets that is paid out in expenses. Expenses include management fees and all fees associated with distributing shares and literature and administration of the fund. The expense ratio for most funds ranges from as low as .2 percent of the fund's assets to around 2.5 percent. Expenses can go higher for funds that do an extraordinary amount of trading, but these exceptions are few.

Fixed annuity Annuity that earns interest at a fixed rate, set by the insurance company.

Fundamental analysis The study of a company's assets, earnings, sales, products, management, and markets—the ''fundamentals'' of the company—for the purpose of predicting whether its stock price will rise or fall in the future.

Global funds Mutual funds that invest in stocks of companies or bonds of governments all over the world, in the United States as well as in most other countries.

Government National Mortgage Association (GNMA) Agency of the Department of Housing and Urban Development, known as Ginnie Mae.

Growth investment An investment that has as its primary goal long-term appreciation or increase of principal. Common stock and mutual funds that invest primarily in common stock are growth investments.

Guaranteed investment contract Contract between an investor and an insurance company that guarantees return of premium and that pays a set rate of interest. A popular investment for 401 (k) plans.

Hedge Transaction used to offset the risk of another transaction or position. An investor with a large bond portfolio might use interest rate futures contracts to reduce the risk of loss in the value of his bonds that would be caused by rising interest rates. A U.S. investor with a large domestic portfolio might hedge against a falling dollar by diversifying into Japanese yen or British pounds.

Immediate annuity Annuity that begins paying income immediately. For example, you are 65 years old and plan to retire. You buy an immediate annuity for $250,000 on January 1. On February 1, you would start receiving monthly income of $2,283 if you are a man; $2,073 if you are a woman. The income is based on your life expectancy. Women receive less because they are expected to live longer.

Income investment   An investment that has as its primary goal the generation of income, in the form of interest or dividends, as opposed to growth or capital appreciation. Preferred stock, bonds, money market instruments and mutual funds that invest primarily in these securities are income investments.

Indicators   Signals used by investment analysts to forecast the direction of the financial markets. An indicator is based on a specific measure of information, such as interest rate trends, insider trading activity, or stock trading volume.

Individual Retirement Account (IRA)   Personal account for retirement. Employees who have no company pension plan or who earn less than $25,000 a year ($40,000 as a married couple) can contribute $2,000 a year and deduct it from income for tax purposes. A partial deduction is allowed for single taxpayers who earn up to $35,000 a year and for married taxpayers up to $50,000. Earnings on IRA investments accumulate tax-free until the account holder takes them out at retirement.

Inflation   Increase in the price of goods and services, most commonly measured by the Consumer Price Index (CPI). The average annual rise in the CPI from 1973 through 1988 was 6.6 percent. But during that period, it was as high as 13.3 percent in 1979 and as low as 1.1 percent in 1986.

Insider ownership   Securities ownership by officers or owners of a company.

Institutional investor   Investor that manages large amounts of money for a big organization. Some examples of institutional investors are mutual funds, insurance companies, and pension funds. These investors account for the bulk of trading on the major exchanges.

International funds   Mutual funds that invest in stocks or bonds of companies and governments outside the United States. To be classified as an international fund, a fund must invest most of its assets overseas. The percentage varies with different funds.

Investment Company Act of 1940 Federal law that regulates investment companies. The act requires registration with and regulation by the Securities and Exchange Commission. It requires investment companies to provide investors with complete and accurate information about mutual funds and other investment company products and protects them from abuses.

IRA SEP Retirement account for self-employed persons and employees of small companies. The employer can put in 15 percent of compensation or $30,000, whichever is smaller, for himself and for each employee. The account is in the employee's name and the employee has control over where to invest it. He is vested immediately. That means that if he leaves the company, the money in the account belongs to him. Employees also have the option of taking the contribution in cash, although they must pay taxes on it.

Junk corporate bonds Bonds issued by corporations that have a low credit rating or no rating at all.

Keogh account Retirement account for the self-employed and small businesses. These accounts, which were established by Congress in 1962, allow people to put away a portion of their self-employment earnings in a tax-deferred retirement account and deduct the amount from their earnings for tax purposes.

Large capitalization stocks Stocks of major corporations. Market capitalization refers to the total value the stock market places on a company. It is calculated by taking the value of one share and multiplying the number of shares outstanding. Stocks with a market capitalization of $1 billion are considered large "cap" stocks. These stocks are also very liquid, widely held, frequently traded, and closely followed by investment analysts.

Leveraged buyout (LBO)   Takeover of a company or a division of a company using a heavy amount of borrowed money. For example, management of a company may buy out a company division from the parent company. Or they may buy out the entire company from its shareholders, which means the company would go from publicly owned to privately owned. Typically, the assets of the company or the division are the collateral for the loan. The investors or managers who execute the buyout can go to a bank for the money. But they sometimes issue bonds to raise the money.

Load   Fee or commission paid by the investor when he buys mutual fund shares. Also called a front-end load, *it can be as high as 8.5 percent. Loads between 1 percent and 3 percent are called* low-loads.

Long bond   Generally, any bond with maturity of over ten years. However, when bond traders talk about what "the long bond" did in recent trading, they are referring to the 30-year Treasury bond, the bellwether of the bond market.

Lump sum distribution   Single payment in lieu of a series of payments. This often refers to the payment of pension benefits in a single check rather than in regular monthly installments.

Management fee   Annual fee paid by an investment company to the managers of a mutual fund, which usually ranges from .5 percent to 1.5 percent of all the assets in the fund. Fees can be considerably lower for certain types of funds, e.g., some income funds. And top performing fund managers are often paid more. Some funds, such as index funds or unit investment trusts, are not managed, and charge no management fee, although there are still other administrative expenses the fund must pay. Some funds pay managers a fee based on their performance, giving them more if the fund performs well, less if it does poorly.

Margin account   Brokerage account that allows the investor to borrow money to buy stocks and bonds or "buy on margin." An investor who has a margin account can buy a security by posting only a portion of the purchase amount in cash and collateral. The brokerage firm lends him the rest.

Margin call   Notification to an investor to post more cash or securities in his margin account.

Market timing   The use of economic and technical financial information to guide your decision on when to buy and sell securities.

Money market deposit account   Insured bank account that pays a market rate of interest. Money market accounts were offered by banks beginning in December 1982 as another way to compete with money market mutual funds. Interest is recalculated monthly. Customers have access to their money through automated teller machines. But only a limited number of checks can be written each month.

Money market fund   Mutual fund that invests in short-term debt obligations of governments and corporations. These accounts pay a market rate of interest that fluctuates from day to day. They always maintain a share price of one dollar. They are not insured, but they are extremely safe. They are also very liquid, which means you can get your money out quickly either by writing a check on the account or by transferring money into your bank account.

Mortgage-backed securities   Securities that are backed by individual home mortgages.

Mortgage passthrough securities   Bonds that "pass through" the principal and interest payments on mortgages from the mortgage borrowers to the bond buyers.

Municipals   Bonds, notes, or other short-term loans issued by state, city, or other local governments to pay for projects. All are exempt from federal taxes; many are also exempt from state and local taxes. Sometimes called "munis" or "tax-frees."

NASDAQ Index   Index of over-the-counter stocks prepared by the National Association of Securities Dealers. NASDAQ stands for National Association of Securities Dealers Automatic Quotations Systems.

Net asset value (NAV)   Market value of one share of a mutual fund. It is calculated at the close of each business day by taking the value of all the fund's assets, less expenses, and dividing by the number of shares outstanding.

$$\frac{\text{Current value of total fund assets} \quad \text{minus} \quad \text{Fund liabilities and expenses}}{\text{Total number of shares owned}} = \text{Net asset Value (NAV)}$$

No-load   Mutual fund that charges no fee or commission to buy or sell back its shares. As mutual funds have adopted a variety of new types of fees, there are increasingly fewer funds that do not charge the investor in some way for their marketing and distribution costs.

Nondeductible IRA   Individual retirement account that is not eligible for a tax deduction. It allows higher wage earners who participate in company pension plans to continue to put away $2,000 a year in an account where earnings accumulate tax-free until withdrawal.

NOW account   Bank checking account that pays interest. These accounts were introduced in 1974 to help banks compete with money market mutual funds.

October 1987 market crash   Drastic drop in stock markets around the world on October 19, 1987. In the United States, the Dow Jones Industrial Average dropped 508.32 points—22.6 percent—to 1,738.42. The 1987 crash far exceeded the drop of 12.8 percent on October 28, 1929, which ushered in the Great Depression.

Odd lot   Unit of stock that is sold in other than 100-share lots. For example, 25 shares of IBM is an odd lot. Investors pay a higher commission on odd lots.

One-country funds   Funds that invest in a single country. Many one-country funds are closed-end funds.

Option   Security that gives the owner the right to buy or sell the underlying instrument for a specific price during a specific period.

Over-the-counter market   Decentralized market for stocks that do not trade on the New York Stock Exchange or the American Stock

Exchange. OTC stocks are traded through a regional telephone and computer network by brokers and dealers throughout the country.

Par Face value of a security. For bonds, par is typically $1,000. The bond is issued for $1,000 and it is redeemed for $1,000 at maturity. In between, it may sell at par; less than par, which is called "selling at a discount"; or above par, which is called "selling at a premium."

Passbook account Basic savings account that has no stated maturity. Rates paid on passbook accounts historically have been low. In fact, these accounts had federally enforced interest rate ceilings from 1933 until April 1, 1986, when the ceiling was lifted. Balances are insured by the Federal Deposit Insurance Corp. up to $100,000.

Portfolio Collection of securities and other investments such as stocks, bonds, gold, art, and real estate.

Price-earnings ratio or p/e ratio (also called the *multiple*) The price of a stock divided by its earnings per share. The p/e ratio gives investors an idea of how much they are paying for a company's earning power.

Principal Amount of your original investment. If you invest $1,000, that amount is your principal.

Prospectus A formal, written offer to sell a security. The prospectus is required to disclose important information about the security. A mutual fund prospectus, for example, discusses the fund's history, investment objectives, performance, and management. Every mutual fund is required to publish a prospectus, which is offered free to anyone who requests it.

Real estate investment trust (REIT) Company that manages a package of real estate investments. The portfolio is publicly traded. A REIT is similar to the investment companies that sell shares in mutual funds. But the REIT shares are traded on the stock exchange rather than bought and sold through the management company.

Real estate limited partnership Real estate investment unit that consists of a general partner and limited partners. The general partner organizes the deal and is responsible for managing it. The limited partners, or investors, have liability only up to the amount of their investment. They hope to receive income and capital gains from the deal. Because there is not a liquid market for reselling these investments, they are generally considered a long-term investment, usually at least five to ten years.

Registered rep Securities salesperson who is licensed by the Securities and Exchange Commission and the New York Stock Exchange. Anyone who sells securities to the public must be a registered rep.

Round lot Stock purchase of 100 shares. Other securities, like bonds, also have round-lot trading units, but mutual fund shares do not. When you invest in a mutual fund you decide how much money you want to invest and the fund company allots you shares and fractional shares depending on the price of the fund.

Rule 12 (b) 1 Rule introduced in 1980 by the Securities and Exchange Commission that allows mutual funds to add an annual charge for marketing and distribution. This charge, which ranges from .1 percent of the fund's assets to 1.25 percent, can be used for advertising or to pay additional compensation to brokers who sell the funds.

Salary reduction plan Employer-sponsored plan that allows employees to set aside pre-tax dollars for certain health and retirement needs. Salary reduction plans used for retirement are named for sections of the IRS code that established them: *401 (k) plans* for employees of for-profit companies; *403 (b) plans* for employees of nonprofit organizations, for example, school systems, universities, and nonprofit hospitals; *457 plans* for employees of the federal government and its agencies.

Sales Charge Charge to invest in a mutual fund, which goes directly to the company. It differs from a commission, which is paid to the salesperson.

Salomon Brothers Bond Index Broad index that measures the movement of the bond market.

Secondary mortgage market Market in which individual home mortgages are packaged together and resold. The primary mortgage market is your local bank or savings and loan. Years ago, bankers were limited in the number of mortgage loans they could make because they kept all their mortgage loans on their own books. Today they can package their mortgage loans and resell them to a government agency or to private investment bankers who will then slice them up and resell them as bonds. These bonds, which are backed by mortgages like yours, can be bought and sold in this secondary market.

Sector fund Mutual fund that invests in one segment of the market. The idea of most mutual funds is to diversify investment dollars over a broad spectrum of securities. Sector funds concentrate in one particular market segment, such as energy, transportation, gold, small stocks, or international stocks.

Sector trading Strategy of moving into and out of various industry and asset sectors to improve investment returns.

Securities Publicly traded financial instruments such as stocks, bonds, and shares of mutual funds or limited partnerships. Securities are regulated by the Securities and Exchange Commission.

Securities and Exchange Commission Federal agency that regulates the securities industry. The SEC regulates the investment companies that manage mutual funds as well as the securities they offer and the salespeople who sell them.

Short sale Stock trading technique whereby the investor borrows stock and sells it, hoping that its price will fall so that he can buy it back at a lower price and repay his loan, pocketing the difference as his profit.

Short-term paper Short-term loans to corporations or government that can range from overnight to 90 days. Interest rates fluctuate to reflect current market conditions. Short-term paper is one of the basic investments of money market funds.

Standard & Poor's 500 Index (S & P 500) Index of 500 widely held stocks that is often used as a proxy for the stock market. Included are the stocks of 400 industrial companies, 40 financial companies, 40 public utilities, and 20 transportation companies.

Statement of additional information   Document provided by a mutual fund company that elaborates on the information found in the prospectus and provides additional information. The prospectus and the statement of additional information were once combined in the same document. Several years ago, in an effort to simplify the prospectus, fund companies put the additional information that they are required to provide to shareholders into Part B of the prospectus or the statement of additional information. Although the mutual fund company is required to send you a prospectus before you invest, it is not required to send you the statement of additional information. This information must be available to you, but it will be sent only if your request it.

Systematic withdrawal   Plan that allows you to withdraw a specified amount from your mutual fund account at regular intervals, usually each month. Systematic withdrawal plans, which are most often used for retirement, are a method of converting your investments into regular income.

Technical analysis   Study of patterns of trading activity of a particular security. Technical analysts chart price changes and trading volumes, for example, to develop trading patterns. They use this "technical information" to predict what the market in general or a particular security will do in the future.

Term life insurance   Policy that offers a death benefit for a specific period of time. The premium increases as the policyholder grows older. There is no investment or savings element in these policies.

Total return   Return on an investment that includes both the income it produces and the change in the value of the principal.

Trailing commissions   Commissions that are paid to the sales agent each year that his clients' money remains in the account. These commissions usually range from .25 percent to .75 percent of total assets, or 25 to 75 basis points.

Treasuries   Debt of the U.S. government. When the government needs to borrow money, it may issue TREASURY BILLS (T-Bills), which range in maturity from 91 days to one year. Two other types of debt instruments issued by the U.S. Treasury are TREASURY NOTES, intermediate securities that range from one year to ten years, and TREASURY BONDS, which range from ten years to 30 years.

Turnover rate Frequency of trading of assets in a portfolio, expressed as a percentage. Although there are many other things to consider, a high turnover rate and heavy trading can result in high transaction costs. Every time securities are bought and sold, the fund must pay commissions.

Underwriting Method of examining risks that are to be insured, classifying them, and setting the proper premium. Insurers use formulas and tables to determine how much premium each person should pay based on how substantial the risk of loss is.

Uniform Gift to Minors Act Law that establishes rules for assets that are held in the name of a child. Since the Tax Reform Act of 1986 all earnings over $1,000 a year are taxed at the parents' highest marginal rate until the child reaches age 14, when they are taxed at his own lower rate.

Variable annuity Annuity that offers the investor an option of different mutual fund investments. In contrast to a fixed annuity, which pays a set interest rate, a variable annuity allows the investor to select his own investments and shoulder the investment risk and reward.

Variable life insurance Policy that combines cash value life insurance with a tax-deferred investment, usually a stock or bond mutual fund. It is a type of whole life insurance. But instead of paying a fixed interest rate on the savings portion, this policy allows the policyholder to make his own investment choices and to take the additional risk as well as the additional potential reward.

Volatility Tendency of a security to rise or fall sharply in value.

Whole life insurance Policy that combines insurance coverage with a savings or investment account. These are sometimes referred to as ''cash value'' policies, because they build up a cash value over the years that the policyholder can borrow against.

Wilshire 5,000 Equity Index Index of all stocks traded in the United States. Although the index, which is published by Wilshire Associates of Santa Monica, is called the 5,000, it actually contains 5,900 stocks.

Acknowledgments

Grateful acknowledgment is made for information provided by:

Jane Lajoie of the Fidelity Publishing Group.

Jack Cahill and Mary Melaugh of Fidelity Research Services; Susan Johnson of the Fidelity Fixed Income Library; Jeffrey Todd and Robert Tanner of Fidelity Information Resources; Jeff Schlinsog and John O'Sullivan of Fidelity Life Insurance Company.

Dr. Mort Baratz, *Managed Account Reports,* Columbia, Maryland.

Sharilynn Duncan, Twentieth Century Investors, Inc., Kansas City, Missouri.

Plymouth Investments, Boston, Massachusetts.

The Investment Company Institute, Washington, D.C.

Brian Mattes, Vanguard Group of Investment Companies, Valley Forge, Pennsylvania.

John M. McAllister, Keystone Massachusetts Inc., Boston, Massachusetts.

Steve E. Norwitz, T. Rowe Price Investment Services, Baltimore, Maryland.

Index